THE FLITTING

THE FLITTING

BEN MASTERS

GRANTA

Granta Publications, 12 Addison Avenue, London W11 4QR
First published in Great Britain by Granta Books, 2024

All photographs are either author's own or from author's family collection.

A CIP catalogue record for this book is available from the British Library.

1 3 5 7 9 10 8 6 4 2

ISBN 978 1 78378 971 9 (hardback)
ISBN 978 1 78378 972 6 (ebook)

Typeset in Caslon by Iram Allam
Printed and bound by CPI Group (UK) Ltd, Croydon, CR0 4YY

www.granta.com

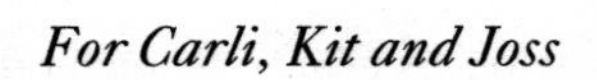

For Carli, Kit and Joss

'Strange scenes mere shadows are to me
Vague unpersonifying things
I love with my old hants to be
By quiet woods and gravel springs'

JOHN CLARE, 'The Flitting'

Contents

III THE BLUES

IV WOOD WHITE

V CLOUDED YELLOW

Prologue

I'm sitting at my desk, in front of my computer, flitting between websites that are dealing with your death: government guidelines (who to notify, how to apply for probate, how to value an estate . . .), banking pro formas, requests for death certificates. It's strange, processing your death through websites when I cannot process it myself. The strangest thing about it though – stranger than all the rest – is that you are in the room with me.

You were very specific with your wishes. Cremation. Under no circumstances were you to be buried. I know all about your mild claustrophobia, stemming, you reckoned, from the time you got trapped at the bottom of your bed, your duvet tucked so tight by Grandma that you couldn't get out (Grandma was a maid at a boarding school; things that got tucked by her stayed tucked). When I recalled this anecdote to Mum, the other day, she corrected me – there's no way you would've had a duvet. Rough ex-army sheets from the surplus shop up the road. I must be mindful of details; they can be distorted so easily.

You wanted your ashes to be buried beneath an oak

tree. (Did I ask whether your ashes are just as likely to feel claustrophobic as your dead body?) Your wish was to be in nature, amongst the birds, butterflies, trees, wildflowers, and all the other things that never meant much to me. But instead, you are on top of my bookshelf in a wooden box, in an overcrowded room surrounded by books, pop culture artefacts, and all the other things that never meant much to you. Immediately beside you, in a lime-green Ted Baker shoebox, is my first novel, safely entombed where I can't see it, poor reading for the afterlife. Underneath that is a plain blue box, inside which it is permanently 2005–8, i.e. my undergraduate years, a random jumble of blank discs for burning playlists, old notes that probably should be burnt, a black and orange Sony Ericsson, one of the earliest iPod models (broken) and unused stationery (Tipp-Ex, highlighter pens, a ball of string). Further down the shelves are my records and stacks of DVDs and CDs, waiting to be archived in the attic, where Carli tells me they belong in 2020. The rest is books.

You should be in the natural world, where you were happiest, but you are trapped in mine. Having you oversee me doesn't help with the guilt. I add another tab to the web browser: *how to plant an oak tree.* I read a bit more about probate. The banal administration of loss isn't something anyone can prepare you for. I can't imagine Mum making sense of all these links and online forms and logins, as if losing her husband isn't already a sufficient demand. Don't worry though. I'm trying to take care of it all.

Sort of. What I'm really doing is reading your diaries. I know you wouldn't mind. They're game registers for documenting what you've shot, field diaries for noting what you've seen, a butterfly diary. I see that you've let in a few titbits of unrelated news. For instance, not only did you kill two pheasants in the first fortnight of December 1986, but also I was born.

Mixed with reports of what you have shot and fished (activities about which we disagreed and rowed) are records of the first Swallow of the year, the first Nightingale's song, the first Blackbird's nest, the first wild violets in flower – all these ways of measuring time that are alien to me, second nature to you. What moves me, though, is how your diaries capture a one-way conversation. Their pages are the space for all the things you knew we, your family, didn't have time for. Did you imagine that one day I would read them? *11 April 1999: found a male Green Woodpecker on the verge [. . .] I brought it home to show the family, but they were not very interested.* I read about a Buzzard teaching its young to fly, Long-eared Owls nesting in the woods, a male Sparrowhawk plucking a bathing sparrow from the garden pond, a single Swallow flying north being coursed by a Hobby Falcon (you report this to the RSPB, something my adolescent self would instinctively want to rib you for, and they confirm it is the earliest sighting of a Swallow that year (congrats)), and how you sat on the lawn in shirtsleeves during an unseasonably warm February and watched butterflies coming out from hibernation. All these experiences, all this time, spent alone. I read about how you used a Dictaphone to record what you thought might be a Nightingale down the lane, and how you played it back to itself to encourage it to sing. But instead of wanting to take the piss out of you, I now find myself proud of your curiosity, your interestedness, your commitment, ashamed of my younger self's dismissiveness, regretful that he didn't share the experience with you. I read about how I found a Sparrowhawk with two broken wings by the village pub when I was twelve, and how you took it to the vet's in the hope they might save it. (They put it down.) I also read about how I stumbled upon a snake's skin at the edge of the garden – you found the snake and observed it for several days (sunning itself in the compost heap, crawling through the vegetable patch, eating the biggest frog from the pond), presumably with no further input from me. Why can't I remember any of these things?

My whole life you have tried to gloss the natural world for me. Binoculars, butterfly nets, books identifying birds and trees and fish – all were common birthday and Christmas presents. But they were up against stiff competition. If you were steeped in natural history, I was a devotee of popular culture – American popular culture in particular: movies, rock music, hip hop, video games, and above all basketball (playing it, watching it, planning an unlikely career in it) – things that were low on your agenda. I could tell you all about the Smashing Pumpkins' 'Bullet with Butterfly Wings' or Kendrick Lamar's *To Pimp a Butterfly*, but we'd be talking two different languages. We never got far on a walk without you pointing out a butterfly or quizzing me on the name of a tree or bird. But I always got the answers wrong – my theory was if I stuck with the same ones (Ash or Chiffchaff or Red Admiral), I'd be right at least some of the time. You must have wondered what you had done to deserve such magnitudes of ignorance in your indoor-dwelling offspring. But then *you* couldn't say who the all-time leading scorer in the NBA was, so which of us was inadequate, really?[1]

I was far more responsible than you for our failure to communicate the things we held dearest. An example: I don't know how to explain to you that at work I have just been discussing a Zadie Smith essay that I love with my students, my notes for which are on my desk, on top of a chaotic stack of papers, including some you left for me to help make sense of your affairs. It's a personal essay about the knotty relationships between identity, taste and understanding. Smith writes of the transformation that turned her from someone who heard the music of Joni Mitchell as 'just noise [. . .] generally annoying the hell out of me' to someone who, later in life, was moved to 'uncontrollable tears' by the 'almost intolerable beauty' of that same music.[2] What I wish I had said to you is that 'Some Notes on Attunement' is an essay I value because it is a writer I admire writing about an artist whose music has meant so much to me – a meeting of two quite different sensibilities that are important elements in the nexus of my own sensibility. I also love that essay because it gets to something I have felt but never satisfactorily been able to articulate: a *change* in sensibility.

I take sensibility to mean more than just one's taste or interests. It is how we respond to emotional and aesthetic experience, our perception of things, our receptiveness to that which is other. Smith talks about 'that mysterious word "sensibility", the existence of which so often feels innate'.[3] Sensibility certainly does feel hardwired. Compelled by involuntary affinities, we appreciate certain things without knowing why; we discover aptitudes that we don't seem to have any influence over; we make instinctive judgements. But one's sense of self is also more everyday than an enigmatic term like 'sensibility' might suggest. Often we are sensitive to particular things simply because of opportunity: we come to them because they are valued by people with influence in our lives (it is no coincidence that *your* father was an outdoors man and naturalist like you), just as things are made possible by circumstances (our identities, where we live, what we have access to). It isn't necessarily any more mysterious than that. Sometimes, of course, we go in the opposite direction from what is on offer. Maybe that was why I hadn't followed you into the natural world. Rebellion, pure and simple.

I turn to your butterfly diary. A pocket-sized blue hardback, with a matter-of-fact record of the butterflies you have seen, dating back to 2000, when I was thirteen and all these beguiling names meant nothing: Purple Emperors, White-letter Hairstreaks, Marbled Whites, Gatekeepers, Silver-washed Fritillaries, White Admirals.

In her attempt to describe how selves change, Smith alludes to the structure of feeling. The cultural theorist and literary critic Raymond Williams, a Welsh working-class boy who became a professor at the University of Cambridge, coined the term 'structure of feeling' in the 1950s, when you were born, and continued to develop it in his essays and books through the 1960s (when you were probably up a tree looking for birds' eggs, or poaching with your dad, or trying to impress Mum at school) and 1970s (when you were leaving school and going to work on the building sites, getting married, trying to figure out what you wanted to be). He used it to analyse how new formations of thought, new kinds of consciousness, new modes, emerge within cultures, often in contradistinction to the dominant ways of thinking. The thing I especially like about the structure of feeling as a concept is how it accommodates the indescribable: those subtle though often foundational transformations that occur beyond comprehension, so complex and multifaceted in their happening that we cannot explain them (maybe even perceive them) in any straightforward way. Williams applied the phrase to how the values and practices of whole societies change, but I find myself applying it at a personal level. If my relationship with you was a structure of feeling, it was prone to evolve and on rare occasions upheave.

Another moment that strikes me in Smith's meditation on sensibility is when, describing her relationship to the visual arts (less familiar ground for her), she says:

> *All the difficult work of attunement and acceptance has already been done by others. Smart critics, other painters, appreciative amateurs. They kicked the door open almost a century ago – all I need do is walk through it.*[4]

That was part of the problem. When it came to the natural world, you had done the work for me, so I went in search of other openings – books, music, film, art. And then I found myself, in your final months, tentatively knocking at your door, hoping it wasn't too late, that it wouldn't close shut. I couldn't have known then that each door would open to yet more doors and an infinite expansion of unfamiliar territories.

And now you overlook me, from your screwed-shut box, stuck inside another man's sensibility, the thought of which makes *me* claustrophobic. I play music to you, including Joni (not your cup of tea). I read poetry to you too. Stuff we would never have spoken about, stuff I never dreamed we could share. Let me read you something now. It's from Thomas Hardy's uncanny 'Wessex Heights'. The speaker is on top of a hill, looking down from the wilderness at past selves in town, in society, creating that paradoxical self-haunting so peculiar to Hardy's poetry, where the self is at once deferred, suspended between past and future states of being, yet also utterly present, immanent, like a structure of feeling:

Down there I seem to be false to myself, my simple self that was,
And is not now, and I see him watching, wondering what crass
cause
Can have merged him into such a strange continuator as this,
Who yet has something in common with himself, my chrysalis.[5]

Which is the chrysalis, which the butterfly, I'm not sure, as you look down at me from atop my bookshelf, strange doubles companioning one another. I just wish I had shared all these things with you when I had the chance.

I
Lulworth Skipper

I
The Unknowing

That shrill, hard pecking sound that seems to be excavating every bad experience you've ever had from the depths of your pillow. I end it with an involuntary reflex, slapping around for the iPhone on the floor to the side of the bed, before it can wake Carli.

There is someone in the next room whose sleep is to be guarded even more fiercely. I light up the monitor on my bedside table and find an unconscious superhero lying flat on his back, fist punching the air above his head like he's soaring through his dreams, vanquishing noisy iPhones. Kit, our baby boy. I check my watch, as if the alarm needs confirming: 5 a.m. But the sunlight gilding the curtain's edge reminds me that it's going to be a beautiful day (I've been tracking the weather for a couple of weeks now; this morning has been carefully chosen for my escape) and my spirits lift. My rucksack is packed by the front door, ready to flee. An autoreply lies in wait in my work inbox for all pursuers. July 2019, the year before everything changed.

Fifteen minutes later I am in the car, driving south to Dorset, alone. Another thirty minutes and I am passing Mum and Dad's house in south Northamptonshire, from where we set off with the caravan every summer on the same journey. Next, the Peartree Interchange into Oxford where, years after our summer holidays had ceased, Dad would drop me off for the new term, and I would be aflutter with butterflies and social anxiety, overwhelmed by impostor syndrome (though no one was calling it that back then), the car loaded with clothes, books and CDs; then the chalk escarpment on the M3 at Winchester, by which time on those long summer-holiday drives I would be feeling travel-sick and achingly impatient for the beach; then the service station on the M27 where we always stopped and Mum would go for a pee in the caravan; then the transition into the prickly heathland of the New Forest, by which time I'd exhausted every Michael Jackson tape I owned on Dad's car stereo. Different selves, haunters and phantoms, hovering at checkpoints for memories on the way to other memories.

By 8 a.m. I can almost taste the ocean as I drive past the military training grounds that colonise the Purbeck coast, with their barbed-wire fences, red warning flags and signs advertising sudden gunfire like it's something for the family to do if Monkey World and The Tank Museum are sold out. And then it's there, the ocean, a blue haze of deep time sandwiched between ancient hills, as I wind through the idyllic village of Lulworth, thatched cottages pressed up against the narrow road so that you can't miss how affronted they are by holiday traffic. I park in the Lulworth Estate car park between Lulworth Cove and Durdle Door. It's empty this early in the morning, but it will be full when I return at lunchtime. Chalk puffs around me as I step out, giddy with childlike excitement. The air is different here, salted, electric.

This must be the fourth or fifth consecutive summer that I've made this solitary pilgrimage, returning to the scene of so many childhood holidays just for one day, seeking something, I'm not sure what. From the car park I make my ascent up the first hill of the morning, figuring things out as I go: how I will attempt to keep Kit entertained during my five months of parental leave when Carli goes back to work in two weeks' time, problems that need resolving with the novel I'm working on and how to finish it while failing to keep Kit entertained, whether I really want to continue doing academic research, how soon is too soon to start eating the sandwiches in my bag . . . Above all, ironically, I am thinking about how to be in the moment.

Already my muscles are tight when I reach the top, my shirt sticking to my back, and I look out across the sea. For a moment my work emails feel as distant as the dissolving horizon. I turn my gaze to the right, where the coastal route peels away, miles of undulation and shimmer, the top of each peak visible like a possible freedom that continually recedes. The names of the hills, headlands and valleys are a shot to the imagination: Scratchy Bottom, Swyre Head, Bat's Head, White Nothe and Hambury Tout, where I stand now. I knew none of these things when I carried my plastic bucket and spade on Dad's shoulders down to the beach at Durdle Door. Nor did I sense the immortal poet, around the promontory of Dungy Head, embraced by Lulworth Cove, taking one last look at England while the boat that would transport him to Italy and death made a brief stop. (Looking up he sees a bright star and makes a composition in his burning head: 'would I were stedfast as thou art'. But he does not see the other immortal poet looking back at him from the future, Wessex-dreaming atop Bindon Hill: 'A hundred years, and the world will follow him there, / And bend with reverence where his ashes lie.')[1]

The first time I returned as an adult to do this walk, I printed a set route from the internet, like it's possible to get lost on a coastline. I ended up inland, lost, panting around some crop fields with Google Earth open on my phone. I could imagine my dad's distinctive chuckle, tickled by my lack of common sense and outdoorsy wherewithal. Just the thought of it made me bristle. Now at least I know the terrain by heart, so I can be in the moment and enjoy the natural beauty: the sea shine, the white time-stamped trail, the thirsty grass, the sharp gorse popping like Rice Krispies, the Los Angeles Lakers purple and gold of heather and furze.

Scratchy Bottom, a clifftop valley just ahead, is where Gabriel Oak watches helplessly as his dog runs the sheep off the cliff in John Schlesinger's 1967 film adaptation of Thomas Hardy's *Far from the Madding Crowd.* The director of photography on that movie was Nicolas Roeg, who would become one of Britain's most visionary directors (*Performance, Walkabout, Don't Look Now, The Man Who Fell to Earth*). Roeg is the type of filmmaker I love (idiosyncratic, experimental, stylish) who makes the kinds of movies Dad would hate (idiosyncratic, experimental, stylish). Seven months ago, upon Roeg's death at the end of 2018, I dispatched an already written appreciation of his movies for the *Times Literary Supplement* from the maternity ward at Kettering General Hospital, while Carli rested and Kit slept next to her in a Perspex box like a guinea pig she had brought into the vet's. Dad, ever reliable, was at our house getting a carpet laid in the new nursery. (He was less reliable when I realised I had overwritten the final draft of my article and, in a panic, had to instruct him over the phone how to log on to my PC, do an auto-recovery and email the piece across. Computers are a great source of consternation and bewilderment for Dad, but then he would never get lost on a coastal walk.)

I carry on hiking. Just below me is the limestone arch of Durdle Door, unfolded from the crumpled coastline, which I used to swim through with Dad and Matt, my brother, while Mum watched from towels laid out over the pebbles and shingle. I picture the slow formation of the coastline in rapid time-lapse as the sea pounds the Portland limestone, undoing its baroque folds and sculpting the rock face into caves, then hollows, then arches and stacks. It's like Roeg is directing the projection room inside my skull, rushing the image from solid cliff face to picture-postcard archway in seconds. The sequence jumps to the burial of a Bronze Age worthy in the bell barrow humped behind me, and cross-cuts between images of his body being dug up by archaeologists over three thousand years later, his hands still clutching his special bit of pottery, and the eighteenth-century smugglers scampering down White Nothe to getaway boats on the shore, leaving chalky zigzags in the cliff face.

I know snippets of the history, the kind of thing attainable by reading (I write and teach literature, a reader by profession), but I'm totally ignorant of the present life around me – the birds circling overhead, the flowers on the slopes, the butterflies. Dad would know the names of all these things.

He is always on my mind when I make this return, seeking nostalgia but finding something closer to disruption. I take a picture of Durdle Door and send it to him. I've not walked far when my phone pings.

I wish I was there with you! Have a lovely time xx

I check my watch: 8.30 a.m. He'll be having his breakfast – a bowl of grapefruit, followed by Alpen, always, in his favourite chair at the kitchen table, a benign creature of habit.

I look around. Just in front, worrying more flowers that I don't know the names of, is a mass of black-and-white butterflies, like a chessboard that dissolves here and reforms over there. I must have seen them before as a child running for the ice cream van at the top of the hill, back when I could take it for granted that Dad had all the wildlife taken care of for us. For the first time they arrest my attention.

Since Kit was born last year, I find myself hyperaware of areas of ignorance that never used to bother me; and here, on the Jurassic Coast, a place that I see through the palimpsest of memory, I am surrounded by the unknown. The black-and-white butterflies are certainly beautiful. I'm mature enough now to see that at least. But I feel self-standing here in the sharp sea breeze, watching them. They stir something vague and incommunicable, and they remain resolutely other. To quote Hardy, 'They know Earth-secrets that know not I.'[2] Why do you find them here, in this spot, at this time of year? Surely there are logical answers to these questions. And why *that* purple flower in particular? (I might be looking at more than one kind of purple flower, I'm not sure.) I imagine Kit in a few years asking me questions I don't have answers to. Will he think me a disappointment for not knowing the names of the trees or the difference between a Swift and a Swallow or what Cuckoo spit actually is? (I always wondered why you never see these Cuckoos casually flobbing everywhere like footballers.) It bothers me that I'm conforming to the kind of stereotypically masculine characteristic (I MUST NAME, CONTAIN AND POSSESS EVERYTHING!) that in polite conversation I would disavow. But Dad always had the answers to these things, and suddenly that seems to matter. Carli would say that I am becoming my dad. Or, if she really hopes to wind me up, that I *want* to become him. I always thought I wanted to do the opposite, to go to university, unlike my parents, and pursue a literary life. Yet here I am on the edge of a cliff, wishing I had the name for the black-and-white butterflies that I am watching flutter around a purple plant that I also can't name. A dedicated reader who can't *read*. I feel useless.

A man and woman around my parents' age pass from the opposite direction in hiking boots with walking poles and other bits of professional-looking kit that I don't have (I am wearing trainers, denim shorts and a Lakers T-shirt). The man points at the butterflies and says to his partner, 'So many Marbled Whites this year!'

I am already unlocking my phone and writing a message to Dad:

Literally hundreds of Marbled Whites around. You'd love it! X

I feel a bit fraudulent, but I know it will fill Dad with pleasure (and surprise) to read my message over his cereal and see that I have named a species of butterfly I assume is plausible to see in this location at this time of year.

Again, the response comes fast.

I bet! Keep an eye out for the Lulworth Skipper. You only get it there! xx

The Lulworth Skipper. I'm struck by how he makes it sound like there's only one in the world, like the Liverpool FC skipper (I can at least identify Jordan Henderson with confidence – can Dad do *that*?). Have I gotten myself in too deep with my Marbled White deception? Maybe Dad figures I've been reading Jeremy Thomas and Richard Lewington's *The Butterflies of Britain & Ireland*, which he bought me in another futile act of encouragement. Or maybe he has seen through my performance and is calling my bluff. Either way, I am drawn by the challenge.

But looking for a Lulworth Skipper is difficult when you haven't got a clue what a Lulworth Skipper looks like, especially when there aren't other walkers within earshot pointing at butterflies while saying things like, 'So many Lulworth Skippers this year!' I turn to Google, but all signal has dispersed into the ocean. Vladimir Nabokov, the only famous lepidopterist I know (more on my side than Dad's), once said: 'It is astounding how little the ordinary person notices butterflies.'[3] I know this to be true because butterflies are suddenly everywhere now that Dad has set me the task of seeing a Lulworth Skipper. There's only one strategy for it: photograph every butterfly I see and identify them when I get home.

I complete the walk in just over three hours, heading inland at the halfway point and looping back round to the car park. I'm exhausted, satisfied with the ache in my legs and the photos on my phone, dissatisfied with the more nagging ache of my ignorance. As I approach the car, my black trainers now white, the signal returns and there's a message waiting from Dad.

> *It's a small olive butterfly with a pale horseshoe on each wing of the female. It's a bit furry. The males are duller. You'll probably think it's a moth xx*

I note the glimmer of doubt – that I'll probably think it's a moth. How he overestimates me. I'd need to know the difference between moths and butterflies for that.

At home that evening, with *The Butterflies of Britain & Ireland* laid out before me, I examine the exquisite illustrations alongside my photos. I've definitely not seen a Lulworth Skipper – looking at the drawings of them now, I realise I probably thought they were moths and didn't bother to photograph them. But I've done something much better: I have snapped one of the country's rarest butterflies! The almost extinct High Brown Fritillary! I recognise it straight away from the drawing. I hastily skim-read its entry in the book, looking for keywords like 'exceptionally rare', 'the Holy Grail of butterflying' and 'never before encountered by humans'.

I'm ringing Dad. I've hit the big time on my first attempt.

'Dad,' I say, impatient to blow his mind. 'I saw a High Brown Fritillary.'

'I don't think so, son,' he says without hesitation, which really pisses me off.

I send him the picture, but it's as he thought: a Dark Green Fritillary. A common enough sight in those parts.

In my defence, it's almost impossible to tell the difference between the High Brown Fritillary and the Dark Green Fritillary in the wild, and it's not much easier to do by photograph unless you really know your stuff. Dad cannot conceal the excitement in his voice as he talks me through the distinguishing features – the High Brown has a row of white spots not far in from the tip of the underside of the hindwing; and on the upperside of the forewing, where both the High Brown and the Dark Green have a row of black dots, the High Brown's third dot is slightly out of line with the rest. Then there are the sex brands ('The what?!'), which are more prominent on one than the other, I can't remember which . . . It's all a bit pedantic. It's all a bit Dad. But I can't believe how consistently detailed each species is, and how such a minor difference offset against such remarkable sameness (three marks here, one dot there) justifies a whole distinct species.

The key clue that mine is a Dark Green Fritillary and not a High Brown Fritillary is far simpler than all that. You don't get High Browns in Dorset.

In another case of mistaken identity, Nabokov once thought he had *discovered* a species of butterfly. At least I haven't gone that far. But I like to think this gives us something in common, me and Nabokov. (To be fair to Nabokov, *he* was nine years old when he rebranded an already named subspecies of the Poplar Admiral as *Limenitis populi rossica* Nabokov.) I'm pleased with the photograph nevertheless. My Dark Green Fritillary is a beautiful tea-stained amber with jots of black ink, its four wings fanned out like a hand of cards of the same captivating suit. But the game is already over. Butterflies are for Dad, like the rest of the natural world.

That evening, on the phone, Dad says if I keep showing an interest (even he's a realist about it . . . he knows my curiosity will not see the end of the week) there are so many places we could visit together. Maybe next summer we could go down to Dorset and spend a few days searching for butterflies, check out the old haunts. An opportunity he would cherish deeply. Maybe, I think. If I'm not too busy. It's unlikely though. You can't reverse a lifetime of indifference.

2

4-4-2

Six months later, January 2020, still groping around in my thirty-three-year-long larval state. My uncharacteristic morning of butterfly-chasing in Dorset the previous summer already a distant memory.

We are sat around the kitchen table at Mum and Dad's, a family of four again. My older brother has flown six thousand miles from Japan, where he lives with his family. I have driven forty minutes from up the road where I live with mine. I've lacked the imagination to put any greater distance between myself, my parents and my childhood home.

We have not been all together for over a year. We are waiting for Dad to speak, clasping our mugs of tea, demonstrating that naively English conviction that a hot drink can improve any situation. But we already know the worst of it – that Dad's cancer has returned after an eight-year hiatus, and that tomorrow he will undergo surgery to remove a kidney and have further biopsies taken from his makeshift ureter (part of the ingenious waterworks that replaced his cancerous bladder back in 2012). Of course, this might not prove to be the worst of it. And that is why we are here.

It's a sunny winter morning and Poppy, my parents' ten-year-old springer spaniel, is undergoing a crisis of bliss beneath the table, moving from one lap to the next, unsure whose trousers to dribble on first, presented with more options for attention than she can remember. Without comment we have taken up our original mealtime seating plan, like a football team whose manager has clung doggedly to the same formation since the 1990s even though the game has evolved and moved on. Mum and my brother sit at the heads of the table, and Dad and I are on the opposing lengths. Ever the baby of the family, I sit slightly off-centre so that I am closer to Mum (a legacy from always needing my face wiping or a spillage cleaning up). On reflection it seems reassuringly progressive of us how Mum takes the head, though also irritating how my brother takes the other head by mere virtue of being the elder, as if he is less likely to make a mess than me.

But we all know where the power really lies. Dad even has a better chair than the rest of us – bigger, with arms and a cushion tied to it. Ostensibly this is because he has had a niggly back since his rugby-playing days, but it is also simply the best place to sit, facing the window and the view of the front garden. The quiet conservatism this privilege suggests has irked me increasingly as I have grown older, but I would gladly swap for that chair, so long as I can shift it off-centre to be nearer to Mum.

The traditional assumptions of my parents' home are unspoken rather than insisted upon. That just two weeks ago I completed a five-month period of parental leave while Carli was at work, or that Carli kept her surname when we married, has never been spoken against, at least not in any strong terms, but there is an implicit bewilderment all the same. It does strike me that our table formation reveals something of the dynamics of the home I grew up in though: kind of traditional and patriarchal, but open to progress at the same time.

'It's time to get my affairs in order,' says Dad, which is ironic because he has always had his affairs in order. 'Just in case.'

He holds a piece of paper in front of him which reduces his sixty-five years on this planet to details of bank accounts, important contacts and a legend spelling out where to find necessary documents (*LHSD* for left-hand study drawer, etc.) The doctor has warned him of the risks of the surgery, has stressed all the possible outcomes. Even if the surgery goes smoothly, there is a chance of cancer being discovered elsewhere. The diagnosis is not terminal though, and Dad is a fighter who will take any option available that might extend his life. He is also a realist.

'I thought you should all have a copy of this. It will make things easier when the time comes.'

Things are worrying him, and he has been losing sleep. What is he leaving behind? Has he done enough for us all? Will his death create burdens that could be averted through careful planning now? But I'm sure there is a kind of stocktaking going on too that gives him some small comfort. He grew up on a council estate and is proud, I think, to have built a successful small business for himself and amassed things (mostly a naturalist's paraphernalia: high-end versions of all those Christmas and birthday gifts that were meant to interest us in the natural world) that might be passed on.

'I haven't named any possessions in the will. Is there anything any of you want in particular?'

My brother and I both shake our heads.

'Dad, you haven't been told that you're going to die,' I remind him.

'I know, but it all needs putting in place still. Would you like to have my watch?' Dad asks my brother.

'Maybe. I don't know. Probably not, thanks.'

'What about the butterfly collection, Ben?'

He has remembered that day in Dorset and the very brief conversation it yielded, has probably been clinging to it ever since. His butterflies are in a special cabinet in the room next door, pinned into white foamboard in sealed drawers, perfect creatures in undisturbed fields of snow, a habitat in which no sun-loving butterfly belongs. Mostly antique, I think, bought at auction, but probably not all of them. The thought makes me uneasy. In the same room are other sources of unease. Accoutrements of a rural upbringing, of a working-class boy who trespassed and poached and collected with his dad, trying to be the version of masculinity passed down to him.

I stare at the table, which is glazing over and starting to look unmistakably wobbly. Dad notices my change in composure. He's always had his eye on me.

'How about we take a break from all this,' he says, and I flee the room.

I slip into Dad's study. It's a small room, and there is something vintage about it. The furniture is old – the partners' desk with the faded leather top and columns of drawers, the mahogany cabinets and cases containing collectibles and curios, the unsettling taxidermy (an owl bought from an antiques fair; a Sparrowhawk whose life, ironically, Dad had tried to save). The photographs too are reminders of times gone by – Grandma and Granddad as youngsters, probably half the age I am now but looking much older; black-and-white photographs of Dad's school rugby XV, back when he had a curly mop and didn't quite fit his own Mick Jagger features; secondary-school photos of my brother and me – one where I've got two lines like speed indicators shaved into my eyebrow, as if the thoughts going on above were especially quick; another where my brother has 1990s boy band style curtains, the photo sitting on the window sill by the room's curtains in a double-curtain effect. We are both in the same green school blazer, the uniform of an underperforming state school that was, in the end, closed down. Even the PC in here is a novelty – an indestructible tower from the early noughties that sounds like it is going to take off when you turn it on, still running on the fumes of Windows 7, still thinking like Encarta 98.

Dad isn't old-fashioned generally, but there is something old-school about his connection to the natural world. He has spent his whole life in the fields and woods of Northamptonshire and seems to have contained them between these four walls. Dead birds, dead butterflies, his own father's collection of pressed four-leaf clovers. It is the sporting element of this relationship that has always bothered me, from the oxidised fishing trophy that my great-granddad won in 1923 to the wooden pigeon decoys on top of the book cabinet, eyeballing you with their unsettling sideways stares. The study is sensibility embodied. Even the smell of leather from the coats hanging behind the door and the aroma of polish are the scents of a confusing manliness.

The strongest smells come from behind a locked cupboard door. The key for this is hidden on the ledge above a row of coat pegs where, as a kid, I couldn't reach it. Now that I *can* reach it, what it leads to doesn't interest me: a tight space that smells like WD-40, lit by an exposed bulb. Wooden clubs, leather satchels, bubble wrap, ear defenders, cloths, chemicals in jars. Standing tall in the middle of this are two steel cabinets, the keys for which Dad keeps on his person at all times. Inside are his guns. He has owned countless shotguns over the years, using them to shoot game and clays, but also doing them up and selling them on for a profit, keeping five or so at any one time. For everything that we have in common, this cupboard is the aporia in our bond, hidden away like something unspeakable.

I turn my back on it. On the other side of the room, in the corner, is the butterfly cabinet. I have no interest in butterflies beyond the confused respect felt by most Nabokov admirers (denizens of the reading room rather than the outdoors). Why did Dad just mention his collection at the kitchen table? It's like he keeps faith, after more than thirty years, that one of his sons might come into his naturalist's passions before his time is up. But where did the contents of the collection come from? Is it ethical? Is it even legal? It must contain so much that I don't know or understand, like inscrutable Lulworth Skippers that I won't be able to recognise. What makes me most uncomfortable, though, is that I am attracted to it without being able to say why.

It's easier to move on to the book cabinet. I know books. I have dedicated my adult life to them. Even here though things are alien – still it's all guns (books on gun collecting and repairing) and natural history. I was going to say that there is no literature in the artistic sense of the word – no fiction or poetry – but then I would be dismissing the shelves of Denys Watkins-Pitchford books.

Better known to his readers as 'BB' (a nom de plume taken from his favourite lead shot for shooting geese), Watkins-Pitchford, the naturalist and children's writer, is better known to me as Dad's favourite author (possibly second-favourite, behind Wilbur Smith). I can see he wrote *a lot* of books – some sixty or so by the look of things – of both fiction and non-fiction. The titles on Dad's shelves range from the intriguing (*Wild Lone*; *Dark Estuary*) to the daft and twee (*Mr Bumstead*; *Be Quiet and Go A-Angling*). I begin taking them down at random and perusing the information on their jackets. I learn that BB was born in 1905 and studied art in Paris and at the Royal College between the wars, after which he taught for eighteen years at Rugby School, and that he spent the majority of his life in our home county, Northamptonshire, born and raised. The book blurbs paint the portrait of a famous naturalist who was sensitive to the rhythms of the countryside; an observer of the secret lives of the creatures that inhabit it. He has 'no contemporary equal as a writer, illustrator and compiler of books about the English countryside', claims one.[1] What strikes me more than dust-jacket hyperbole is the apparent sense that he was writing for a nostalgic mid-century readership that felt threatened by the aggressive onrush of modernity. 'There is a growing need for the "quiet fields" in this noisy, restless world,' declares the book flap for *The Quiet Fields*, and the foreword to *A Summer on the Nene* reassures the reader that 'in my story you will find no hazardous adventures, no frantic endeavours'.[2] Well, that's a relief, I think. 'It is a simple account of the voyage of three people in a river cruiser, who found in the meandering stream a peace and silence which is now unknown upon the roads of England.' In a similar vein, *The Idle Countryman* is 'guaranteed to make the reader homesick' (like the reader should be grateful for *that*!). Sometimes the imagined reader is comically exact: 'This latest BB book is for those who love the countryside and country pursuits, although through force of circumstances they may be townsmen, or temporary exiles from these shores.'[3] Not for me, then.

Running my eye along the shelves, I want the books in Dad's collection to tell me something I don't already know about the man I love. The titles that are familiar are the children's ones – *The Little Grey Men* and *Brendon Chase* made BB's name (the former was awarded the Carnegie Medal and the latter was once immensely popular and adapted for TV in the 1980s), but the ones about Bill Badger also ring a bell. I trust Dad recognises that books like *Monty Woodpig & His Bubblebuzz Car* are intended for children, though even the books for adults imply a reader yearning for a childhood spent rambling, climbing trees, collecting birds' eggs and butterflies. Basically, my dad's childhood.

The only BB book I remember Dad talking about specifically was some kind of bedside companion. Now I can see that BB published several such companions: *The Sportsman's Bedside Book*, *The Countryman's Bedside Book*, *The Fisherman's Bedside Book*, *The Shooting Man's Bedside Book*, *The Naturalist's Bedside Book.* Evidently BB is the man for putting other men to sleep (one book claims to be 'designed for casual reading', and here I can feel Dad's and my sensibilities diverging again),[4] but they are not at Dad's bedside at all, standing sentry in his study, looking out for the unlikely approach of a reader. There are anthologies on Dad's shelves too, and I learn that BB wrote reams of journalism on country matters, including butterflies, the majority published in

Shooting Times (a magazine that my brother and I always teased Dad for purchasing from the newsagent alongside, for us, issues of *Slam*, *Basketball XXL*, *Kerrang!*, *Q*, *NME*, *The Source*, *Empire* and *Official UK PlayStation Magazine*).

If the countryside and nature belong to Dad, literature belongs to me, at least in the ecosystem of our family. Books are *my* obsession – reading them, studying them, writing about them, even writing a couple of them myself. In fact, I can see my books on the top shelf of Dad's cabinet resting above *Modern Wildfowling*, *The Complete Book of British Birds* and *The Millennium Atlas of Butterflies in Britain and Ireland*. My work as a literary critic and lecturer is opaque to Dad. He didn't go to university (not the done thing for a young man of his background in the early 1970s), and his unmerited pride in what I do is only increased by its foreignness, though ultimately I reckon he thinks it all a bit mysterious, maybe even a little suspect. I feel guilty that I have not done a better job of sharing my love of literature with Dad, that I haven't tried turning him on to the stuff that has changed *my* life, like he has tried to do with me. I have preferred to keep it all a secret instead. It's easier that way. On the rare occasions that we have attempted talking about literature, we have got into arguments born of miscommunication and suppressed judgement. And yet Dad is the only person I know (possibly the only person in the world) to read my first academic book in its entirety. I had no idea he was reading it and was stunned when, in the middle of a conversation about something else, he casually mentioned that he had finished it. 'You mean you read the *whole thing*?' 'Every word.' It perhaps reveals my lack of scholarly conviction that my immediate reaction was to apologise to him. I cringed at the thought of Dad slogging his way through it.

Dad thinks that I relate to literature in ways he will never understand, but he also feels that I overthink it. He says things like 'I just want to enjoy a book. I read for pleasure', which is meant antagonistically, as if I am up to something else. 'I like a good story,' he says, as if I don't. In our discussion of my scholarly book (a conversation ten times more uncomfortable than my PhD viva voce – the oral examination where a doctoral student defends their thesis in front of other academics) he asked what I meant by 'the ethical value of literature', something that I had made claims for in my book. Rather than offer any useful response, I crumbled and put the impossibility of clarification down to the fact that we were coming at it from such different angles. Really, of course, the failing was all mine. I think I said something clichéd about literature embodying a peculiar kind of thinking and how it makes us see anew. 'I don't understand how that works,' he said, swiftly puncturing my already insecure intellectual pretensions. 'I can honestly say a book has never changed how I view the world.' 'Then you're not reading very good books,' I said, defeated.

But I'm not holding my book when Dad startles me by coming into the study, not at all looking like a man in need of surgery. No, I am holding *Confessions of a Carp Fisher* by BB (which begs the pressing question: what does a carp fisher have to confess?).

'Would you like those for your collection one day?' he asks.

What's with this sudden urge to give everything away? I have too many books at home already and too little space. I also have no interest in natural history, or in how to fit a new stock to a gun, and I certainly have no interest in BB. For Dad, I guess, BB is an enchanting writer of rural pursuits, while to my mind he is a nostalgic documentarian with low literary value.

'No, thank you,' I say.

But, of course, I have never even read him.

3

Our Fathers' Studies

Another son in another father's study. One year after his father's passing, at sunset, Dmitri enters the study in his parents' suite at the Montreux Palace Hotel and closes the window. It is September, but the temperature drops fast in the hills of Montreux, Switzerland. This is where he sleeps now when he visits his mother. The room holds phantoms of his father's quiddity: a beautifully detailed butterfly hidden in the design of a lightshade on an old floor lamp (you have to be a close reader like his father, a fondler of details, to spot it); a dusty print of Fra Angelico's *L'Annunciazione* leaning against the back of the desk, which if you look closely reveals a note in pencil, in his father's hand, describing the angel's baroque wings in butterfly terms:

> *A recollection of* Iphiclides podalirius *with a slight dash of* Papilio machaon *and perhaps a hint of the day-flying moth* Panaxia quadripunctaria. *The two blackish stripes of each 'wing' correspond to the pattern of* I. podalirius *in the natural position of rest.*[1]

Dmitri finds reams of undeveloped film and boxes containing sketches for scientific studies, notes for an unwritten book on butterflies in art, and most of an unpublished novel. Gone is the lectern at which his father used to start each day, writing on his feet until gravity nibbled his calves,[2] at which moment he'd move into a horizontal position on the couch in the corner, filling scores of made-to-order Bristol index cards with sublime prose. There are boxes of blank cards in the room, hinting in their pristine whiteness at stories that could have been.

Dmitri's father, rather than mine, was responsible for any short-lived gleam of interest I might have shown in butterflies. Vladimir Nabokov was a writer who could change how you viewed the world. Stylish, experimental, aggressively literary and intellectual but funny with it, provocative, morally complex, a dandy – the antithesis, at least I assumed, of BB, Dad's favourite butterfly-loving writer. But if Nabokov was obsessed with butterflies, then there must be some merit in thinking about them. Or so I thought for a passing moment in my twenties, when I first consumed his work and became intrigued by the butterfly themes and imagery. But the connection between butterflies and literary inspiration was not assured. Being interested in Lepidoptera had never given Dad any literary inclination; more dispiritingly it would never give me Nabokovian talent. So I didn't follow up on this potential meeting of our sensibilities.

Butterflies were something that Vladimir Nabokov did share with *his* father. As a boy growing up in the splendour of the family's country estate near Siversky, south of Saint Petersburg, Nabokov was surrounded by butterflies, living and dead. 'There was a magic room in our country house with my father's collection,' he writes, 'the old faded butterflies of his childhood, but precious to me beyond words'.[3] His own father's study and library haunt his work, whether described in the non-fiction and interviews, or emerging in pupal form in the private rooms of his fictional characters. The most direct depiction comes in Nabokov's strikingly original autobiography, *Speak, Memory*, where he recalls 'the *objets d'art* of crystal or veined stone [. . .] the glinting family photographs; the huge, mellowly illumined Perugino; the small, honey-bright Dutch oils'.[4] Whereas my dad's study is decorated with generic watercolours of rural scenes bought from car boot sales, Nabokov's father's study had a portrait of his mother painted by Léon Bakst. To say they came from different worlds would be an understatement.

It's almost comic now to read of this privileged boy raised with private tutors and beloved nannies, collecting specimens in the family's meadows by day, cracking impenetrable chess puzzles by night, being woken at 8 a.m. in their city house in Saint Petersburg and taken down to the large family library to greet his father after his regular morning fencing duel (he sparred *in* the library).[5] Here they were ringed in by fat armchairs, boxing gloves and a punching ball, and book-lined walls holding an eclectic collection, ranging from expensive works on Lepidoptera to the novels of H. G. Wells (a family acquaintance whom Nabokov met as a boy).[6] Nabokov's father was a prominent member of the Constitutional Democratic Party, and the Bolshevik revolution sent the Nabokovs fleeing Russia, never to return. Twelve years later, Nabokov would find his father's copy of Wells's *The War of the Worlds*, with his *ex libris* pasted inside, in a Berlin bookstall.[7] This is like something from one of his fictions, where pattern and fate are artful facts of life, where life and art are inseparable.

From the window of *his* father's room – another magical room of private sensibility where time is traversed and the life-worn past folds into futures unlived – Dmitri can see a small group of mountains, which he had planned to walk one day with his father. They wanted 'to sample the panorama at close quarters at last, to see what butterflies were available, and to look back on Montreux from those slopes'.[8] But they were never to make this imagined excursion.

4

Dance with My Father

Later that evening, I'm sitting in the living room with Dad, just the two of us, pretending to watch TV. He is in the chair nearest the telly (even here he has *his* chair) and I am slumped on the sofa with my feet stretched out, in my early thirties but never able to feel like anything other than a child in this house. I've been hanging around all day trying to tell him how I feel about him, but I can't find the right moment or the right words. I think it might give him strength ahead of tomorrow's surgery if I say something; and it will haunt me if something goes wrong and I haven't said it. I run through how I might put it while we talk about everything else and people do some cooking on the TV.

'Sometimes, in bed at night,' says Dad, 'I play that Luther Vandross song on YouTube on my iPad. "Dance with My Father".'

It's quite a bit of information to compute: Dad using his iPad after a lifelong struggle with computers and technology, Dad navigating YouTube, even just Dad in his bed. Dad listening to Luther isn't so strange. He loves soul music and

R&B – the only stuff he listens to, one of his few concessions to American popular culture. (Just before Christmas, when I bought a new record player, he let me pinch his old vinyls from the attic, a decent collection of Marvin Gaye, Stevie Wonder, Earth, Wind & Fire, Isaac Hayes, Gladys Knight, Al Green, the original Motown Chartbusters compilations and others.)

'I know the one,' I say.

'It reminds me of when your granddad was in the nursing home.'

It's a hard connection to make – Luther, a Black man from America, the king of smooth R&B, and my grandfather, a white bricklayer from Northants with a notorious temper, quick to aggression, slow to anything American or contemporary. I remember Granddad as an unpredictable man, hard as nails, his cheeks corpuscle-red and a gnarled scar on his forehead from where he got hit by shrapnel in the war. He always seemed to wear the same clothes – dirty work jeans and a tired knitted jumper, scruffy because if he wasn't doing odd jobs then he was poaching in the fields and woods with the dog. I can remember visiting him in the hospital (I would've been eleven) after a series of strokes, this bull of a man reduced to baby-like vulnerability, yet still frightening somehow.

'I thought he was in the hospital in Milton Keynes,' I say.

'He was, but they moved him to a home for the final few weeks. You saw him there.'

I can't remember, but it was twenty-one years ago.

'He wanted to try sitting up in an armchair, so I gathered him in my arms and lifted him from the bed.'

Dad continues to stare at the TV screen as he says this.

'I held him and we just danced. I'll never forget it. Holding him close like that. He had no say, really, but I like to think he enjoyed it.'

There is so much more to be said – about longing for his father's love and approval, about the confoundments of masculinity, about a history of violence – but now isn't the time. I don't know whether to laugh or cry at the image of Granddad in my dad's arms, dancing, something that could only have occurred when he was in a state of total helplessness.

'All I wanted to do was dance with him. I think that's what I'll want to do with you.'

Or did he say 'I think that's what I want to do with you,' as in right now, here in the living room? I'm not sure which would be worse: that he is starting to imagine his own end, or that he might be suggesting we start dancing.

The thought of picking *my* dad up without his co-operation is impossible to me. He is so much bigger – at least a couple of inches taller, at least three stone heavier – an imposing man, robust and powerful. He has always been the larger and stronger of us, even with chronic fatigue, which began in his forties, and then cancer. I have spent my whole adult life in universities questioning gender roles and stereotypes, sceptical of constructions like 'masculinity', and yet I have to confess that I wish I was as big and strong as him, like it matters even though I tell myself it doesn't. I'm stupidly proud of the photos in the family albums from his rugby and boxing days. Handsome and masculine. (I used to play rugby too and Dad never missed a match, but I was never going to surpass him when it came to matters of physicality.) Even if I try to imagine Dad hospitalised like Granddad, I can only picture *him* picking *me* up for a dance.

'I listen to that song and think of him.'

I can feel the words I want to say like a physical compulsion welling up from my chest to the back of my throat, where they get stuck. *I love you.* I want him to know how I admire him. *I love you.* I want him to know how fortunate I feel to have had a dad like him. *I love you.* It is all so much more straightforward than his relationship with his father was. Yes, we have fought and argued, butted heads, but we have also loved intensely.

Maybe none of it is straightforward though, because I find I can't speak. Perhaps that is part of what I am trying to tell him.

'I know that I don't need to say it,' I start.

'I know,' he says, still looking at the screen.

Well, that simplifies things. But still, I need to say it.

'The surgery will go fine tomorrow, and soon this will be behind you, so I'm not saying this like it's the end, because it isn't. But you've been the best dad and I am so grateful.'

He closes his eyes for a second, still facing the TV, as if he is trying to lock it all in for future sustenance.

'Thank you.'

5

Terminal

On the last day of March, just a week after the UK has entered a national lockdown in response to the outbreak of a new disease no one had heard of before, our worst fears are confirmed. We're not allowed to leave our houses, so Dad breaks the news on FaceTime, sitting beside Mum on the living room sofa, wearing braces over his shoulders, the weight already starting to fall from him. The details are lost in a fog of despair: despite the successful surgery in January, the diagnosis is terminal. A matter of months to live if he responds well to treatment . . . if he doesn't, weeks.

I cry. Dad cries. Mum cries. Everything falls apart.

6

The Early Spring Fliers

In May the government eases some of the lockdown restrictions. Now you can meet one person from another household, outdoors, for recreational purposes. I am quick to take advantage of the opportunity to sit with Dad in the garden. There isn't anything very recreational about it though – no recreational sports, even the drugs (of which there are suddenly a lot) aren't recreational.

'How is Kit doing?' asks Dad, sitting on a patio chair several metres from me, like we are about to conduct a job interview, to which, bizarrely, I have decided to wear a mask.

'He's fine,' I say. 'You know, he adapts to anything.'

Truth is, I'm wondering if we are failing Kit. Carli and I have transitioned online for our work, so we are home full time; and with the nursery closed, Kit, sixteen months old, is with us around the clock. Life is uncanny: our home is our office, CBeebies is Kit's childminder, and my parents (ordinarily one of the main sources of Kit's childcare) now require *my* care. In some ways it is a relief to have him out of nursery though, what with Dad's immune system in the process of being obliterated. I am Mum and Dad's lifeline to the outside world, responsible for getting Dad to the hospital for treatments and appointments, and generally on call in case of an emergency. If Kit was to pick anything up from nursery, I'm not sure what we would do.

Carli and I have Kit on a rota – one of us works for an hour or two while the other looks after him and then we swap, though most of the time he has his face glued to the TV screen just as we have our faces glued to our computers.

'I wish I could see him,' says Dad. I try calculating how many weeks it is since he last held his grandson – sixteen, more? But the most difficult thought travels in the opposite direction: will he ever hold him again?

'How are you, Dad?'

'Ah, you know. Not as bad as I was a couple of weeks ago, before the chemo.'

He was started on a course of immunotherapy but deteriorated so quickly that they switched him to chemotherapy. The rapid change might just have saved his life, for now.

I attempt to read his face for the things he isn't telling me. I can't get past how tufty his thick white eyebrows are (making him look a bit like the owl in his study), and how red his cheeks. We chat for a while, but I can see he is flagging. He bows his head, catching a breather. I'm not sure what to say. It's hard to know when to turn to ultimate discussions – there are so many questions only he can answer, things about the past that I want to record before it's too late, and deeper questions about his thoughts and feelings, about his experiences, that I want to understand. But how to start?

I pass him my phone.

'Here, take a look at these.'

Dad picks his glasses out of his coat pocket and rests his chin in his spare hand.

I have been taking photos for him. An unexpected by-product of a new routine. Around 3 p.m., when Kit wakes from his afternoon nap, I strap him to my front in a baby carrier and we go for a walk. It's my government-sanctioned dose of daily exercise, but it is also an attempt to break Kit's imprisonment and convince myself that we aren't failing him. Strolling the fields near to home I have found myself doing something strange. It was involuntary at first. Each time a butterfly fluttered into view I gravitated towards it until I realised I was pointing it out to Kit, who showed about as much interest as I ever had towards my dad's persistent pointing (the difference being that Kit was physically held hostage, a length that even Dad never resorted to). Kit is like a butterfly himself on these walks, facing frontward while pinned to me – the sling's pouch is the thorax and abdomen, his legs and arms splayed outwards like four wings. Each day that we returned, the urge to spot butterflies became more pressing, until we were catching askance looks from dog walkers as we waded into stinging nettles or stood staring, seemingly without purpose, at a hedge, scared of missing anything, as if some exceptional species might be right in front of us without me realising, like the unseen Lulworth Skippers on the Dorset coast last summer.

'The first one is a Peacock, right?'

'Yes,' he nods. 'One of the most beautiful of our common species.'

Oh, common is it? I think.

'See how the eyespots on the upperside of the hindwings look like big old owl eyes if you look at it upside down, and the abdomen and thorax look like a beak? Predators think it is an owl looking out from the hedge or tree and back off. Nature is ingenious like that.'

He shows the picture to me from across the patio. I had thought of it more as David Bowie than an owl – its glam-rock eyespots smudged in purplish-blue eyeliner like Ziggy Stardust. They are everywhere this spring, doing their hazy cosmic jive, getting down in my internal soundtrack to 'Starman'. Searching around online, trying to confirm what species it was so that I could announce it to Dad, I had found a super-close-up image of the scales on the wing. Seen at that magnification they are like the pixels on a television screen and made the Peacock look like the opening shots of the cityscape in *Blade Runner*. But I don't say any of this to Dad.

He scrolls across to the next image.

'Ah, beautiful,' he says. 'Do you know what this is?'

'A Brimstone,' I say, like it's nothing, a short time spent on Butterfly Conservation's website starting to pay off. (Dad introduced me to this, first guiding me to the local branch's page, where there is an ongoing record of members' sightings – he checks it most days. It was on the main website that I discovered that what I had always thought was a Red Admiral is in fact a Small Tortoiseshell. I keep that to myself.)

'Well done.'

I take a triumphant sip of my tea.

'Male or female?'

I sigh, unsure whether I have said 'for fuck's sake' out loud or kept it in my head.

'There's a difference?'

'Oh yes. A lot of species are sexually dimorphic.'

'Right?'

'It means the male and female appear different. This is a male. They are more yellow.'

What I *had* noticed was how its pale-green complexion and jagged wing perfectly mimic a leaf.

'It's the yellowy male that some people think inspired the name butterfly.'

'Why?' I ask and feel stupid straight away. 'Butter,' I say. 'Got it.'

I assign the Brimstone 'Walk on By' by Isaac Hayes, from the album *Hot Buttered Soul*, which I have recently discovered in Dad's vinyl collection. Walk on by is exactly what the Brimstone's melted camouflage is hoping you will do, but once spotted its freshness only inspires you to stop and stare.

'The first Brimstone is always a sign that spring has sprung, at least in my mind. It will sound daft to you, but I'll miss the seasons.'

It doesn't sound daft at all.

'You can't take these things for granted,' he adds.

The seasons have been much on my mind too. I'm busy reading Ali Smith's quartet of novels, each named after a season, in preparation for a review I have been commissioned to write of the last instalment (*Summer*), but also for an academic paper I have been working away at for months. The latter is about the affinities between the work of Smith and H. G. Wells and how they write about sublime experiences. Again, I don't know how to explain any of this to Dad. It would require a degree of self-reflection that I can't handle, a dispensing of self-consciousness and embarrassment that I have never come close to achieving, and a way of expressing myself that I have never managed to compose outside of my head or on the page.

But then I am myself a total beginner when it comes to the natural world, if not quite illiterate. To me, entering the fields, meadows and woodland around my house is a similar experience to the one I would imagine Dad encountering if he opened a page of *Ulysses*. The habitat is recognisable (there are words and sentences and paragraphs and chapters and dialogue and description), just as in the field I can see trees and shrubs and hedgerows and flowers and birds and butterflies. But where one sees the general, the other sees the particular. Description is vision, and without the terms for these things, how can I grasp their particularity? The overlooked Lulworth Skippers on the Dorset cliffs last year are like missed allusions and intertexts that might give life to a larger, richer text, if only I could see them. Nabokov once referred to his encounters with butterflies as a kind of reading, or rereading.[1] I know nothing of appropriate habitats or larval foodplants or nectar sources or hatching times, the key components of informed butterflying as outlined in the few bits I've read. As far as I'm concerned, a caterpillar's main sources of nutrition include lollipops, cupcakes and salami, as per Eric Carle's entomological primer, *The Very Hungry Caterpillar*, which Kit and I have been devouring during our long days at home.

'I guess nature has a way of telling us that time must pass,' says Dad.

'But it comes back around,' I say, hopefully.

'What's next?'

He looks at my photos of various white butterflies, all of which I would lump together as Cabbage Whites. But he describes the subtle differences between the Small White, Large White, Green-veined White and Orange Tip. He shows me how the veins on the underside of the Green-veined White's wings show up green (the name is very literal), like someone has carefully drawn around them with a felt-tip pen. I figure the whites as the John, Paul, George and Ringo of the British butterfly kingdom – from a distance they're the uniform Beatles of the early teenybop years with their matching haircuts and outfits, while on closer inspection they become the four distinct characters on the rooftop of the Apple Corps headquarters in 1969, playing 'Don't Let Me Down' to the crowd gathered on Savile Row. And, like the Beatles, they're *everywhere*. (Dad was never a rock and roll man. But it turns out there is a forgotten Beatle too, the Wood White, one of Dad's favourites, though apparently I need to go to special locations to see the Stuart Sutcliffe of the whites.)

The last two images are the ones I am really excited about. Orange Tips. An attractive white butterfly that has dipped the tips of its forewings in the marmalade pot (Kit and I have been watching the first Paddington movie at least once a day) and dresses the underside of its hindwings in one of those floral Ted Baker shirts that middle-aged men wear to feel a bit funky.

'You know what this is?' he says, showing me the final image. I have been waiting for this moment.

'Yes, a *female* Orange Tip.'

'Well done,' he says. 'You do know about dimorphism then.'

'I guess.'

The female doesn't have the orange tips of the male on its forewings, so it looks just like the other whites when its wings are open. But when closed they show the same Ted Baker design as the male and have the same exquisite off-white marbling on the upperside of the hindwings. A thing of beauty, like a glitter of snow out of time with the seasons, dancing in my mind to Prince's ethereal 'Sometimes It Snows in April'.

Tramping around the fields, trying to forget about work and COVID, mostly thinking about Dad, I glimpse something unexpected, a possible way forward. I chant new names like Orange Tip and Small Tortoiseshell under my breath, the surprising celebrities of our spring, while Kit, in a parallel world, quietly chants 'bus', 'digger-tractor' and 'bin-men truck'. Sometimes he disarms me by exclaiming 'buttie-fly', pointing with the wet L of sucked thumb and index finger. An actual celebrity has been on the wing this spring too – Britain's most famous vicar, Reverend Richard Coles. We live in his parish, and he gives us a smile as Kit and I pick our way out of some thorn-and-nettle trap and step into his path one sunny morning. Fleeting distractions from the sudden pounding realisation that Dad is going to die.

'Fantastic,' says Dad, leaning forward and grimacing as he passes the phone to me. He sits back and takes a few seconds, eyes closed.

'You okay?'

'Fine.' He opens his eyes and smiles at me unconvincingly.

I'm tense with unspoken thoughts and desires, my chest aching with things I want to say, things I want to ask, without knowing exactly what they are. Inside is a chaos of questions that I want to distil into a simple three-word statement – *I love you.*

'I saw there's a book coming out soon about the Purple Emperor, by Matthew Oates,' he says, 'if you need any gift ideas for Father's Day or anything else.'

Father's Day. I'm glad to hear him talking of the future, even if he isn't going to acknowledge how tenuous a future it is. Maybe he is also trying to engage me in books, once again attempting a meeting of our interests.

'I'll make a note,' I say, typing it on my phone. 'The Purple Emperor. Is that a good butterfly then?'

His eyes fill with more life than I have seen in a while, as if to say *you don't know the half of it.*

'Oh yes.'

'Okay, cool,' I say.

For a minute we relax quietly into the background score of the walnut tree rustling on my parents' lawn.

'There's something I want to talk to you about,' says Dad, breaking the spell. I sit up, alert.

'Okay.'

'I've been thinking about my shotguns.' This catches me off guard. 'I need to figure out what to do with them.'

'Just get rid of them,' I say, like it is so simple.

'The thing is, only someone with a licence can keep them.'

'Sell them to people with licences,' I say, wanting to leave it there.

'I did wonder if you would want to keep any of them, seeing as they are so meaningful to me.'

'I think Carli would have something to say about that,' I say, passing the buck.

'And if you got a licence, it would mean you could keep them until new owners were found. Otherwise, they'll just get taken away. Or I suppose I can arrange for one of my shooting friends to look after them until they can be sold . . . '

'Do that then.'

We both take sips from our tea (I have to lift my mask every time I do this), which has gone cold. Dad is frowning.

'Don't bite my head off,' he says, a leading statement that I find makes a person's head look instantly biteable, 'but why wouldn't you just get a licence and safeguard them? What's your issue with it?'

Ordinarily this is the point where we would go at it. I'd blast Dad with my muddle of semi-formed convictions, he'd say whatever the contrary thing to say is, and we'd go around in circles, neither of us willing to retreat. But I glance at him and just think how impossibly vulnerable he looks.

'I don't want them in the house,' I say.

'That's okay,' he says, his energy spent. 'I understand.'

7

The Gift (i)

One thing you will find in both my father's study and Vladimir Nabokov's father's study is a Browning – a shotgun in *my* father's case, a revolver in Nabokov's. In *Speak, Memory* Nabokov recalls 'the heavy black Browning my father kept in the upper right-hand drawer of his desk. I knew that pistol as well as I knew all the other, more salient, things in his study.'[1] Guns were ever present in Nabokov's life, from the pistols loaded with sticks he used in duels with his all-action cousin Yuri to the handgun (likely a Browning M1900) carried by Véra, his wife, in her handbag during their Weimar years, in case the Bolsheviks came for her husband (but also, she claimed, to kill Trotsky). She also kept a Browning .38 calibre in the glove compartment of their car as they drove across America in the 1950s searching for rare species of butterfly (on her pistol licence application she wrote, 'For protection while travelling in isolated parts of the country in the course of entomological research').[2]

Guns are tightly coiled in the logic of Nabokov's work – whether it's Margot turning Albinus's gun on him in the dénouement to *Laughter in the Dark*, or Humbert Humbert tracking down the seventeen-year-old Lolita with a pistol in his pocket and shooting his nemesis, Quilty (Nabokov researched gun catalogues in preparation for writing *Lolita* and was especially interested in the history of the Colt revolver).[3] Nowhere is a gun more significant in Nabokov's fiction than in *Pale Fire*, where the murder of John Shade evokes the murder of Nabokov's father, V. D. Nabokov, who on 28 March 1922 was shot dead at the Berlin Philharmonic Hall. The assassins were in fact there to kill the liberal historian and politician Pavel Milyukov, but V. D. fought one of the gunmen to the ground and took his weapon, only to be fatally shot by the other. Nabokov, twenty-two years of age, was reading the Russian poet Aleksandr Blok in the family's Berlin apartment when the unthinkable news was delivered over the phone. In a diary entry, he remembers how earlier in the day on which his father was killed, he 'had traced on the fogged-up carriage window [of a train] the word "happiness" – and every letter trickled downwards in a bright line, a damp wriggle. Yes, my happiness has run . . . '[4]

Nabokov's recollection of the words dripping down the windowpane is of course a recognition of transience in the immediate wake of his father's death, but it is also the dawning of a new unstable relationship to language. How to write now that the anchor points of meaning will never be the same? In May of that year, Nabokov wrote a letter to his mother from Cambridge, where he was completing his studies: 'At times it's all so oppressive I could go out of my mind – but I have to hide. There are things and feelings no one will ever find out.'[5] Eventually Nabokov would face the conundrum of how to write about his father, and he would find the answer in butterflies.

*

Perhaps butterflies had always been the answer. In 1908, when Nabokov was nine, his father was sentenced to three months' solitary confinement in Saint Petersburg's Kresty prison for signing the Vyborg Manifesto against the Tsarist government, as well as an additional charge relating to his editorship of the Constitutional Democratic Party's newspaper. From there he sent secret missives to Elena, Nabokov's mother, scribbled on toilet paper and conveyed by a paid-off guard. Rather than the usual kinds of contraband, the young Nabokov sent back the other way a butterfly in one of his mother's notes. 'Tell him,' V. D. Nabokov wrote in response, 'all I see in the prison yard are Brimstones and Cabbage Whites.'[6]

Thirty years later, Nabokov netted a pair of blue-washed butterflies at an altitude of four thousand feet, above the village of Moulinet in the Alps. He had just completed his Russian masterpiece, *Dar* (translated into English as *The Gift* in 1963), the last novel he would write in his mother tongue, regarded by many critics as one of the greatest Russian novels of the twentieth century, and now he was fulfilling his childhood dream of discovering a new species of butterfly. Two years later, in 1940, he would narrowly escape the Nazis as he fled France for the US (Véra was Jewish, and the ship they fled on was the *SS Champlain*, which was blown up by a German mine on its return trip). Once there, Nabokov was able to confirm via the American Museum of Natural History in New York that the specimens he had caught that day in Moulinet had indeed never been named before. He called them *Lysandra cormion*.

Brian Boyd, Nabokov's biographer, suggests that it was this discovery in the Alps in 1938 that prompted Nabokov to return to *The Gift* in the spring of 1939 and write an addendum, in which he extends the narrative and themes of the novel's second chapter, and writes indirectly about his father and their shared love of Lepidoptera. This was published over twenty years after Nabokov's death, when it was named 'Father's Butterflies'. This time, however, the act of naming an original species was done by his son, Dmitri, who in the final years of the century named and translated Nabokov's addendum from Russian into English – what Boyd calls '*his* longest tribute to *his* father's butterflies'.[7] Dmitri – an opera-singing, mountain-climbing playboy with a passion for fast cars and aeroplanes – had been groomed to be his father's English translator from a young age and translated a number of his Russian works, feats of literary artistry in themselves. But we all spend our adult lives translating our parents one way or another, making sense of them in new contexts, asking them to communicate across time, to speak to and for different selves.

Dmitri was a great defender of his father, taking on even the most subtle slights against him, sometimes with comic disproportion. Like the applicant in a job interview who answers the classic question, 'What is one of your weaknesses?' with a strength ('I'm too organised . . . I work too hard . . . '), Dmitri confesses that 'if Father had a defect, it was an openness to and trust of others, a goodness bordering sometimes on ingenuousness, an instinctive assumption that others were as good as he until proven otherwise'.[8] He also says that his father 'was the most totally honourable individual I have ever met' and (justifiably) counters criticisms of his father's work by pointing out the offending party's literary inferiority. Every child has either said or heard another child say, 'My dad could beat up your dad.' Dmitri could in full sincerity say, 'My dad could *write better* than your dad' and win the argument every time, not that it would carry the same weight. I say all this here now because I know I too must avoid the risk of idealising my father, and I will probably fail. For example, my dad could definitely have beaten up Dmitri's dad.

II

Purple Emperor

8

If You Go Down to the Woods Today

Once upon a time, at the edge of the deep dark forest, there was an old house as round as a stone, where the toll-keeper who guarded the way used to live. Down at the bottom of the garden, beyond the shimmering pond and the bowing willow tree, stood an enclosure of nets the height of a grown-up. Inside the enclosure were twigs and leaves, and on these leaves were some jewels. The jewels were the shape of a jelly mould, but you wouldn't see them unless you knew where to look, for they were no bigger than a grain of rice.

They were put there by the mysterious creature who lived in the round house (not the toll-keeper, for this was many moons later). If you had gone to the woods that morning you might have seen him. A gnome-like man without collarbones carrying a walking stick curled like a wizard's staff. He used this stick to part the branches of a very particular kind of tree in which the treasure was hidden. You might have seen him peering into the foliage, murmuring and chortling, picking amongst the leaves. Every now and then, when he found what he was looking for, he would let out a cry of '*ai ai!*'[1]

He had dreamed of this treasure ever since he first laid eyes upon it in a book written by a fantastical being called Frohawk. Curled up in front of a fire on wintry evenings in the vast manor house where he grew up, he discovered an other-worldly purple creature. It mesmerised him with its regal sheen, and the greenish whorls and marblings on its underside, and the rich coloured eye on the tips of its forewings. He wanted nothing more than to possess it. But no matter how he searched the woods he could not find one. He began to wonder if it truly existed at all.

Years later, when he was a young man, he saw it, the insect of his dreams, flying towards him down a woodland ride and settling for a moment on a leaf. Then, as he advanced, trembling with excitement, it soared heavenwards to the top of an oak. There he watched it, flitting round one of the topmost sprays far out of reach, mocking him, the Unattainable, the Jewel, the King of butterflies![2] Even later still, he found some of this majestic creature's eggs in another woodland further from home. He took them back to the round house and nurtured them in the special nets at the bottom of the garden. And there, in the light of the moon, they hatched.

Immediately the creatures ate their own eggs. Then they gorged on the sallow leaves the man had placed in the enclosure. Then they shed their first skin and grew horns; they even changed colour, from green to brown, so magical were these pieces of blind ingenuity. As winter drew in, they each found forks in the twigs of their home, or the shelter of a bud, where they built beds of silk on which to sleep through the cold of winter and early spring. When the April sun made the gnome-man's garden twitch with new life, they awoke and resumed their feast, turning green all over again, and then a paler green, before finding a leaf under which to hide.

The man from the round house watched all of this with great interest. He noted how they suspended themselves from silk and transformed into the perfect imitation of a sallow leaf, making a puzzling optical illusion – plump from the side, slim from the back. But so brilliantly camouflaged were their disguises, you would never notice them unless the man pointed them out to you. Finally, in the warmth of late June, they broke the walls of their chrysalises and emerged. 'Wahoo!' he cried when he heard them tapping the nets of the enclosure with their powerful wings.

So it might surprise you to find him collecting the purple butterflies in jars and carrying them back into the depths of the woods to release them. But he is clever, for he has delivered them to a place rich with oaks (their lofty perch) and sallow (their magic ingredient) where they will hide new eggs for him to discover next year with his curled stick, crying '*ai ai!*' all over again. And he will take them back to the round house and the nets at the bottom of the garden in a cyclical love affair that will last the rest of his life.

I arrive at my parents' house on a Friday in June to collect Dad.

Since he had his kidney removed at the start of the year, I find myself looking after Dad in ways that were unimaginable before. He is beside me, a cowed man in the passenger seat with a bucket between his feet. Even having gone through major surgery in January and coming close to death at the start of May, before the chemotherapy commenced, there remains a residual strength in him (still he has a bigger frame than me), and so far he has avoided the hair loss he dreads so much. Determined to retain standards, he is dressed the same as ever – an Oxford shirt, chinos, his tan leather jacket that swamped me when I tried it on – only now he has to wear braces to keep his trousers round his waist. The bucket is a precaution, as is the surgical mask on my face.

It isn't lost on us, the irony. How he has driven me around most of my life, the two of us in the front together (I always got front seat privileges over Mum and my brother due to persistent motion sickness, one of countless similarities with Dad), and how when I was young I too used to have a bucket, an empty ice cream tub in my case, at my feet for emergencies. It's a cliché that our parents become our children though. I am not the parent and he is not the child. That's what is so difficult about all of this. You cannot reverse the relationship of a lifetime.

'They love nothing more than shrimp paste,' I say. We are driving through Silverstone village, past the racetrack, but I am going very slowly. 'That and dog poo.'

I have been reading Matthew Oates's new book about the Purple Emperor, *His Imperial Majesty*, which arrived in the post yesterday. It's the reason I was early this morning. It was meant to be a Father's Day gift, as requested, but I can't wait until Sunday. I want to talk about it on the drive to the hospital. Nothing can be delayed anymore. Dad teared up when I gave it to him. Since the cancer, emotions are quick.

'And fox poo,' Dad says. 'Steady, son.'

I try to drive as smoothly as I can, easing my way around the incessant roundabouts on the A43 between Northants and Oxford, working the pedals gradually, avoiding sudden changes in speed, every bump and turn and rub of the brake a trial. I feel tense. Even in his reduced state, Dad is unable to commit to the role of passenger, making characteristic comments and recommendations – 'It's fifty miles per hour along here', 'You need the outside lane for this roundabout', 'Have you seen the police car ahead?' – all of which make me feel a little less sympathetic.

'Have you heard of Fermyn Woods?' I say. 'According to the book it's *the* place for the Purple Emperor, and it's only nine miles from my house. I had no idea!'

This is what I am most excited to tell him, as if it reflects well on my life choices; as if I have played some part in the Purple Emperor's presence, like it is part of my ecosystem.

'Of course,' says Dad, shifting in his seat. 'I went on to there from your house a couple of years ago. I asked if you wanted to come with me but I think you were busy. Saw my first ever Black Hairstreak.'

Another opportunity missed. I do remember him going to Twywell Hills and Dales, even closer to home, to look at the butterflies in the wild meadows there, hoping I might accompany him. Another time, I had said, though that time never came, always too busy.

'So you've seen a Purple Emperor before?'

'I've bred them,' he says.

'Really?'

'Yes. Don't you remember the net enclosures at the end of the garden?'

Vaguely, now that he says it. I remember my brother and I joking that we had seen butterflies outside with Dad's face on them. Breeding insects was an embarrassing perversion as far as we were concerned, but then we never paid much attention to what Dad got up to out of doors.

'Apparently BB was obsessed with Purple Emperors and reared loads every year,' I say. 'This book says he played a big role in bringing them back from the brink in Fermyn.'

Dad shuffles up in his seat, wincing, catching his breath. 'He showed me his nets when I visited him. They were no bigger than mine.'

This could just be an entomological dick-measuring contest (Nabokov, incidentally, made a scientific career out of comparing butterfly dicks), or a typical instance of Dad being sceptical of whatever others are saying. I had forgotten that he once visited BB's home, though I know he has told me about it. The dust-jacket blurbs I browsed in his study failed to mention it. From what I can recall, BB expressed an interest in *Shooting Times* for an unusual kind of gun that Dad happened to own. What was unusual about it, I can't say. I'm sure he must have shared more detail about this, but it escapes me.

'Maybe he was winding down then,' I say.

I wonder if he has told me about BB's butterflies before. Is it something else that I have tuned out?

'He only lived down the road from your house,' says Dad. 'A funny place – a seventeenth-century round house. It used to be the toll-keeper's cottage, I believe.'

'Oh yeah?'

'There are Emperors in these woods here,' he says, nodding out the car window at Hazelborough Wood, which borders Silverstone. I went there with him as a child, but I have no recollection of what we got up to, nothing I will be able to cling to once he is gone. 'That's where I released the first Emperors that I bred.'

'Is that legal?' I ask, hoping we aren't about to have an argument about ethics (though at least this time it won't be about literary ethics). Our arguments can be monumental, and since the diagnosis I have been doing everything in my power to avoid them.

'Yes,' he says. I haven't a clue if he is being straight.

I wonder if some found their way into his killing jar too, but I don't want to ask. Instead, Dad tells me about 'master trees' – the large old oaks that Emperors colonise – and how the male comes down for just an hour or so a day to feed from an array of disgusting sources including faeces and puddles.

'Steady as you can, son,' he says, reminding me of his frailty.

'Sorry,' I say, slowing down. We drive a few more miles in silence.

'Thanks for doing this,' he says. 'I know it takes a lot of time out of your week.'

'Don't be daft,' I say.

'What a sorry state of affairs, eh?'

That earlier description of the Purple Emperor (*Apatura iris*) soaring 'heavenwards to the top of an oak' is from BB's beloved *Brendon Chase* (a scene that Oates credits with making him an entomologist) and was written before BB had even seen an Emperor outside of the coloured plates in Frohawk's *Natural History of British Butterflies* (1914). But in the twentieth century Purple Emperors were endangered by forestry management policies that devastated its foodplant, sallow. Hence the delirium of the vicar who finds them in *Brendon Chase*, a tale of escape and adventure in which a group of children go feral in the woods.

The Purple Emperor is still uncommon. According to Oates there are 'only four or five genuinely strong Purple Emperor populations in the country',[3] largely confined to the south of England, though he also notes that the Emperor is perhaps not actually as rare as we think, but rather 'heavily suppressed by prejudice against its larval foodplant, sallows, and [. . .] significantly under-recorded'.[4] It *feels* rare though because it is so elusive, even in its strongholds. Purple Emperors are only on the wing for approximately three weeks of the year, and within that time frame only likely to be seen at two points in the day – from mid-morning for an hour or two, and possibly again late afternoon after a siesta. At these times the male descends from the canopy to gorge on animal droppings and muddy puddles. For such a lofty butterfly, its tastes are in the gutter.

This is why in July you'll see men and women guarding piles of poo in certain ancient woodlands, the only time people actively discourage dog walkers from scooping up their mess. This is excusable given the limited window of opportunity for seeing an Emperor, a window that will quickly snap shut in the face of the casual. The devotee, on the other hand, will not allow it, and so in the month of July Purple addicts descend on hotspots like Fermyn Woods near my house in Northamptonshire.

The Purple Emperor is *the* butterfly for photograph-hungry butterfliers. They long to snap an Emperor with all four wings showing purple. In Fermyn, people line the rides (a ride, it turns out, is what the initiated call a woodland track, though there may be more nuance to it than that), clutching their long-lens cameras and binoculars, some even cycling back and forth through the labyrinth, spreading news from person to person, turning the forest purple with gossip ('Some were seen over in the next wood thirty minutes ago', 'There's one sunning itself by the green gate where the path forks', 'I just spoke to a man who spoke to a woman who bumped into a man who saw seven this morning somewhere in that direction').

BB saw himself as responsible for the regeneration of the Emperor in Fermyn, where he released an average of twenty-five every year from 1972 until 1990. 'They really *were* mine,'[5] he says in *The Naturalist's Bedside Book*. Later, in an article for *The Field*, speaking of the particular area in Fermyn where he focused his efforts, BB says: 'I introduced this rare and most prized of all our British butterflies to the reserve' and, in case we missed the point, 'There were no *iris* (purple emperors) in my reserve until I introduced them; at least I never saw any.'[6] It is open to debate whether BB was solely responsible, but there is no doubting he played a pivotal role in making Fermyn Woods purple once again. Oates calls this BB's 'true legacy'.[7]

It was in fact in another ancient Northamptonshire forest – one even closer to where I grew up, the inspiration for the forest to which the children of *Brendon Chase* escape – that BB first glimpsed the Purple Emperor. As he recounts it:

> *I suppose my first brief view of my long-sought prize was one hot July afternoon in Salcey Forest near Northampton. I had cycled there from Lamport – a distance of some dozen miles or more. Tantalising as ever, and so typical of the butterfly, it was only a fleeting glimpse of a large black butterfly, far larger than a Red Admiral or Peacock, which appeared briefly soaring round the top of an oak.*

> *I only had it under observation for a matter of seconds but there was no mistaking it, or the bold gliding flight which was almost like that of a partridge.*[8]

The open-eyed, joyful style of BB's writing has often been attributed to his innate childlike wonder for the natural world. But when it comes to his writing about butterflies the subtext often seems more young-adult than childlike. The sultry summer days, the burning desire and fretful yearning, the breathless chase, the glimpses of bliss that are over prematurely, the ejaculations of hyperbole (like on the day in 1946 when BB finally encountered an Emperor and one settled on his knee, sending him aquiver) – such sublimations are everywhere in BB's writing in which his attention keeps returning to the Purple Emperor. (Salcey Forest was just three miles from where I went to school, and to many of my peers its significance was as a place of discreet lay-bys for young lovers making fleeting night-time pull-ins in cars that had only just shed their L-plates . . .) I'm sure my dad wouldn't have seen it like that. Maybe it is a Nabokovian reading of BB. Either way, the Emperor clearly excites in a way that no other British butterfly can.

When we arrive at the Churchill Hospital in Oxford, I wrap a tissue around my finger and reach out of the window to press the button on the car park barrier. Already prone to neurotic behaviour, I am being forced into advanced levels of fussiness and fear by the pandemic. But it's the thought of having to separate myself from Dad's support bubble if I were to get ill or, worst of all, pass COVID onto him, that has me almost paralysed with obsessive risk assessments, drafting ever more refined strategies for not making contact with the world and its contents. At least today the wheelchair won't be necessary, Dad being in relatively decent condition this week. I drop him at the door and go to park.

The car park is filled with helpless loved ones, sat in our cars opposite each other, barred from the ward, hoping for miracles. It must be almost thirty degrees and the car is stifling, even with the windows down, but I carry on wearing my mask to prevent the build-up of aerosols ahead of the return journey. I attempt to mark some student work on my laptop, but I end up searching the internet for information on the Purple Emperor. Oates is on Twitter telling people to make their excuses and head to the woods next week: Emperor season is about to begin. Those in the know are trembling with anticipation, like the Emperor pupae on the sallow leaves in Fermyn, poised to burst open.

I look up and see Dad walking towards the car. Two hours has vanished. He was supposed to call me when he was done, so that I could pull up outside the building and collect him from there. But he likes to challenge himself, to remain independent. It makes my heart skip, watching him walk across the car park. You could convince yourself he is a strong and vibrant man, but I see the details that give him away: the slower than normal pace; the slight drop of the shoulder; the sadness in the eyes, newly topped up with poison. He is carrying his NHS-issue red pouch with additional medication inside. I feel like a father collecting his son clutching a terrible goody bag from a birthday party. Maybe roles can be reversed after all.

Dad smiles as he gets nearer, a smile purely for me.

9
A Momentary Vacuum

I park at the start of the bridle path and enter Fermyn sideways on, perpendicular to a bizarre reality where a pandemic is raging and my father is dying.

It's the second time in three days that I've been here. Both days were scorchers. The first time, walking the same path and thinking of turning around because I felt like an impostor, a man had come round the bend, armed with butterflying ammunition with which to expose me: long-lens camera, equally expensive-looking binoculars, proper walking boots and one of those sleeveless adventurer jackets that Kit has at home in a playset along with explorer's hat and toy binoculars. (There is something of the overgrown child about the butterfly hunter, like the famous image of Nabokov gripping his net in long socks, shorts and hat.)

'I've just seen a beautiful Emperor,' he said, stopping in the middle of the path. 'About six hundred metres down the track there, at the intersection.'

At any other point in time we would have looked an odd sight, the way he was talking to me while I kept an antisocial distance and fidgeted awkwardly. As of the end of the last month, groups of six are permitted to meet outside, and we are no longer restricted to one activity of outdoor exercise. But that hot weekend had yielded scandalising images of teeming beaches and enraged traffic queues, which provoked conflicting views on what was acceptable conduct. There was no sense that the man with the expensive kit and I were doing anything wrong (well, maybe there was a residual sense that we were), but the fear of contagion remained.

'Super,' I said, eager to demonstrate my enthusiasm.

'If you keep going 'til you get to the crossroads of two rides, you'll see I've placed a banana skin soaked in soy sauce at the foot of the oak there,' he said excitedly. 'You might still catch sight of one yet.' He looked at his watch.

I looked at mine too to give the impression that I was alert to the schedule. It was already getting towards midday.

I thanked him. It was the first of many gifts; a pure gift in that no reciprocation was expected. He could tell just by looking at me that I had nothing to offer in return. Like all pure gifts, it didn't seek recompense or any kind of end product at all. I was simply being invited in. Maybe soon I would be offering information to others and the exchange would enlarge its value through an uncalculated kind of circulation.[1] But it shouldn't be this easy, I thought. BB had spent decades fantasising about the Purple Emperor before he ever saw one. Without that man on the path, I wouldn't have known where to start – I wasn't even sure I knew how to identify an oak, the Emperor's resting and mating place, and I certainly had no idea what sallow looked like.

Looking back, the man doesn't quite seem real to me. Too fortuitous. I like to pretend he was the ghost of BB, traipsing the woods like a talisman for the butterfly he had regenerated there, ushering a novice into the fold of a future obsession. BB thought of the natural world as a hauntology (though he wouldn't have used such a term) where the presence of past naturalists is woven into the texture of time and space. In *Fisherman's Folly* he recounts the story of Father Angelus, a Catholic priest who used to fish at a secretive lake in Devon that BB called Beechmere (now infamous as a suicide spot), arriving each summer and staying in the neighbouring village for two months. One year he simply didn't appear and was never seen again. '[W]henever I tread that winding path under the beeches at that rare hour when the world is hushed and dim,' writes BB, 'I think that any moment, at any turn of the way, I shall see him before me, tall and black in his medieval habit, burdened with basket and rod and moving with noiseless tread towards his special pitch.'[2]

BB's connection to realities deeper than the here and now extended back to his childhood, which was noisy with omens and visitations. He was chilled by the parlourmaid's account of her vision of a small black monkey perching on the shoulder of the coachman who had brought the doctor to deliver him and his twin brother.[3] When he was four, he woke in the night to see 'a diminutive Being' with 'a round, very red, bearded face about the size of a small crab apple' standing between the twins' beds before vanishing underneath one. And on the lead-lined balcony that ran around their bedroom at the top of the house was 'the Peak', a 'pointed pyramid which glided past the windows' of their bedroom, 'hideously black' and malevolent.[4] The woods, fields and lakes outside were equally eerie, though in a more hospitable way: palimpsests of time where the rambling naturalist could connect with spirits of the supernaturalists that had come before. The quiet of these places was underscored by the silent clamour of invisible companions, gift-givers, possibility-makers.

Just dipping my toe into the cryptic depths of Fermyn Woods, I sense the rustle of conversation between its spirits. Is it friendly or hostile? Can I merge myself with it, or will I drown? I imagine Dad walking the same bridle path, swallowed by the density of trees. For some reason I haven't told him about coming to Fermyn – not the other day, nor today on my return. But as I continue down the ride I can't help thinking how the man who had pointed me to an Emperor location *wasn't* my dad. The absent presences of Fermyn are a reminder of imminent departure.

I have resolved to head to the same oak tree today. The first time there, I had seen a large butterfly weaving through the foliage. It seemed a dark, almost blackish blue but it complicated into a rarer heaven-spun purple. And then like a conjuring trick it was gone. I doubted my own senses. I couldn't quite persuade myself that I had seen an Emperor at the very first attempt. But I had seen *something.*

This time I have to know for sure. The track turns slightly, bringing another man into view. He stands in a large clearing before a giant oak. An expert, armed with a comically long high-spec camera, a backpack slumped in the shade behind him. There is a frisson of competition, like there isn't enough nature to go around. He keeps his eyes fixed on the tree and mercifully ignores me. I creep past.

I feel uncanny, out of place, terrified of being seen by butterfliers using obscure butterfly slang and talking expertly of sophisticated lenses (I only have my iPhone, an insult to the Purple Emperor), who will identify me straight away as an impostor. But the path to my oak is clear, so I keep moving, time working against me.

But what *had* I seen last time? I know from reading about the Purple Emperor that it is sometimes confused with the White Admiral, especially by the less experienced. They differ in size, but the White Admiral is still a relatively large butterfly. The male Emperor is, unlike the White Admiral, purple, but only from certain angles, riddling between black and purple depending on the light, while the female is a dark brown, almost black, without any purple sheen at all. And like the White Admiral, the Emperor has striking white bands on its upperside. Will I be able to decipher the evidence?

But often you find the thing you need when you're looking for something else entirely. On my first visit to Fermyn, in the exact same spot where I stand now, I was anticipating a flash of purple in vigorous flight, not knowing what such a thing might actually look like, half-expecting to see Prince at the height of his Purple Rain pomp flying overhead, when I saw a slice of shadow cutting the grass in front of me. I looked up and, instead of a purple butterfly, found an ingenious piece of orange origami powering above and disappearing into the hedgerow. It stopped me in my tracks. It took my breath away. I was bowled over. Cliché then dissolved and complicated into a glorious confusion. I thought I knew what I had seen – I had read about it in advance in the sightings records on Butterfly Conservation's website – but such knowledge was insufficient for the felt experience, for which I had no terms. I stood still, overwhelmed for the first time in my life by the butterflier's paradoxical feeling of regret for what has been missed and excitement for what might be about to come. Then it exploded from the bramble.

Seeing a species for the first time is both rapturous and rupturing. There is the shock of the new, which is pleasurable, but also painful, shifting the familiar and the known into new configurations. I chased the Silver-washed Fritillary with a determination that I hadn't felt for anything – at least anything that didn't relate to Kit – in years. The challenge was to keep my eyes attached to it, following its rollercoaster dips and turns like I was the hoop on the buzz wire of its trail. (A piece of rugby wisdom Dad once imparted came back to me: run diagonally to where the breaking player is going and meet him there rather than chase him.) It was one of the most stunning things I had ever seen. The perplexing combination of strength and elegance. The rapid shimmer of orange and silver. How it could shift so effortlessly from muscular flight to moments of delicate drifting, like an out-of-season autumn leaf falling through the air. Who knows if I had accidentally seen one in my butterfly-blind past, but I had certainly never *seen* one.

The woodland ride felt like a parting in the ocean, the swash and timpani of the deep forest beating all around me. The ground didn't quite feel certain, like I was being loosened at the joints, ready to be taken apart and put back together again. There it was, vanishing and reappearing as it sought thistle and bramble. Each disappearance hurt and each return was a powerful reconnection, an exhilarating romance of loss and relief played out in infinite regression. Sometimes I would lose sight and it would materialise in a different spot metres away, like a Roegian jump cut, skipping whole intervals of time and space. I was surprised how much it mattered to me, like I was chasing Dad's health and happiness, if only I could catch it.

'Are you seeing this?' I found myself saying under my breath to the person who was not there.

This time I will not leave the forest without knowing for sure that I have seen a Purple Emperor. But before I reach my oak, under the intense spotlight of the sun, the Silver-washed Fritillary bursts from the foliage and we are reunited. Could it be the very same one from the other day? Is such a thing likely? I have no idea. It certainly feels like the continuation of a tryst. I watch it racing down the ride when, as if by returning to Fermyn so soon the woods are recognising me as a worthy, I am gifted an exquisite White Admiral. It glides through my periphery and settles on the floor ahead, displaying its shimmering black and white like the most romantic of old movies. There is no mistaking this one for a Purple Emperor.

As enthralling as these butterflies are, they are not Purple Emperors, which I am doubtful of seeing for sure. What I need is know-how and hunch, a talent for nature like BB and Nabokov. I need Dad. He would talk me through it all if he was here. In *Ramblings of a Sportsman-Naturalist*, BB describes how 'as soon as I entered the forest on that hot July afternoon I felt that [the Purple Emperor] certainly was to be found there'.[5] I feel the same way (largely because the internet has confirmed as much), but unlike BB I have no confidence that I will actually see one. For BB the natural world was a kind of intuition, a metaphysical connection beyond logic or explanation, whereas all I feel is a great unknowing.

At last, I reach my oak. Now that I have a verified spot, I'm not going to give it up easily. I root myself and stare resolutely at the tree. I scan the canopy for soaring black specks until my neck aches. I watch the forest floor in case one has already come to ground and is feasting. BB claimed that one summer he searched so fixedly for the Emperor that he got conjunctivitis. Will I go so far?

At regular intervals the man from the clearing emerges from beyond the kink in the ride and peers into the bush along the edge, reminding me that I'm not alone. He seems to get a little nearer each time, but always returns to his bigger oak (he must know something I don't . . .), leaving me to sizzle beneath mine.

I keep checking my watch, conscious that I should be working, convinced the minutes are moving too quickly. I alternate between feeling that I am in a preternaturally intense present and feeling that I am so far out of the moment

I might never grasp it. I experience a nostalgia for things I can't know: the secrets of Dad's past and the time *he* spent as a young man in similar woods; an aching nostalgia for a future that Dad and I will not share – enchanted expeditions for Purple Emperors and Black Hairstreaks, flights of fancy into Nabokovian territory. 'I confess I do not believe in time,' writes Nabokov in *Speak, Memory*:

> *I like to fold my magic carpet, after use, in such a way as to superimpose one part of the pattern upon another. Let visitors trip. And the highest enjoyment of timelessness – in a landscape selected at random – is when I stand among rare butterflies and their food plants. This is ecstasy, and behind the ecstasy is something else, which is hard to explain. It is like a momentary vacuum into which rushes all that I love. A sense of oneness with sun and stone. A thrill of gratitude to whom it may concern – to the contrapuntal genius of human fate or to tender ghosts humouring a lucky mortal.*[6]

One cannot help thinking that Nabokov's father is at the centre of the oneness he describes here, rushing into that momentary vacuum created by the dissolution of time. Maybe by being here, amongst (I hope) the Emperor's food-plant, I am trying to create a timelessness that might be hospitable to *my* father once he is gone.

The closest BB comes to sounding like Nabokov is when he describes the Painted Lady's mind-boggling long-haul flight from Africa to England as 'one little thread in the vast pattern of Life's coloured carpet'. He continues: 'The laws which must govern "chance" are strange, yet these same laws influence our own lives at every twist and turn. The shuttle moves, perpetually weaving our lives in the pattern of the whole.'[7] These words were written in the middle of the Second World War in a book called *The Idle Countryman*, published just a few years before Nabokov first published the 'Butterflies' chapter of *Speak, Memory* in the *New Yorker*. For Nabokov's magic carpet, swap BB's coloured carpet of life. Did BB's 'vast pattern' also contain the sublimity of loss, like Nabokov's contained his father's? BB's life was certainly confounded by loss, just as it was interrupted by moments of disturbance that seem other-worldly. Take this momentous passage from his memoir, *A Child Alone*:

> *Some years before my father married, in 1903, he visited the Holy Land – a pilgrimage often undertaken by Edwardian clergymen. When visiting one of the holy places, he was asked for alms by a deformed and hideous old beggar man. My father refused. The old beggar cursed him with some vigour.*
>
> *Rather unwisely perhaps my father asked the guide what the old beggar man was saying and was told that a curse had been laid upon him – that his first-born son would die (I and my twin brother Roger were his second sons), and that the first-born son of his second son would also die before manhood.*[8]

True to the terms of the curse, BB's older brother passed away when they were just children. In nature BB found a way of making sense of such tragedy, all part of the pattern of the whole. But would he have felt the same about life's 'vast pattern' if he had known that the rest of the beggar's curse would also come true? That 'the first-born son of [BB's father's] second son would also die before manhood'? BB was a young writer, flush with the early successes of his career, newly committed to full-time writing and illustrating, having given up his day job as art master at Rugby School, when he was struck by the blind cruelty of nature. Not long after writing *The Idle Countryman* he lost his only son, Robin, to Bright's disease. Robin was seven years of age. BB vowed never to write of his family's crushing tragedy. The only direct comment can be found in his letters: 'My dearest son died in my arms in the early hours of November 6. I do not think life will ever be the same again for me.'[9]

Yet it is with butterflies that BB and Nabokov, forever altered by the fragility of the father–son bond, seem to feel a consoling oneness with all that has been and all that might be. Standing at the crossroads, gazing up into a burning sky, I am struck by an intimation of what will be lost when Dad dies. At the same time, I feel the exhilaration of a burgeoning connection with him through the butterfly I am yet to see, so I am cocooned in paradox – both absent and present; neither subject nor object of my own experience; past, present and future all at once.

'It is probable,' writes Matthew Oates, 'that the [Purple Emperor] has stimulated a number of heart attacks, seizures, apoplexies, terminal winebibbings and the like, not to mention divorces and separations, only these have not been recorded in entomological history.'[10] At least it doesn't spread COVID, I think. But I witness the truth of Oates's diagnosis first hand when a man passes my oak, half-acknowledging me but gone behind the eyes, transfixed by what might be in the bushes and the grass. Five minutes later a beleaguered woman appears, perspiring and breathing heavily. She asks if I have seen her husband.

'He went that way,' I say. 'Towards the road.'

She rolls her eyes and then smiles despairingly.

'He always does this.'

She says it with such tired forbearance that I can't help feeling sorry for her. My mum, just like my brother and I, would not follow Dad so patiently. When I was growing up, my parents' hobbies and pastimes split along clear lines. Dad's were outdoors, Mum's were indoors. If Dad was out rambling, certainly if he was out shooting, we would be with Mum, often shopping in Milton Keynes, my favourite pastime as a kid: getting lunch; browsing the CDs, computer games, movies, books; trying on clothes; always wanting more of everything than our pocket money could allow. None of us wanted to hear about Dad's natural-historical interests, which were available for free.

A beautiful butterfly lands on the ground just a couple of feet away. Another White Admiral. I get a good photo and compare it to images online on my phone. Presenting itself to the sun, it looks like a rockabilly shoe; and then it closes its wings to reveal a leopardish underside. It sits a while, trembling in the heat, and then takes off, gliding suavely into the canopy, flashing black and white like some blinds being riffled open and shut.

More minutes melt in the heat, and an older couple, probably my parents' age, are expelled by the woods. The man clutches a long-lens camera, ready to fire. 'Seen much?' asks the woman. She is careful not to get too close, wary of COVID I presume. 'Not today,' I say, like I've been seeing loads every other day. They tell me that I'm not in the best place. Too late now. Not long after they have gone, I am startled by another wanderer, the labyrinth of rides producing Purple enthusiasts by the minute. He has the well-earned tan of a committed naturalist and, despite the heat, wears trousers – suddenly I swear I can feel insects biting my legs. This one's weapon of choice is a pair of binoculars. We don't speak, but there is an acknowledgement.

The leaves, whose shapes I am sure Dad decoded for me when I was a child, and the trees, whose names I know these shapes are the keys to, continue to absorb time until there is none left. The Emperor's ideal flight window has closed for the day and my window for getting some work done is narrowing. It's time for home. Reluctantly I leave my station without an Emperor to report to Dad. I turn the corner and grass gives way to gravel. The clearing in front of the large oak is empty. I look right and there is the man's rucksack still slumped in the shade at the edge of the path, but no one is there to guard it. I look ahead and see my car glistening in the distance. I also see the loiterer, just up the track, standing over something. At his feet, lying on his front in the dust and dirt, is another man – the one with the trousers and binoculars who has just passed me at the crossroads. They are frozen. It is a bizarre scene and I find myself running towards it.

As I near I can see what they are worshipping: a large hunk of dog poo. It is so old and sun-dried that it has mineralised, encrusted with tiny diamonds. But the real jewel is the butterfly at its centre.

The man who owns the rucksack looks up.

'It's just come to ground,' he says, a little breathless. The trousered man with the binoculars is prostrate on the ground. He doesn't look up at all, stuck in an *Apatura iris* trance, as if he might be able to get close enough to give the butterfly (and, by collateral, the turd) a kiss.

'Stunning,' says the rucksack man, inviting me into the fold.

'Beautiful,' I say. 'The first I've ever seen.' I add the latter involuntarily. I no longer care about covering up my ignorance. The integrity of the Emperor seems to elicit truth.

The Emperor closes its wings tight and I see its owlish eyespot staring at me from the tan, white and black folds of the underwing. It is the largest butterfly I have ever encountered. There is something individuating about being in its presence, each of us under its spell.

I hear a crunch and turn to see the couple with the long-lens camera power-walking towards us, like a signal has been sent through the woods. The rucksack man, excited by my obvious inexperience, says, 'Once it's feeding it takes some disturbing. You can get really quite close.'

Now there are five of us gathered around the shit, kind of sharing the moment, but also enclosed in our private reveries, no one really talking or acknowledging one another. All notion of social distancing has dissolved. This is the closest I have been to human beings other than my family since early March. Will we stake our lives for the Purple Emperor?

I hold my iPhone ready, but I wonder if there is a strict etiquette in these situations. Would it be indecorous of me to start snapping pictures, like an influencer in the wild?

As if reading my mind, the man says: 'Get some photos. Then I'll see if I can coax it into opening its wings.'

I bend down, nervous of getting too close, the other man still on his front eyeballing the butterfly, not saying a thing. It all feels a bit undignified, but I take a few shots, anxious not to scare the Emperor off and end the moment for everyone else. When I look up, I find the rucksack man with one hand up his shirt, rubbing at his armpit.

'I've not worn deodorant or washed for a couple of days,' he says proudly. 'They like the salts.'

He crouches and nears his finger to the Emperor. Sure enough, the exquisite creature sucks in its party-streamer proboscis and walks onto the finger. 'There is to many of us a mysterious element of near-deity about this species, a *mysterium*,' writes Oates.[11] Mystery, yes, but near-deity? It is hard to see. Shit and body odour are no nectar of the gods. But then, attached to the man's hand, suspended in mid-air, the Emperor parts its wings and suddenly I know what Oates means. The purple is almost a shock when, as the Emperor re-angles itself, it emerges from the black of the wing, like liminal time coming out of night, a shimmer of colour that defamiliarises anything I have thought of as purple before. It only takes a couple of seconds before the Emperor flies away, its wings cutting a butterfly-shaped hole through the surface of the present so that what we are seeing is no butterfly at all but the beautiful underside of 'Life's coloured carpet', as if alternative worlds have been folded against one another.

We behold something far more than a butterfly. It is the tangle of personal associations it weaves around each of us as it flies about our heads and away. For me it is no longer the insect of a specialist's natural history, of my dad's world. It is the purple of the 1980s Los Angeles Lakers running a flashy but aggressive fast break through the green of the Boston Celtics; it is Prince in purple suit and New Romantic ruffles tearing a solo from his stave-shaped guitar amidst the purple rain; it is Nabokov's purplest prose.

The five of us follow this angel of the wood, half-waddling, half-running. We look absurd. The man who was on the ground stops still and tracks it with his binoculars.

'There!' he exclaims. 'On that bramble.'

We all dash for it, homing in on the hedge, five gawping faces.

'Yes, there it is,' says the man with the long lens to his partner, pointing.

I nod, pretending I can see it too, but I'm lost. No matter, because several seconds later, the Emperor takes flight again, sending us all running back in the opposite direction like joke figures in a skit.

'It's back on the turd,' says the rucksack man.

Yes! I think with total sincerity and elation. *It's back on the turd!*

The man with the long lens is already on it.

'Now's a good time for photographs,' says the rucksack man, as if he was the one who sanctioned it. Somehow, he has adopted the role of guide and I notice the couple, possibly regulars of these woods, doing their best to ignore him.

'You can get right up to it,' he says.

We all take our photo opportunities. With semi-concentration, slightly dazed, we look for the words to describe it: *remarkable . . . beautiful . . . regal . . . majestic . . .*

Oates has commented on the clichéd application of the term 'lofty' in writing on the Purple Emperor. 'In the month of July he makes his appearance in the winged state, and invariably fixes his throne upon the summit of a lofty oak,' writes A. H. Haworth in *Lepidoptera Britannica* (1803); 'As befits his rank, the Emperor has lofty habits,' says Richard South in *The Butterflies of the British Isles* (1906); 'By universal suffrage,' declares W. S. Coleman in *British Butterflies* (1860), 'the place of highest rank among the butterflies of Britain has been accorded to this splendid insect, who merits his imperial title by reason of his robe of royal purple, the lofty throne he assumes, and the boldness and elevation of his flight.'[12] It's the measure of the Purple Emperor that it can seem lofty while grounded on a turd. Surely this is superiority at its most effortless. Rather like the tripodal Martians in Wells's *The War of the Worlds* – a novel that interrogates the very imperialism implied by the Emperor's nickname, His Imperial Majesty – serene in their supremacy as they feed on the helpless humans of the Home Counties, the Purple Emperor (in its own Martian-like stance of legs and unfurled proboscis) could not care less about the circle of enthusiasts gazing at it. Unlike most butterflies that flee from the minutest disruption, the Emperor will stay put for protracted feeding sessions even with the snapping cameras of its superfan paparazzi breaking the taut quiet of the woodland around it.

'If you've all got some photos,' says our ringleader, 'I'll give it a little tickle. See if we can get it to open its wings.'

Now he is just showing off. He kneels down and caresses the Emperor with a blade of grass and we wait, tense, poised with our cameras, fearing that our precious moment with this special creature is about to end. It twitches and tilts, minutely re-angling itself. Here is a being of another order, and here we are breathless and sweating (some doing more than others to combat their perspiration), desperate for a flash of its gorgeous scales. Does it despise us and our efforts to satisfy base obsessions? The man tickles it again and the large wings part. You can almost hear the forest gasp.

Still, no one quite knows what to say in our small band of

strangers. We struggle to name the ineffable quality of the Emperor. It exceeds language somehow; silence is the only way of honouring it. Our ringleader, however, is *not* lost for words. He tells us how he has travelled from afar and how he has spent all morning in the woods looking for Emperors.

'I even filled a bottle with piss,' he says, like it's nothing. 'I poured it around the oak tree down there to entice them down. They love it.'

Months of lockdown and obsessive hand sanitising for *this*. 'It is a mindset,' says Oates, 'but so is the Purple Emperor.'[13] In a weird way, I am grateful for this man and his smelly armpits and his bottle of piss.

The Emperor, though, has had enough. With a powerful beat of its wings, it soars towards the clearing. The older couple are content. They smile, nod goodbye and head off. The two men will stay all day. I check my watch. Somehow forty minutes has passed in their company, as if the Emperor can bend and warp time. I thank them. Something has been shared. But the person I need to share it with isn't here.

Breathless, prickled with perspiration, buzzing with adrenaline, I collapse into my car and close the door. I scroll through the images on my phone and send one to Dad. I want him to know what has just happened. A gift from me to him, but really from him to me.

As always, the response is instant.

Well done. Keep it up. I'm living through you now xx

10

Dad the Obscure

Dad and I are in the field behind the house. It's a small field that my parents bought in 2007, after I had left home. They got it cheap as arable land and Dad quickly set to creating a conservation area. He dug a pond; planted apple trees, pear trees, plum trees, oaks, Silver Birches, willows; fixed up an owl box; laid ground shelters for snakes; seeded wildflowers; and allowed large sections to go wild for the butterflies.

'Marbled White . . . Large Skipper . . . Green-veined White . . . Meadow Brown . . . ' He names each one and points. It's the kind of thing that would have pissed me off a treat when I was a moody teenager (and moody twenty-something and, shamefully, moody thirty-something too), walking ahead or behind in my own moody world. But now, fresh off my Purple Emperor success, I am more open.

Since the terminal diagnosis Dad has hardly been able to get out of the house. But today, another sunny afternoon in this unusually hot summer, he is game for a short stroll into the orchard at the top of the field. Out of necessity we move slowly, but the pace helps us spot more butterflies.

'You don't know how much it pleases me that you've seen a Purple Emperor. You beat me to it this year!'

'Not quite a fair competition,' I say.

'I used to report my first sightings to your granddad,' he says. 'Not just butterflies – the first Swallow, the first nest, that sort of thing.'

He pauses and points at something else.

'Ringlet,' he says.

I nod.

'I still do,' he carries on. 'Report back to your granddad, that is. I have a little look up to the sky and speak to him. When he passed away, I lost the person I shared these things with, but he is still with me in a way. But now that you're interested, I can share them with you.'

He must know that he is unlikely to have anything more to report: that he will be confined to the house from here on. What I think he is really trying to tell me is that *I* will be able to continue the conversation with *him*, if I like. He is preparing me for the time after he is gone.

'See how the Ringlet has those hypnotic eyespots on its underside? You find Ringlets everywhere, but they're special in their own way.'

As he describes the subtle beauty of the less exceptional butterflies in the orchard, I sense a quiet lesson taking place. Celebrity butterflies like the Purple Emperor are all well and good for encouraging a new interest, but I need to go back to fundamentals.

'Was it busy in Fermyn?'

'Not really.'

I wonder if he thinks there is something slightly crass about fixating on the most glamorous species in butterfly tourist spots, a sign of the dilettante. Not that he hasn't spent time doing exactly the same himself.

'I'd love to take you to some of my favourite butterfly locations,' he says. 'There's a small wood near here with Emperors. You'd have them all to yourself. Maybe if things improve, eh?'

He is wearing a coat despite the heat and he is the thinnest I have ever seen him, like he's waiting to grow back into himself, his face drawn, wearing replacement expressions. His hair is still thriving, albeit wild and wispy. He is overdue a cut, but so is everyone thanks to the pandemic in this summer of dodgy hairdos.

'I think that's when it's really going to hit me that you're gone,' I say, slowing almost to a halt. 'When I want to pick up the phone to tell you something or ask for some advice.'

That's going to happen a lot. I always call Dad, seeking his counsel, sharing news.

'Can you just give me all the advice you've got now?'

I'm being facetious, but I can see Dad is taking the question at face value. He stops and concentrates.

'We're similar, you and I. I see myself in you all the time, good and bad. I know I could have done many things better. But you've got every chance to not repeat my flaws.'

Which flaws exactly are we talking about here? Our short tempers? Our obstinacy? Our susceptibility to stress? The way we let things consume us when it would be better to just let things go? A predisposition to be alone rather than in company? I've seen them all play out in him, and I recognise them in myself. But our circumstances are different. So much of Dad's life has been shaped by ill health, at least in my living memory. In 2000, after a couple of collapses and generally feeling low on energy, he was diagnosed with chronic fatigue syndrome (ME). Ever since then he has been plagued by pain and tiredness – a hammer blow for a man who always prided himself on being active, whether outdoors or simply by being hands on with practical work. If you had met him during the last twenty years, you might not have noticed his ill health at all. He could put on a front to an extent, but he would pay the price in private. His chronic fatigue is one of the reasons he bought this field in the first place. Sceptical about his diagnosis, he wondered if the spraying of agricultural chemicals on the other side of our garden fence might have had something to do with his fatigue. He spent several years in his twenties selling sprays for a large agricultural company and recalled car journeys that would end in awful headaches, dizziness and nausea. So he knew. Buying the field was an important step in putting some distance between himself and the substances that he had learned could harm his family and the other creatures he loved.

In *A Child Alone*, BB remembers a time 'before the advent of the accursed toxic sprays' when 'the English summer meadows were as flowery as any alpine pasture', 'dazzling gold with buttercups and flowers innumerable'. He goes on to say:

> *Some sixty years on, those agricultural sprays, so deadly and destroying, might well have been responsible for killing my lovely wife, and for wiping out untold millions of wild creatures, flowers, insects and trees, but that is part of my life I shall never write about.*[1]

In a life distorted by unexpected losses, the death in 1974 of Cecily, his wife of over thirty years, was a seismic event.

While she was gardening, a wind had blown the farmer's spray over the hedge and covered her. Illness was almost instant and just a few weeks later she passed away.

This only strengthened BB's resolve as a conservationist and coincides with the early stages of his Purple Emperor period, when he committed himself to protecting the Emperors and their habitats in Fermyn. But like Dad, he held a perspective on life and suffering that might seem contradictory to a modern sensibility. BB was a great conservationist and, in some ways, a proto-environmentalist, yet he was devoted to the sport of rural life too: shooting, fishing, even dabbling in collecting butterflies and birds' eggs in younger years, common pastimes for naturalists up until at least the 1960s. Some of the most poignant moments in his writing come out of this very conflict. Watching one of his Painted Ladies pupate, he writes: 'It was unbelievable that so large a butterfly could have been compressed into so small a space. I had meant this specimen for my collection, but after witnessing this miracle of birth I could not bring myself to put it into the killing bottle.'[2]And after failing to net a Purple Emperor in the forest, he writes: 'I felt rather bad about missing this chance for this *iris* was in perfect condition. But I am glad now that it is free to breed, still a living beauty.'[3] There are powerful instances in his writing where the cruelty is not stated but implied, maybe unconsciously, like when he is describing his efforts at rearing: 'I have placed these two new victims on a thistle, complete with turf beneath, and have protected them by a fine net, so I defy them to give me the slip.'[4] This is a contorted sentence that has conservation at its heart yet cannot camouflage a tyrannical impulse in the endeavour: the butterflies are his victims, unable to escape his omnipotence.

I have never quite been able to square my father's love of shooting, and his lesser interests in fishing and collecting, with his intolerance for suffering. I have such vivid memories of him trying to rescue animals. Like when we were driving down the A5 – the old Watling Street that runs past the field – and saw something sticking up like a leaf in the middle of the road. Dad recognised that it was an injured Bullfinch. He pulled over and ran out amongst the traffic to collect it, passing it to me in the passenger seat and driving away. I held it in my cupped hands, unsure whether I could feel the tiny creature's heart pounding or whether it was the nervous beat of my own. We set it up with a quiet bed in the garage, but it passed away within the hour.

He was also decisive in dispatching wild animals in anguish and unlikely to survive. I remember him giving peace to birds and rabbits in the fields around our home which had either been left for dead by disrupted predators or ravaged by disease. A common discovery during my childhood was rabbits blinded by myxomatosis, which in severe cases Dad would kill swiftly. Once, as a very small boy, I ran home in tears, distressed after witnessing Dad break a rabbit's neck. Later he explained to me how the disease was painful and fatal, and that if we had left it alone it would have only met a slower, crueller end. What he spared me was that it would probably have been eaten alive by a fox or picked apart by a bird of prey. For this very reason he would leave such dispatches exposed for their predators. 'Otherwise,' he told me later, 'another one will be taken in its place.'

I also remember Dad returning home from shoots, incensed by other shooters' lack of care for the animals, especially when they didn't do everything in their power to reduce suffering by making the quickest kill and pick-up possible. (In his diaries I find complaints about 'dangerous and greedy' shooters, and an account of how Dad 'climbed a 20-foot tree to retrieve a woodcock shot by another gun. It was caught in the branches and would not move'.) It all seemed such a muddle of convictions. In some ways I came to view him as a modern-day Jude the Obscure who, in Hardy's final novel, hears the 'shrill squeak' of a rabbit caught in a trap one night and goes outside to 'put it out of its pain'.[5] (Also like Jude, Dad wanted to go to university but had the odds of class stacked against him.) It is memories like these that make a photograph I once found in his study all the more confusing: Dad standing in the middle of a crescent of dead pheasants, smiling for the camera.

Earlier, I mentioned the stuffed Sparrowhawk in his study. One of my primary-school teachers had phoned him when she found it lying injured at the side of the road. Dad was known in the community as the sort who could be depended on in these situations. He collected the bird and took it to the vet's. They put it down. He was upset by the outcome, but where he differed from how I would have responded was in his decision to take the dead bird home and get it stuffed. To him it was a thing of beauty and he was proud to have it displayed in his study, on the same side of the room as the butterfly collection.

'I can't go any further, son,' he says.

We are at the end of the small orchard, where a narrow path I have mown into the long grass for him begins. The field is heavy with seed, billowy and velveteen, teeming with life and summer snow. The cruelty of this beauty hits me hard, looking out at so much possibility, teased by what Dad knows will be there, right in front of us, but might never see again. You can almost hear the applause of a hundred butterfly wings, beating the air above the wildflowers, untroubled by our viewing.

We turn and head back towards the house.

'What if I drove you to Wicken Wood or somewhere and we just went in for a couple of minutes?' I say somewhat desperately. 'Anything would be better than nothing. Or maybe I could try pushing you on your bike? I'd just love to do some proper butterflying with you before it's too late.'

Dad closes his eyes and shakes his head. An uncharacteristic admission of defeat. The gifts that have been on offer for thirty years, the gifts I have consistently rejected, are no longer available.

II
The Gift (ii)

I'm back at my desk, surrounded by a pile of your BB books (*A Child Alone*, *The Countryman's Bedside Book*, *Ramblings of a Sportsman-Naturalist*) and a pile of my Nabokovs (topped by *The Gift*, which I have just finished reading for the first time). How can I write about you? How can I translate you so that you don't become distorted by my own sensibility? I don't know if I can get this right.

This is something Nabokov was conscious of when writing about *his* father, though he was talented enough to do it through the transformative mirror-world of fiction. He even has the protagonist's mother in *The Gift*, upon hearing that he plans to write about his father, say: 'Remember that you need a great deal of exact information and very little family sentimentality.'[1] But Nabokov knew the difference between sentimentality and sentiment. If sentimentality is recycled emotion, generalised and clichéd, then sentiment is

> *the real thing, keen, subtle, specialized compassion, with a grading and merging of melting shades, with the very accent of profound pity in the words uttered, and with an artist's choice of the most visible, most audible, most tangible epithets.*[2]

The Gift vibrates with sentiment. It is a vivid portrait of the artist as a young man – one Fyodor – who is, like Nabokov once was, an émigré writer in 1920s Berlin. When Fyodor decides to write about his beloved father, Russia's leading entomologist who disappeared on a butterflying expedition in central Asia in 1916, he is transported to the bliss of his childhood in pre-revolutionary Russia. Once again, we find ourselves in a refraction of Nabokov's father's study when Fyodor describes his father's 'home museum, in which stood rows of oak cabinets with glassed drawers, full of crucified butterflies [. . .] where it smelled as it probably smells in Paradise'.[3] But as ever in Nabokov, it is the particulars that render the quiddity of experience. On remembering a period of illness during which he devoured his father's life work from his bed, a book called *Butterflies and Moths of the Russian Empire*, Fyodor writes: 'How I luxuriated in it in the blissfully languorous days of my convalescence, with a crumb of toast tormenting my buttock.'[4] That crumb is Nabokovian sentiment for you – the small detail that makes the whole thing vibrate with a peculiar human vividness.

If Nabokov wanted to commemorate his father but feared exposing or failing him, he could use Fyodor and Fyodor's father as proxies, and butterflies could provide the wings for his filial desire. 'When I fell under the spell of butterflies,' narrates Fyodor, 'something unfolded in my soul and I relived all my father's journeys, as if I myself had made them.'[5] In the novel's remarkable second chapter, which collapses time and space in a singular declaration of love, Fyodor imagines himself accompanying his father on the central Asian expedition from which he never returned. What follows is prose of authoritative lucidity, a style that combines scientific precision with baroque artfulness – a prose that no other twentieth-century novelist could have written. But every writer is a unique meeting place of different sensibilities. The second chapter of *The Gift* is the kaleidoscopic re-angling of, on the one hand, Nabokov's love of technical entomological literature (of the kind his father introduced him to), and, on the other, the fictional romances of Wells, Robert Louis Stevenson, Jules Verne, Rudyard Kipling and Oscar Wilde that he read as a child. But unlike either of these strands of Nabokov's reading, *The Gift* is freighted with longing and pathos.

What Fyodor soon comes up against is the dreadful unknowability of the man he loves. Perhaps worse than the dawning of his father's fundamental otherness is the realisation that his own writing might take him even further away from him: 'I have realized, you see, the impossibility of having the imagery of his travels germinate without contaminating them with a kind of secondary poetization.'[6] This is the central conundrum of Nabokov's art: is reality made more real by the artist's lucid particularisation of it, or is it simply made artificial? Indeed, is there a distinction between reality and artifice? A perilous, even painful, question when the subjects of that art are the people that you love.

Eventually Fyodor backs out. He cannot do it. This is compensated for by his meeting Zina, with whom he falls in love, and the strange sense he has of his lost father playing a shadowy part in their convergence. This is his father's gift, which, in combination with Fyodor's own literary gifts, brings him to the point at the end of the narrative where he is ready to write *The Gift*.

Reading *The Gift* after you had died was an uncomfortable experience – largely because I had already made the decision that I would write about you, which distorted everything I read. There is a fear of misrepresenting you, of falsifying our relationship, of confronting the loss. But what I think really troubles me is the realisation that in leaving this life, you have presented me with a confounding gift: the possibility of this book. After years of toiling at unpublished novels, I now have something urgent to write about, something that connects me to a wellspring of feeling that my writing has lacked to this point. It was Mum who pointed this out, and she meant it in an entirely sincere and approving way. 'This is the book you have to write,' she said. But I would give this book back, and all the butterflies in the world, if it meant you were still here.

I'm getting ahead of the story though. Perhaps, for me, the gift of *The Gift* is the advice the narrator's mother offers him when *he* is doubting whether to write about his father: 'Only if you imagine him reading your book and you feel it grates upon him, and makes you ashamed, then, of course, give it up, give it up. But I know this cannot be, I know he would tell you: well done.'[7]

I think you would tell me the same.

12
Magic Carpet Ride

I could have considered early retirement from my butterfly career after photographing the Purple Emperor. A one-off achievement, enough to surprise Dad and satisfy a competitive filial itch. And yet five days later I find myself parking at the same pull-in to the same bridle path on the same single-track country road on the edge of Fermyn Woods.

The woods are a-roar with things I don't know or understand: the larval foodplants and nectar sources of specific species that I can't differentiate, the particular trees they colonise that I can't identify, and the multitude of things I sense I don't know without even being able to say what they are. Rather than seeing light through the interstices of trunk, branch and leaf, I see the darkness of my own ignorance. But maybe, to adapt Saul Bellow's arresting line, my ignorance is the dark backing that a mirror needs if we are to see anything at all.[1] It is only by accepting the unknowable complexity of the forest that, paradoxically, I might begin to see it for what it is.

I pass the oak where I had first glimpsed the forest's Imperial Majesty, the Purple Emperor. I glance up but keep going. The track narrows and the trees close in overhead. By chance I disturb something in the grass. I only realise this when it lifts off, as if issued from my foot, and settles in some high bramble. I can't get a good view of it, hidden in the tangle like the whisper of a love affair, but it is there alright, and at last I have a moment by myself with an Emperor.

Just a few metres down the ride, I find another purple shape darting scattily in the grass, too small for an Emperor. I track it until it settles in the forest's carpet and get a blurry photo on my phone. My reading around is starting to pay off, because I know what it is even though it's the first Purple Hairstreak I have ever seen. I send the picture to Dad. He texts me straight back, thrilled. *Unusual to see them at ground level, unless they've just emerged*, he writes. But the one I have photographed is worn, missing a small bit of its hindwing like a clipped ticket.

As if the Purple Emperor and Purple Hairstreak have sprinkled the trees with purple angel dust, the forest comes alive. The bushes vibrate with the electric thrum of insect life, like the producer at the forest's mixing desk is sliding all the dials up, and the leaves and grass have a new sheen, glossy to the touch, glazed like you could eat the forest whole. I know I should probably turn around and go home, return to Carli and Kit and my work; I could ring Dad on the way and see how he is doing. But instead, I take the corner onto a crosswise track and impossibly there you are.

'This looks promising,' you say.

'How so?'

I follow in your footsteps, though of course you're not really there. You stop so that we're side by side. You peer up.

'Blackthorn, lots of privet, Ash trees. Just what the Black Hairstreak needs. See?' Your phantom points at a tree. 'Ash. Look how the leaves are made up of opposite leaflets, like mirror images of each other, and then one leaflet coming off at the end.'

'Sure,' I say.

'You'll get the hang of it.'

The grass is longer here and the edges feel closer. I wish I had taken the opportunity five years ago to come with you when you made this trip, but I was too busy and uninterested.

'You know, for years I've been looking for Black Hairstreaks down at the woods near Grandma and Granddad's. Your granddad reckoned he used to see them there. I've never managed to.'

'Have you got any in your collection?'

'Yes. They're incredibly rare.'

I look at the ground uneasily. You put your hand on my shoulder.

'I'm so glad you've come with me. I know you're very busy, but it's—'

You stop abruptly and stiffen, alert, like when you're watching TV at night and you hear a noise from the other end of the house.

'What was that?'

I have seen nothing.

'Where?'

'There.'

There could be anywhere as far as I can tell.

'There it goes!'

Now I see it. Something tiny spiralling from one side of the trail to the other, brisk and elusive. You look so alive. This is the thrill of the chase you're always talking about. You're pointing your binoculars.

'Yes! It's on that leaf there!'

I see literally hundreds of leaves in an unreadable kaleidoscope of green.

'That's it alright,' you say, passing the binoculars to me. 'See the squiggly white line on its underside? On the White-letter Hairstreak that looks more like a W than it does on the Black Hairstreak – that's how you tell the difference. Aren't its delicate tails beautiful?'

I can't even get the binoculars into focus, seeing only a smudge where you would have seen clarity. It will be gone before my point of view adjusts to yours.

'It's off!' you say. You carry on walking and I falter forward, following.

We reach another intersection of tracks. I follow you left onto a wide ride where the bush at the edges is sparser. The sun vanishes and the air turns wintry. The trees lose their leaves and the geometry of the space is blown open as the seasons change.

There is a man examining the edges. He is elderly and small. He wears a chequered flat cap and thick-rimmed glasses and has a solid white moustache. He is holding a curled walking stick. 'Good morning,' you say.

'Hello there,' he says with a slight delay, like we've just lifted him from deep contemplation. 'What a travesty.' He motions at the edge of the ride. 'All the sallow has been cleared from one end of the forest to the other.'

You shake your head.

'Food and shelter for hundreds of hibernating Purple Emperor larvae,' you say. 'Gone.'

'And after such hard-won progress,' he says. 'For decades the Emperors have had to contend with such human stupidity. You know, after the war, huge swathes of the native broadleaved trees were felled to make space for Norway Spruce and other conifers, destroying the Emperor's habitat of sallow and oak. But spruce doesn't like the heavy clay this forest is built on, so now the conifers are in ill health. The Forestry Commission have started to clear them, which means . . . '[2]

You complete the thought for him: 'More space for the sallow to regenerate and flourish.'

'Yes,' says the man. 'Which is why it ties one's stomach in knots to see this.'

There is an innate sadness to him, but he seems to invite our company, so the three of us walk together slowly.

'Do you know these woods well?' he asks.

'No,' you say. 'This is my first visit. My son has recently moved out this way.'

'It is a palimpsest of time,' says the man. 'Centuries of division and deforestation.' Here he pauses, checking us for interest. 'This all used to be part of the ancient Rockingham Forest, William the Conqueror's royal hunting ground.' (I remember learning that William the Conqueror built Rockingham Castle near here and wonder if he played any part in the Rockingham Triangle athletics ground, where I proved myself a mediocre high-jumper in year nine.)

We keep walking, reading in Fermyn's scars the injuries of a long history of exploitation and enclosure.

'I'm not for this world much longer,' says the man, 'but I like to hope my dear Emperors will continue on without me.'

'I'm sorry to hear that,' you say. I don't speak. Even as a thirty-three-year-old I assume the child's role of silent companion whenever we meet strangers together.

'This forest is a palace of transience,' he says. 'My whole life I've known change and loss. When I was a child I was very ill and thought I was going to die, and then my older brother *did* die, just a boy. I realised then that the birds, plants, trees, insects, every living thing however large or small, had been burning, like my own life flame, since time began, and all around me these existences were being snuffed out completely, every second, every hour, as time went by. It is true life still went on, and this perhaps was the most painful thing – the knowledge that all this wonderful world, with its light, colour, sounds, feelings, smells, would remain after I had gone, and I should have no further part in it.'[3]

As if you're ignoring what he has said, or maybe in direct response to it, you say: 'Quick, Ben. This way.'

I look to the strange man but he is fading. You pull me by the sleeve and I follow you through a narrow gap in the hedge, ducking beneath branch and twig, to a portal backlit by the sunshine of an elsewhere far beyond these Northamptonshire woods. The boulder clay underfoot gives way to chalk; grass and nettle transform into gorse and heather; winter turns back into summer. The ground slopes towards a heaving ocean two hundred miles from home. We are in Dorset, where you longed to chase butterflies with me.

'That'll be one,' you say.

'One what?' I say, lagging behind.

'A Lulworth Skipper.' You stop, pointing again. 'Yes, it is! See the pale semicircle on the wing?'

I catch up, panting, and see it: a faded horseshoe, just like you described it.

'A female. You only get them here. Keep up.'

I chase you and the grass mixes into sand and downland becomes dune. We're sifting through a heavier element altogether now, our feet flicking the ground about us in a spray of memory. Deep time fills our shoes and lodges between our toes, where we will transport it home and it will vibrate in the footwell of the car and the corners of the laundry basket. We're on Studland Beach, Dorset, and I am in your arms. I reckon I'm three or four, which puts you in your mid-to late thirties. You're topless, wearing your cheap black plastic sunglasses, and we're standing at the edge of the water where the sand is sludgy. It's late in the day, the sun is dipping, and I can feel that pleasant tightening of the skin as it meets the breeze. But your shoulders and neck are warm. I cling to your hair (no greys to be found there yet) and find its curliness strange in my fingers, the clinch of your skin against mine, the silver chain around your neck, the faded smell of Aramis. But all I can think is how impossibly big you are. The sensation is a paradoxical one: that simultaneous feeling of reassuring sameness and alienating otherness. We have the same limbs, we seem to function the same, I somehow belong to you – and yet through that same intimacy I realise (only subconsciously, but I will recognise it painfully later in life) our insurmountable difference.

What strikes me most is more a feeling than a physical fact. It's a feeling of complete safety. That as long as I'm connected to you, I won't come to any harm. I will always feel that, even as you struggle with chronic fatigue in about ten years' time, and even as you battle cancer for the first time ten years later again. Because no matter how much we might like to valorise strength, power and size, the feeling of safety has nothing to do with these things, all of which can be taken away in an instant. It's something much deeper. It's the feeling that you're not alone because there's someone for whom nothing is more important than protecting you.

But I know that when I return to the woods, you won't be there and I must continue on, alone.

13

The Lowick, Sudborough and Slipton Parish Newsletter

There is a note in the Lowick, Sudborough and Slipton parish newsletter for December 1985. It reads:

> *Despite valiant efforts to get the sallows in the woods spared I was horrified the other day to find there had been a great clearance from one end of the forest to the other. This means that many hundreds of hibernating larvae have been deprived of food and shelter during the winter [. . .]. What a desperately hard business it is to preserve our countryside against greed and ignorance! Many years of hard work have been set at naught. I'm sorry this country note is a sad one.*[1]

Until the very end, BB released fresh Emperors in Fermyn Woods. In 1990, in his eighty-fifth year, he was travelling from Northamptonshire to the Churchill Hospital in Oxford – the same hospital where Dad received his treatment – for weekly dialysis. Often, he was driven by his friend, Badger Walker, and on one occasion he encouraged Badger to go to nearby

Bernwood Forest while the dialysis was underway in order to look for Purple Emperors. They had just hatched, he said, and would be on the wing. After an hour without success Badger saw one in the lay-by where his car was parked, on his way out. 'I knew you'd find one, Badger,' said BB when he reported back. 'I just had a sort of feeling.'[2] A couple of months later, in September 1990, BB died in Northampton General Hospital, the same place I was born four years earlier.

There is a moment in *Speak, Memory* where Nabokov describes being a child going beyond the limits of the family estate on one of his butterfly hunts, and spying some 'peasant girls' skinny-dipping in shallow water. But his attention is reserved for the butterflies, and so he continues until he reaches a bog where he explores the butterflies. And then in a moment of narrative magic he is transported to the American Rocky Mountains, decades in the future. The transition is not flagged to the reader and is only indicated, at first, by a change in flora, before the locale is named:

> *At last I saw I had come to the end of the marsh. The rising ground beyond was a paradise of lupines, columbines, and penstemons. Mariposa lilies bloomed under Ponderosa pines. In the distance, fleeting cloud shadows dappled the dull green of slopes above the timber line, and the gray and white of Longs Peak.*[3]

Longs Peak, some readers will know (I certainly didn't), is in Colorado, USA. Between that one step from the bog in Russia to the mountainside in America, Nabokov loses his childhood home and the family's wealth, flees Russia, loses his father and escapes the Nazis from France. It must have been difficult to think that paradise might still await after all that. But it is easier if you have a magic carpet, like Nabokov, or believe in life's colourful carpet, like BB. Maybe for both these writers, vastly different in so many ways, butterflies *were* the carpet, or at the very least an integral part of its pattern, a conveyance to carry them through the abyss of memory and desire, where time and space might be re-coordinated – a tempting notion for anyone who has loved, lost and grieved.

14

The Purple Prince

I'm back at my computer. I should be working – either university work or my novel in progress – but instead I am messing around on YouTube. I feel like the character in Ali Smith's sublime *Artful* (one of my favourite books) who is caught by the narrator watching clips from old Greek musicals when they are meant to be writing an academic lecture. I wish you had read it – a book about loss and grief, but also about gifts and shapeshifting and love. Another transformative reading experience I never shared with you.

I also wish I had shown you this. I am watching Prince's performance at the 2004 Rock & Roll Hall of Fame induction ceremony. This is my idea of a Purple Emperor. I want to tell you about it, even if it is too late. A gift from me to you.[1]

You'd barely know Prince was there for the first two-thirds of the performance, standing at the far edge of the stage in the shadows, nonchalantly strumming non-Prince chords, while Tom Petty and Jeff Lynne and Steve Winwood and Dhani Harrison (George Harrison's son) make their way through a faithful rendition of 'While My Guitar Gently Weeps', one of Harrison's most famous Beatles numbers. Prince was inducted to the Hall that year too (hence why he is there on stage), but it's his contribution to Harrison's induction that everyone remembers. A whole legend has grown around it on internet forums and in the comments section on YouTube, where the video has over 120 million views.[2]

The story goes that Prince had been invited to participate in this ode to Harrison by Joel Gallen, the director of the Rock & Roll Hall of Fame ceremony, with the suggestion that he would take the solos originally played by Eric Clapton on the studio recording. But during the dress rehearsal, Marc Mann (a frequent collaborator of Jeff Lynne's) ploughed on with the solos, leaving Prince to play the chords in the background, like he'd ever been backup to anyone in his life! Gallen apologised to Prince after the practice, who told Gallen not to worry – let Mann play the main solo and let him do a solo at the end. No rehearsal needed, no fuss.

So, on the day, while Mann plays imitations of Eric Clapton's leads, complete with lead-guitarist gurning and shoulder spasms, Prince is the chrysalis offstage, biding his time. And then, around the 00:03:30 mark, he bursts out of his cocoon, the full-blown incomparable imago, and takes over centre stage. (Prince, the ultimate shapeshifter, a master of metamorphosis, was wearing red that night, not his customary purple . . . but you see purple no matter what he's got on.) He then proceeds to play one of the most electrifying pieces of improvisation you could hope to witness, soaring with the justified arrogance of the Purple Emperor, mixing grace with aggression to create the same dazzling aura I saw that day in the woods when I chased the butterfly of BB's dreams.

The thing I love most about this video is the look on Dhani Harrison's face just as the butterfly emerges, like he is the only lepidopterist on stage and knows exactly what is about to happen. (If you want to talk about father–son relationships, imagine being the son of a Beatle! Dhani is another Dmitri Nabokov, translating his father's work.) There's a spine-tingling moment when Prince turns his back on the audience while shredding the fretboard of his guitar and just lets himself fall. He is caught by a security guard who props him up while he continues to rip through the solo, back arched like gravity's got nothing on him, and Dhani beams from ear to ear. On a stage of people being a bit like his father, Prince is the one person there doing totally un-George-Harrison-like things. You can tell Dhani loves this, because it's the most fitting tribute possible.

Like the Purple Emperor, Prince knows he is good. There are at least two moments where he casts an impish glance across stage, presumably at Marc Mann, the guitarist who stole his solos, as if to say: 'Can you believe this shit?' Which seems a very Purple Emperorish thing to do. (My hunch is that the Mann vs Prince dynamic is an overplayed part of the mythology – repeated by me here – as Mann seems pretty thrilled by what Prince is doing in the video . . .) Finally, and this is the bit that has the internet commentators in fits, at the end of the song Prince throws his guitar in the air and *it simply disappears.* As in: it *disappears.* Like the other-worldly Emperor flying back into the canopy, it has ascended, never to come back down.

This, to my mind, is aesthetic experience in its purest form. A momentary realisation of your own discontinuity as you're taken out of yourself, out of time, and presented with something *beyond.* I wish you could check it out. From me, to you, with love.

15

Emergency

The phone call comes just as another day working from home is ending.

'Ben,' says the voice. Mum talks quickly. 'Your dad isn't good at all.'

She sounds panicked.

'His temperature has gone through the roof and his pulse is really fast. I think he needs to go to hospital, but . . . '

The *but* is their nightmare. The hospitals are over capacity due to COVID. And to contract it would likely be fatal, with Dad's compromised immune system, just as Dad is starting the treatment they hope will extend his life.

'I've called the Churchill Hospital,' says Mum, 'but they won't send an ambulance. Do I need to call the General?'

Hospital politics. Dad's consultant works at the Churchill in Oxford, but it's technically not his local hospital – it's across county lines and just under an hour away by car – so they won't send an ambulance to bring him in. If it's an emergency, they tell Mum, he should go to Northampton General. This would mean sitting in A&E where the doctors won't know anything about his case. Mum is convinced he will catch COVID and never come home.

'Can I speak to Dad?' I say.

'Yes.' Mum passes the phone.

'Hi, son,' says Dad. His voice is weak.

'Are you okay, Dad?' A stupid question. 'If I come and get you do you think you'll be okay to go all the way to Oxford?'

'Yes,' he says. 'Possibly. I don't know.'

'I'm on my way.'

'Thank you.'

It's a forty-minute drive to Mum and Dad's from mine, plus the hour to the Churchill from there. I call Mum on her mobile as I pass the junction for Northampton General.

'I'm twenty minutes away,' I say.

'I'm just on hold on the house phone with the emergency services,' she says.

'I'll take him,' I say.

'Are you sure? Is it too far? I've spoken to his consultant. He says if you can get him there, he would much prefer him to come to Oxford. He really doesn't want him ending up in A&E in his condition.'

'If he doesn't feel he can go all the way to Oxford,' I say, 'I'll take him to A&E.'

'Okay. Thank you.'

Fifteen minutes later I'm letting myself into my parents' house, wearing a surgical mask. Mum meets me at the door. Her eyes are puffy, terror-filled. I give her a quick hug and go through to the living room. Dad is sitting on the sofa with his shoes and coat on, ready to go. He looks lost. Mum has packed a small bag just in case.

'Sorry, son,' he says. 'I'm so sorry.'

'Don't be silly,' I say. He looks awful.

I help Dad to the car, but before he gets in he turns and gives Mum a cuddle. He tells her he loves her. I know what he's thinking. She's thinking the same. Her eyes flood with tears.

The journey is a trial. Sixty minutes of endless roundabouts and traffic lights, all stop–start, a disaster for Dad in his state. We don't talk. He is too sick and I'm concentrating on every inch of the drive, trying to keep things as smooth as possible while also going as fast as I can. I keep peering at him. Half the time his eyes are closed, focusing on his breathing, bucket between legs, still dressed smartly in buttoned shirt and chinos despite it all.

Forty minutes later, at the Peartree Interchange, we turn off the A34 and join the Oxford ring road. I speed over roundabouts and through traffic lights, taking bus lanes, overtaking, undertaking, attacking any gap I can find. Dad's eyes are fixed open in a disconcerting stare. With his head pinned back against the headrest, his eyes start rolling back in his skull.

'Dad?' My head is swivelling from him to the road and back again. I squeeze his leg. 'Dad?'

'I'm going,' he says. He slaps himself in the face.

I notice Dad is fumbling in his pocket for his phone.

'Dad? What is it?'

He ignores me, can only manage one thing at a time, shakily making a call.

'Jane?' he gasps.

He is saying his goodbye to Mum, I think. I want to stop and put my arms around him, simply be with him, but I also want to get to the hospital.

'Call the oncology ward,' he says to the phone. 'Tell them to meet us at the door. I don't know if I'm going to make it.'

Not a goodbye at all, then. This is a glimmer of the old him, still trying to control things, trying to be prepared.

He drops the phone and keeps his head back.

'It's going to be okay,' I say. 'We're nearly there.'

'I'm going faint,' he says. His eyes start rolling again and he looks like he might just switch off at any moment. I squeeze his leg one more time, driving one hundred miles per hour up a short stretch of dual carriageway.

'We're nearly there.'

As we approach the large roundabout at the top of Headington, I'm overcome by the realisation that Dad might be about to die, there on the passenger seat, while I'm unable to look at him for longer than a second. His breathing is rapid, his face emergency-red; I fear his heart will pack in at any moment. Should I just pull over and comfort him?

We're at the roundabout when his finger feebly points to the right.

'What is it, Dad?' I say, my voice filled with desperation. 'Are you okay?'

'You need the other lane.'

There he is! The old know-it-all that has always known how to piss me off. But he's right: I *do* need the other lane.

We tear round the roundabout and down into Headington, on our final charge for the hospital.

'I'm not going to make it,' he says.

I'm pulling onto the hospital grounds, my heart thumping. We follow the road round the hospital site, turn towards the cancer building and go through the parking barrier. We pull up outside, but of course there's no one waiting for us. It's dead, dusk descending, visiting hours over.

I practically fall out of the car and sprint towards the entrance, my legs no longer beneath me, my feet no longer my own. The automatic door shuffles open slowly and I run into the building. I don't know if I'm even allowed to go in, COVID restrictions, but what choice do I have? The cafe and shops are closed, shutters down, the atrium empty.

'Help,' I shout. 'I need help. My dad is dying.'

III
The Blues

16

The Boxer

Vladimir pats himself down, but he cannot find the key to the trunk.[1] It is a misty morning in 1940 on the French Line pier, New York. Vladimir, Véra and six-year-old Dmitri have arrived after a week's journey across the Atlantic, escaping France just as the German army is rolling in. Véra cannot locate the key either. A trio of customs officers gather round. One of them whacks the trunk with an iron bar. It opens. Pleased with himself, the officer inspects the lock, as if trying to unlock his own ingenuity. Then the trunk snaps shut again.

Eventually the trunk is reopened. Inside, lying on top, are two pairs of boxing gloves. Two of the officers put these on and begin dancing around the family of exiles, fists raised, feinting and jab-stepping. The third officer is drawn to a case of butterflies, which Vladimir opens for him. They talk about butterflies for a bit, while the others continue to prance about, throwing pretend punches. The officer suggests one of the butterflies should be called 'captain'. Vladimir doesn't mention how he is keen to get to the American Museum of Natural History so that he can compare his special catch from Moulinet, in the hope that it is a new species.

The small box of butterflies is but a remnant of much larger collections that have been lost to the perils of personal history colliding with impersonal historical forces. Vladimir's childhood collection of several hundred Russian species was left behind in 1919 when his parents fled the Bolsheviks, and now he has left another substantial collection of rare European specimens behind, this time in a Paris basement. In a couple of weeks, the Nazis will reach Paris and Vladimir's butterflies will be smashed from their glass cases by inspectors, sent blowing down the street with his rifled and tossed papers.

All boxed out, the other two customs officials suggest he close the trunk and move on. Nabokov is touched by this unexpected and faintly ridiculous welcome. 'Doesn't this show how straightforward and kind Americans are?' he will later say.[2]

Boxing gloves and butterflies. He is his father's son. Nabokov's father's library, with its sporting paraphernalia and butterfly collection, still glows in his mind. His father, V. D. Nabokov, is the embodiment of Nabokov's masculine ideal: a man of principle and moral courage, a fearless intellectual, and a man of physical strength too. He is sublimated into Fyodor's father in *The Gift*, who, in the extra chapter to that novel (which Nabokov finished not long before leaving France for the US), figures like a proto-Indiana Jones. In his father's study, Fyodor finds 'the elaboration of [his] father's thoughts, jotted in the hasty hand of a testament in the night preceding a dubious departure, when holster, gloves, and compass intrude momentarily on the sedentary life of the desk'.[3] Weapons, gadgets, midnight escapes – these are the dimensions of a stock manliness that Nabokov derived from his childhood passion for cowboy stories and the derring-do of his cousin Yuri. (Yuri died at the age of twenty-two in the White Army, rushing a machine-gun nest.[4])

But Nabokov, standing on the pier, asking another officer where he can get a good newspaper (one of them fetches him a *New York Times*) is as much Pnin as he is Indiana Jones. Pnin, the hero of his 1957 novel, yet to be written into existence; the confused, pathetic and bathetic émigré, out of place in the United States with his old-world ways and dandified intellectualism. Pnin is the stranger, the outsider, whose conception of manliness will be complicated by the continued pressures of loss and transformation in a strange land. 'After a period of panic and groping,' Nabokov will later say about his family's exile in America (an exile that begins in penury but will end with him becoming one of the most famous and wealthy writers in the world), 'I managed to settle down rather comfortably but now I know what a caterpillar must feel on the rack of metamorphosis, in the straitjacket of the pupa.'[5]

17
Holly Blue

Carli and I are sitting on the lawn with my mum at my parents' house, watching Kit decompose a small picnic. It's early July, another sunny day in lockdown. Kit is excited. He loves the weather, the large green space that we don't have at home, the promise of colourful flowers and distracting creatures, the novelty of his nana. The lockdown restrictions have eased a little, with two households now permitted to meet indoors, though I am the only person other than my parents who goes in the house. The risk is too great for Dad. Kit has probably already forgotten that going inside was ever possible anyhow. To his mind, Nana lives in the garden along with the Robin that keeps jittering towards his crumbs and the occasional butterflies that have me jumping up with my iPhone, always a second too late.

Does he notice the missing person, the absence around the picnic rug whose gravity is threatening to pull me under?

A shimmering blue butterfly has me on my feet again. It is tiny, effervescent, like a secret messenger momentarily glimpsed as it passes through our world on its way to another, a one-in-a-million alignment of different realms. It gleams like some fantastical porcelain, alternating between visibility and invisibility, and then it is gone, leaving only a flutter-by of pale blue in my mind's eye.

I turn back to the picnickers. They're not watching. Kit is toddling around with a stick of cucumber in one hand and half a crust in the other, relishing the bounce of the grass through his socks. Carli and Mum watch adoringly. Nobody else saw. The absence pulls me back towards it.

Other more familiar butterflies add their adornings to the picnic – a Peacock, a couple of Small Tortoiseshells – attractive garden frequenters whose ornateness would make them as highly prized as the Purple Emperor if they weren't so common. They are of a different reality altogether from the small blue butterfly that only I saw, which in comparison seems like a lost miniature from a quantum dimension.

This thought is disrupted by the clatter of the metal stay on the dining room window. I turn to see it opening. There, looking out onto the lawn, is Dad.

After a few nights in hospital and an adjustment to his treatment, Dad is home. But he is both Dad and not-Dad, rendered uncanny by a couple of unusual details. First, he is wearing his dressing gown. When I was growing up, Dad's dressing gown was only the rumour of a hidden life, hanging disembodied on the back of my parents' bedroom door. Kit routinely sees me lounging around the house in pyjamas or sportswear, but I rarely ever saw *my* dad looking anything other than smart. He held to personal standards – always showered and shaved and dressed appropriately before presenting himself to the day, hair combed, aftershave applied, shirt tucked in. You never caught him mid-metamorphosis.

He'd already be at the kitchen table eating breakfast in a polo shirt or an Oxford shirt and chinos (chino shorts if it was hot) when I entered in various forms of undress with bed-hair, a child of the slacker 1990s and an adolescent of the garage-rock noughties. He must have thought me scruffy, turning up later in life in my purple Lakers tracksuit top, like I hadn't ever quite grown into a serious man. Even when Dad was muddy in the fields he was in quality, specialist wear, doing things properly. There seemed to be a moral assumption behind such standards, an old-school sense of masculine pride. But today he just looks degraded – the navy-blue dressing gown, his bare chest and silver necklace, the tufty hair on his head, some scattered stubble.

More unusual than all of this are the tears in his eyes. I can't recall ever seeing him cry when I was a child, even when his chronic fatigue pushed him to despair in his forties and fifties. There was one exception though. I was home from university for Christmas when he opened a present from Mum: a framed photograph of his parents. Granddad had been dead for almost ten years, and Grandma had died just two months earlier. Parentless at Christmas for the first time in his life, raw and caught by surprise, Dad kept his eyes down, the picture in his lap, and wept silently.

My instinct is to run over to Dad, block Kit from the confusion of his granddad crying and spare Dad the embarrassment. I have to check these inherited stirrings – why should his tears be confusing or embarrassing? – this urge to cover up vulnerability, to fend off emotion. But it's hard. To see Dad physically removed from us, too exhausted and weak to come outside, too vulnerable for us to come inside and be with him. This is not the exile of historical forces that remove one from their country, of the kind Nabokov knew too well, but the paradoxical exile of being banished within one's own home. We've all tasted this strange exile a bit these past few months, living through lockdown. But for Dad there is no escape in sight.

'I'm sorry,' he whispers.

'Don't be silly,' I say, standing at the window.

'Is he okay?' asks Dad, looking out at Kit, who is too pre-occupied with the food and Nana and the dog to notice us.

'Yeah, he's all good.'

'That's good,' says Dad, wiping his eyes on his sleeve.

'I've got something for you,' I say. 'Perhaps I'll come inside?'

I put on my mask and meet Dad upstairs in the spare bedroom, off the corridor from my old room. He is lying in bed, waiting for me.

Dad no longer sleeps in what I think of as my parents' room. It's easier now to have his own space and the use of an en suite. The window looks out across the field where butterflies will be busy feeding, mating, egg-laying, their natural cycle continuing without him. I notice the binoculars on the windowsill, which he uses to watch the Red Kites wheeling and the Buzzard that sometimes settles on the fence posts. Dad also likes to keep an eye on the family of geese that have taken up on the pond he dug over in the furthest corner, locked in a sustained conflict with the prowling fox, another frequenter of the land. But I don't think the binoculars are getting much use of late, capped in their dust covers, folded shut like a roosting butterfly.

I can't get used to Dad slumped in bed, this man I associate with nothing but uprightness and rectitude. The position somehow flattens his chin to his chest even though his head is back, making him look compressed and unfamiliar. His hair remains, but its shades of grey and white are complicating. I walk across the foot of the bed and see the plastic washing-up bowl on the floor. It holds a large transparent pouch connected to a tube that runs to the bed and vanishes beneath the duvet. A cloudy pinkish liquid, like freshly squeezed grapefruit juice, sits in the bend of the tube, while the liquid in the pouch is more infernal looking, darker, concentrated.

Dad opens his eyes.

'That's looking pretty nasty, Dad,' I say, nodding at his urine bag.

'Infection,' he says, not even bothering to look at it. 'Just another of the horrible realities of it all.'

'Do you want me to empty it for you?'

I've not emptied his bag for him before, the end result of his first bout of cancer back in 2012. In the eight years since, he has never needed me to, and it's not something he wants me to start doing now. The thought of his son having to empty his piss down the toilet is wounding for a man like Dad. I know this without him having to tell me.

'It's okay,' he says. 'I can do it in a minute.'

I sit on the edge of the bed and squeeze his foot through the covers.

'I don't know,' he says, sighing, a succinct statement of resignation. He's never been a man to resign himself to anything, but in our recent conversations he has started to sound hopeless. He wonders what the point of it all is – the treatment, the physical suffering, the mental anguish, the dependency and need. Can he hold on long enough for a miraculous breakthrough in scientific knowledge? Can he defy all expectations? Can he at least get one more period of relatively good health, no matter how short-lived?

I hand him a piece of paper. He looks at it carefully and the tears come back. On it I've put five images. At the top it says: *A few reasons to keep fighting when it all feels too much.* Each image has a caption beneath. The first is a photo of Durdle Door and the Dorset coast: *So you can see the Dorset sea again.* Below this is a picture of Kit sitting in his pram. He is wearing some funky red sunglasses and a large Spot the Dog bib, holding a teddy bear on whom, for some reason, we've put a nappy: *So you can hug Kit again.* In the middle is a picture of Dad, Matt, Mum, Nan and me at Christmas, in the living room with presents all around us. Must be from the mid-1990s. Dad is heavier (he put on a bit of dad-weight in his thirties and forties) and his hair is oddly dark: *So that we can have at least one more family Christmas together.* In the top right corner is a picture of my niece. She is five. She lives in Japan and can't come to the UK because of the travel restrictions. This, of course, is the case for my brother too, who hasn't seen any of us since before Dad's surgery in January. In the picture, she is holding a drawing of Dad, Mum and Poppy: *So you can see all the family again (more than once!).* The last picture in the bottom right corner is a pristine Swallowtail (one of the many species of butterfly I have never seen) nectaring on a large red flower: *So we can go butterfly-spotting together.* I've left a space in the bottom middle for Dad to add some of his own goals.

'It's a bit corny, I know.'

'Thank you,' says Dad, wiping his eyes. 'I hope I can do all of these things.'

'You will,' I say. There's still so much to live for. But it's too easy for *me* to say that, and therefore crass somehow.

I ask how he's feeling instead. He's tired, in a lot of pain, struggling to eat, occasionally nauseous. It's amazing how these symptoms are so generic – they're what we all expect of cancer and its treatment – and yet so cruelly particular and extraordinary when you see them made manifest.

'I saw a pretty blue butterfly in the garden just now,' I say. 'Didn't see it land though.'

'Ah,' he says, a bit more upright. 'The Holly Blue.'

'Is it?'

'Yes, we get them around the garden. Probably the second brood by now. Interestingly, it's the only UK species that changes its larval foodplant between broods. The first brood lays in Holly and the second brood in Ivy.'

'I didn't know that,' I say, stating the obvious.

'There should be a few Common Blues about as well, mostly in the field, but they tend to fly much lower, at flower level. You'll see the Holly Blue spiral around the hedgerows and even up into the trees.'

'It was tiny,' I say.

'The blues are the kind of butterflies that people overlook – not your common large garden butterflies. A good next step in your butterflying journey maybe?'

My butterflying journey? Is that what I'm on?

'I want to try and see as many of the butterflies as I can this summer,' I declare.[1]

I'm not sure where that came from. It's not something I've

even consciously thought about. Where would I begin?

'I wish I could do it with you,' says Dad.

'Maybe we'll do a bit together,' I say, glancing at the motivation board, wishing for his support in this foolhardy quest that I have just signed up for and for which I am unprepared. Dad closes his eyes for a second.

'You've already missed a few of the species we get in Northants for this year,' he says, sleepily. 'But there's still plenty to see.'

Already I can feel a competitive itch surfacing, plus the obsessiveness of the completist – both traits I get from the man in the bed opposite me. He tells me that there are fifty-nine British species in all, two of which are regular migrants – the Painted Lady and Clouded Yellow – and that we get a good thirty or so of them in Northamptonshire. He tells me some good spots further afield for the various blues. Northants, it turns out, is not that prolific for this particular subfamily, which on the whole prefers unimproved grassland on south-facing chalk grassland slopes. He mentions the Chalkhill Blue, the Adonis Blue, the Small Blue and the Large Blue, the last of which is almost extinct and only present in a handful of cultivated colonies in the south-west. The Holly Blue, Common Blue and Brown Argus (a blue, apparently, despite the name) are all fairly common locally. And there's the Silver-studded Blue, which prefers heathland and dunes and is most prevalent in Dorset.

'Right,' I say. 'Okay.'

'They're all in the collection downstairs,' he says.

'Maybe I'll take a look,' I say. But I won't.

He tells me about a special butterfly at the end of the

garden that should be on the wing any day now. A rare species, not a blue. The White-letter Hairstreak.

'I watch them every year. But the way I feel right now I won't even be able to make it to the garden. They were there last year, just about, hanging on. You'll have to go looking for me.'

I am struck by a desolate sense of responsibility *and* liberation, stuck in yet more paradox. Am I even capable of continuing Dad's routines for him? He seems beyond me in so many ways.

'You'll need binoculars for the job. They rarely come down from the canopy. Just black specks spiralling around the top of the elm trees.'

'Okay,' I say. 'And how do I know which is the elm?'

Dad smiles to himself.

'We've got two – Wych Elms.'

'Right.'

'I taught you this when you were young. The base of the leaf is asymmetric.'

'Rings a bell.'

'Maybe I'll at least be able to point out the trees to you, even if I can't hang around and watch,' he says.

As if the very thought of it is tiring, Dad starts to nod off. I search on my phone for the White-letter Hairstreak. *Satyrium w-album.* I think how the White Album is one of my favourite Beatles records – for its sheer messy eclecticism, that sense of a diamond being formed under pressure. Maybe I'll mention Prince's performance of 'While My Guitar Gently Weeps' to Dad. But he's asleep now, dreaming of delicate blues and scarce White-letter Hairstreaks. I wonder if the latter are in the collection downstairs too.

18

Pictures of You

What if I'm getting this all wrong, Dad? All these made-up conversations, as if I can remember verbatim dialogue. All these contrived scenes, as if I can organise that last summer into neat episodes of time. This false shapeliness of experience, as if there was so much intention and design behind what we did in those final months. How do I find the form to do you justice? Truth is, the summer of 2020 was so formless. We simply staggered from one day to the next, while time misbehaved and conversation dissipated into dust.

I'm looking at pictures of you. A collage in a 50 × 75 IKEA frame that we made for your funeral – something for the thirty guests (the maximum permitted, COVID rules) to look at in the car park outside the crematorium, a poor substitute for a reception (not permitted). It's propped against the butterfly cabinet in your study, this room of such singular sensibility that makes no sense now that you're gone. I nearly vomited putting it together, the night before the funeral, from the fumes of the spray glue. I should have worn a mask. Now you're stuck there fifty-nine times over, behind the glass, like the butterflies pinned in your cabinet. There's a striking, muscular Purple Emperor (you on the beach in trunks pulling an old-fashioned pugilist's pose with fists raised), a precious Small Blue (you as a young boy, dressed smart in blazer and tie), a rejuvenated Brimstone (you holding Kit when he was just a few months old, podgy and soft in his nappy), a distinguished Silver-washed Fritillary (you with your arm around me at my wedding), a proud Swallowtail (you holding Matt as a baby, so small in your arms, on the maternity ward), a stylish Comma (you in your 1970s threads on a date with Mum).

What is this obsession with form, as if I can taxonomise your selves into different periods and species, when really you elude me, like the rarest butterfly running me ragged on a perilous mountainside, rocks tumbling from my feet, the sun blinding me from above? All I can offer in this book, this book you'll never read, are strange hybrid creatures, aberrations of memory and desire, composites, flashes of actuality. When I envision its final form, I don't see an unblemished imago, perfect in symmetry and shapeliness. No. I see one of those tatty butterflies you find towards the end of their cycle, making fragmented motions through the air, or resting time-worn on leaves and petals with their disintegrating wings open, bearing their damaged beauty like exploded umbrellas with twisted spokes and torn-away membrane. That's the form this book will take. But I hope you understand. I hope it would *feel* like the truth to you. Or a flutter of it, at least.

19

Mr Blue and Mrs Woolf

Almost by magic a rare blue materialises in the living room of a refined Bloomsbury townhouse. 'I felt as if a butterfly,' recalls an observer, 'by preference a pale blue butterfly – had settled on the sofa; if one raised a finger or made a movement the butterfly would be off.' That same observer watches from behind a hedge as the butterfly '[flits] through Gordon Square, erratic, irregular, with his bag, on his way to catch a train'. [1] As if a blue butterfly with a bag, catching a train, isn't astounding enough, this exceptional species then flies into the onlooker's diary and transforms into a different species altogether. 'It takes as long to know him,' writes our observer, both fatigued and intrigued by the pursuit, 'as it used to take to put one's gallipot over a humming bird moth.'[2]

Our observer is the great modernist writer Virginia Woolf, and our strange specimen, so captivating of her attention, is E. M. Forster, author of *Howards End* and *A Passage to India*. I'm not sure if the time it takes to catch a Humming-bird Hawk-moth signifies a long time or a short time, but either way Forster should have counted himself lucky not to have encountered Woolf when she was a child, when she certainly would have given the catch a good go. Woolf was a keen entomologist who enjoyed collecting butterflies throughout her childhood, and butterflies and moths flutter in and out of her writing, doing graceful symbolic work.[3]

Forster is 'an attractive character' to Woolf, but elusive, likely to fly away if she tries to engage him. There are conflicting compulsions at play in these two references to Forster-as-butterfly (one of which comes from Woolf's essay 'Old Bloomsbury', the other from her private diary): Woolf wants to catch Forster so that she can know him, understand him, but also so that she can emulate him, which, paradoxically, means be free like him. (Did Woolf know of Forster's sexuality? It seems implicit in her conscious queering of his body; indeed, Woolf's description of the 'irregularity' and 'erratic' style of his movement and his 'fantastic & very sensitive' nature have been read by others as counter-movements against the rigidly normative and hegemonic – as seen from behind a Bloomsbury hedge – values of Georgian society.[4]) This rare Forsterian species is 'whimsical & detached, caring very little I should think what people say, & with a clear idea of what he wishes'.[5] Forster, the butterfly, is mentally and physically liberated. He is an artist.

Butterflies are often a metaphor in Woolf's writing for the possibilities of non-fixed identity. And while this metaphor is used to explore aspects of gender, it has especial resonance as a metaphor for the woman artist. As Woolf's biographer Hermione Lee points out, Woolf liked to describe herself in the early stages of her writing life as 'a butterfly emerging from its chrysalis, still quivering, "apprehensive" and incapable of flight'.[6] The adult imago with its fully pumped wings, able to dart, soar and zigzag, freed from societal and cultural restraints by its irregular movements, is the ultimate goal.

The butterfly's life cycle, from ovum to larva, to pupa, to imago, is again a helpful metaphor – here representing the search for form. This search for form is no fanciful thing. It is a matter of survival. While working on *To the Lighthouse*, one of her most esteemed novels, Woolf wrote in her diary about reading Marcel Proust. He is 'as tough as catgut', she writes, '& as evanescent as a butterfly's bloom'.[7] Tough *and* evanescent. A seeming contradiction. Lily Briscoe, the introspective painter in *To the Lighthouse*, looks at a painting she is working on and sees 'the colour burning on a framework of steel; the light of a butterfly's wing lying upon the arches of a cathedral'.[8] The evanescence of the light of a butterfly's wing, built on the solidity of a cathedral – a confounding image that asks us to look through its stained-glass windows to see the illuminated truth. Not only must the artist attain the almost paradoxical status of evanescence and solidity, but so must every woman, Woolf implies, if she is to flourish in a man's world. Studying her painting, convinced that no one will ever see it, Briscoe hears Mr Tansley whispering in her ear, 'Women can't paint, women can't write . . . '[9] Towards the end of the novel, looking again at her painting, Lily thinks:

> *Beautiful and bright it should be on the surface, feathery and evanescent, one colour melting into another like the colours on a butterfly's wing; but beneath the fabric must be clamped together with bolts of iron. It was to be a thing you could ruffle with your breath; and a thing you could not dislodge with a team of horses.*[10]

Was this the form Woolf wanted too? A form that could gift her people – her Briscoes and Forsters – the environment within which to be free, light, delicate; but a form that could not be broken, formidably protective of its characters' vulnerable sensibilities?

Early on in *To the Lighthouse*, Woolf describes the large party of holidayers who comprise the novel's ensemble cast, locked away in their rooms at night:

> *their fastnesses in a house where there was no other privacy to debate anything, everything; Tansley's tie; the passing of the Reform Bill; sea-birds and butterflies; people; while the sun poured into those attics, which a plank alone separated from each other so that every footstep could be plainly heard and the Swiss girl sobbing for her father who was dying of cancer in a valley of the Grisons.*[11]

If earlier in life Woolf liked to catch butterflies and moths, she knew her characters could never be caught, just as they exceed the confines of the Ramsays' holiday home. Their fate is not to be fixed to her pages like butterflies pinned to a setting board. They must remain contingent and variable, free of the dogmas of form and society. The girl losing her father to cancer cannot be known, only glimpsed.

20

Lulworth Skipper Revisited

I'm woken by the shrill, hard pecking sound of my iPhone alarm, drilling the floor to the side of the bed. 5 a.m. I end it with an involuntary reflex before it wakes Carli.

I look in on Kit in the next room. Usually, I come in just as he is waking, when his beautiful babble starts playing on the monitor hooked up in our bedroom. I love how he grins at me as I unzip his sleeping bag and how he uncoils from his cosy chrysalis, every morning becoming yet another beautiful butterfly that I can't name. But it's too early today, so I watch him sleep for a minute and then sneak downstairs, collect my rucksack from the kitchen, and slip out the front door as quietly as I can. Forty minutes later I am passing Mum and Dad's. I hope they are both asleep too, their nights and days becoming undifferentiated as Dad's cancer continues to erode all the conventions that once gave life its form. I feel a flash of guilt, making this journey that they can no longer make, regretting that we're not making it together.

Forty minutes later again and I am passing the same junction into Oxford where just last month I tore around the roundabout while Dad almost passed out in the passenger seat. Today I don't turn off, continuing southwards on the dual carriageway and the long drive to Dorset.

It's not even 7 a.m. yet, but already the day is bright, auguring well for my butterfly expedition. It is the first time I have made this trip since last summer, when we didn't know that Dad had cancer again, and I didn't have butterflies on my mind. That day Dad had sent me his text message encouraging me to spot some Lulworth Skippers. I failed, but today I hope to put things right. I stayed up late last night reading about this plain yet somehow endearing butterfly in *The Butterflies of Britain & Ireland*, learning its feeding, mating and egg-laying habits, studying its image and varieties, as well as reviewing the Silver-studded Blue, a more enticing creature, which I also hope to see. As if it will bring me good fortune with blue butterflies, I am playing Joni Mitchell's *Blue* on the car stereo. By the time I get to the last track and Joni is singing about breaking free of her dark cocoon and flying away with beautiful wings, I am convinced that Joni is on my side and that today will be a good day.

I at least *feel* more attuned this year as I park my car on the Lulworth Estate and make the first ascent up the side of Hambury Tout. The wildflowers hugging the hillside, hiding a cacophony of crickets, while still mostly nameless to me, are now startling in their individuality. Wild Marjoram (one of the Lulworth Skipper's sources of nectar) and Tor-grass (its larval foodplant, which makes it the place to look for egg-laying females) have been memorised from Google Images, though now that I'm here I am undone by how much quirkier and kinkier everything is in reality. The idea that I will be able to distinguish Tor-grass from, well, *grass*, feels pretty laughable.

Over the years the Lulworth Skipper's numbers on these slopes have fluctuated, depending on the changing fortunes of the grass. Requiring tall clusters of Tor-grass for egg-laying, the Lulworth Skippers were kept in check in the nineteenth century by grazing rabbits and the real-life counterparts of Gabriel Oak's sheep in *Far from the Madding Crowd*, but they had their baby-boomer moment in the 1950s when sheep-grazing was largely abandoned and myxomatosis wiped out much of the nation's population of wild rabbits, enabling the grass to reach the Lulworth Skipper's required height. Numbers have dwindled slightly again since the partial reintroduction of domestic grazing and the return of wild rabbits, but if I'm not going to see any Lulworth Skippers here then, well, I won't see them anywhere else in the UK.

The Lulworth Skipper occurs throughout central Europe, Asia and North Africa, while in England it is only found on the hillsides of a twenty-five-mile stretch of Dorset coast between Weymouth and Swanage, with most concentrated on the hills around Lulworth. And yet everywhere it goes, the Lulworth Skipper is known as the Lulworth Skipper. It was James Charles Dale, squire of Glanvilles Wootton, who found this small moth-like creature at Durdle Door in 1832 and gave it its inapt soubriquet. In fact, it is the only butterfly whose English vernacular name has stuck throughout the world. The butterfly's localised name predisposes me towards it, as if it has been sprinkled with the magic of my childhood holidays.

Having spent over three hours not seeing Lulworth Skippers on these same hills last summer, I've barely walked fifty metres from the car park when I see a couple of promising creatures darting amongst the flowers on the bank. They are tiny, so I pick one to track, keeping the other in my periphery, and follow it to a lilac thistle head. It could be another kind of skipper (the equally diminutive Essex Skipper or Small Skipper, or maybe even a Large Skipper, which isn't exactly much larger), but I have a feeling this is it. I get a banker photograph and then risk getting even closer for a more useful one. Once I have this, I spend a few seconds watching it sway on the thistle until it hops from one flower to the next and weaves off through the growth. I remember Dad telling me last year to look for a pale horseshoe on its upper wings, most visible on the female, and zooming in on the image on my phone I think I know what he was talking about. It's a leathery creature – often described as olive – a bit like an inveterate sun-worshipper of my parents' age. It is fairly nondescript, but it has a certain charm. There is something mischievously cute about its large eyes, and an underdog appeal to its dullness, its teeny stature and its frisky, never-say-die activity (they usually die after a week or so . . .). I send the picture to Dad:

Is this it? I've only just got here! X

I don't have to wait long for confirmation, by which time I think I've seen several more moving between Marjoram and thistle.

That's a Lulworth Skipper alright. Well done! I wish I could be there with you xx

It's almost anticlimactic. I haven't even reached the photo ops of Durdle Door yet, the true starting point of my annual hike. Although it is extremely rare nationally, the Lulworth Skipper is locally common – how did I not see any last year? Indeed, what was I ever looking at in my pre-butterfly days? I could turn around now, conserve my energy, and head straight to the dunes in Studland, where I have a date with the

Silver-studded Blue, but that wouldn't be in the spirit of the venture somehow. I want to see more – more Lulworth Skippers, more other species. I want as much to report back to Dad as possible, to fill him with butterfly energy and compensate for last year's failure.

At the top of Hambury Tout I spot a much larger species speeding around a thicket of briar and gorse. I'm on it with alacrity, like a collector of the past, waving an iPhone instead of net and killing jar, like I might be able to get the butterfly to exchange numbers with me. I watch it dart ahead, trying to keep up, trying not to lose sight. The trick, I am learning, is to fix your gaze and power-walk without care for what might be (or, on this hillside, might *not* be) at your feet. I wonder how many lepidopterists have been sent over the edge for their obsession. Luckily, this particular butterfly waits for me, its wings held open so that I can take a good photo.

It's a fritillary of some kind. Not the Silver-washed Fritillary I have fallen in love with back home in Fermyn, nor quite how I remember the Dark Green Fritillary that I photographed last time I was here (the one I mistook for the exceptionally rare High Brown Fritillary). The name fritillary comes from the Latin *fritillus* for 'dicebox', suggestive of the code-like black-dotted design of all the fritillaries. I roll the dice and conclude that it must be some kind of Dark Green Fritillary. I know from my late-night research not to expect any other kind of fritillary in this spot – so it's not much of a gamble at all. I load up the Butterfly Conservation website: this one has the denser black trimming of the female; last year I must have snapped the male, which is why I didn't recognise it. I'll show the photo to Dad when I see him next.

*

I can now see Durdle Door below and the peaks and valleys of the coastal path opening out in concertina. But something is different this year. A new oddness prevails over these ancient hills. Two paths have been created by a run of white tape unwinding from temporary posts. A sign says 'One-Way System'. The tape wants to take me inland, when I want to operate at the edges, taking the path towards the headland and following the chalk paths up and down the extremities, like I do every summer. 'Edges,' writes Ali Smith in *Artful*, 'are magic [. . .]; there's a kind of forbidden magic on the borders of things, always a ceremony of crossing over, even if we ignore it or are unaware of it.' Edges form thresholds, loaded places, 'framed spaces through which we pass from one state to another'.[1] This is the experience I hunger for, maybe to take me away from Dad as he is now and restore me to the person who used to walk these hills. I have persuaded myself that my intended route is the only conduit to such a transformation.

A couple of hikers approach me on the path I want to take.

'Don't worry,' says the woman. 'There's no one else around and the two paths meet back together on the other side of the hill.'

Durdle Door has been on the news for all the wrong reasons – thousands of people fed up with lockdown, drawn out by the heat, overloading the beach, ignoring police warnings to stay home and safe. Just the other day three people were gravely injured after jumping from the cliffs. Can I claim any moral superiority? After all, I *am* here. I check my watch. It's not even 9 a.m. and the coast is clear. Besides, what do the hills know of one-way systems and social distancing? I'll be out of the way before there is any risk.

'Thanks,' I say and carry on.

I am thrilled to meet the Marbled Whites again, and equally thrilled that I don't need someone else to identify them for me this time. They are out in abundance, swaying on the tops of any purple flowers they can find, showing their gothic underwings like black-and-white Tim Burton sketches, all expressionist lines and angles. I see other species that I know – a solitary Small Tortoiseshell and Red Admiral, some whites. Future selves will see even more here – my first ever Small Blue, Wall Browns, rare aberrations of the Lulworth Skipper, all loaded into the landscape, waiting to be uncovered by the unfolding of continuous time. But not today.

My expectations of the Purbeck coast are, in part, shaped by Hardy. Whenever I visit, I feel like I am walking through the Wessex imaginary of his novels, formed out of the Dorset landscape and the geology of memory. In *The Return of the Native* Hardy writes of 'the strange amber-coloured butterflies which Egdon produced'.[2] Egdon is the make-believe heathland of Wessex, an amalgamation of the various heaths of Dorset. Was Hardy thinking of the Lulworth Skipper when he wrote this line? You wouldn't expect to find one on heathland, but Hardy's description suggests an exclusivity that brings the Lulworth Skipper to mind. Such is the empowering otherwiseness of the novel as an art form. Elsewhere, in *Tess of the D'Urbervilles* Hardy describes how 'gauzy skirts had brushed up from the grass innumerable flies and butterflies which, unable to escape, remained caged in the transparent tissue as in an aviary'.[3] Imprisonment never seems far from butterflies in the artistic imagination (Nabokov has a lot to answer for in this regard, as does John Fowles, author of *The Collector*), where the lethal sharpness of the imagination's edge reveals freedom on one side and capture on the other. Like Ali Smith says: 'Edge is the difference between one thing and another. It's the brink. It suggests keenness and it suggests sharpness. It can wound. It can cut. It's the blade – but it's the blunt part of the knife too.'[14]

I cross over another edge, moving from the dip of one hill to the rise of another. Ahead of me on the steep slope I see a man and a boy. They are out of time, their clothes dated, their behaviour not quite in keeping with the contemporary. The man holds a butterfly net at shoulder height and, as I get nearer, I see that the boy (a young teenager) is following tentatively behind, holding a jar. The man swipes at a tussock and with the flick of his wrist has the object of his desire enclosed in the net. I don't see what he has caught, nor do I stop to enquire. By the time I reach the top of the slope they have disappeared. But I know them, the way that anyone would know a part of themselves being reflected back.

21
Silver-studded Blue

I drive east from Lulworth to Studland, cambering and undulating with the winding lanes, which seem to lead to an overwhelming question. When the ghostly ruins of Corfe Castle rear into view, I think of Dad. He'd always challenge us to be the first to see it as we approached in the car, caravan in tow, and he'd always win, because he knew by heart the exact spot where it would appear.

It feels like I'm passing over another edge as I turn left at the base of the castle's hill, go under the railway bridge and take the Studland Road. *Corfe* comes from the Old English for cutting (*ceorfan*) and refers to the gap in which the hill stands, where a long ridge of chalk hills has been broken over millennia by two streams eroding the rock from both sides. It's the location most pregnant with the aura of our family holidays. The thought of Dad asking if I've seen the castle yet, when he can already see it, brings a lump to my throat. Edge is the brink, it can wound, it can cut. My emotions are quickened by the vertiginous sensation of moving across temporal edges, from a past in which Dad is so dominant, to a present in which he is just about with me, to a future in which he will never cut this landscape again.

I'm listening to Joni's *Blue*, turning my focus from skippers to blues, specifically the Silver-studded Blue, another butterfly we don't get at home, which I hope will be one of the most precious sightings I'll report back to Dad this summer. When I was a kid Dad used to let my brother and me have alternate control over the car stereo, though it felt like I got the most airtime, given that I always sat in the front, Dad's motion-sick rally partner. When I was very young, it was a lot of Michael Jackson (I had all the albums on cassette and purchased second-hand Jackson 5 albums and singles from car boot sales, a committed collector from the start). I didn't come to Joni until I was sixteen, when our family summer holidays had stopped, but I don't think Joni would have lasted long before Dad would hit the eject button and request something else. Too folky and warbling and, well, white, for Dad's musical tastes. They have very little in common, Dad and Joni. All that free love and bohemian culture in the 1960s and 1970s might as well have been taking place on another planet as far as Dad was concerned. Maybe he would have appreciated some of the lyrics though. Like the bombers that transform into butterflies in Joni's 1970 track 'Woodstock', a tribute to Woodstock Festival – which, ironically, she didn't attend. (They have at least that much in common, Dad and Joni.)

My other ally this afternoon is Nabokov. Nabokov dedicated himself to the blues during his American exile, particularly in the 1940s. At a time of hand-to-mouth existence, in which he took up teaching posts, moved between temporary accommodations and struggled to find publishers for his writing, scientific work provided structure and purpose. In 1942 he was appointed Research Fellow at Harvard's Museum of Comparative Zoology – low-paid but rewarding work that satisfied his lifelong ambition to be a professional entomologist. 'Four days a week,' he explained in a letter, 'I spend at the microscope in my wonderful entomological laboratory.'[1] Ensconced in a lab that took up half of the museum's first floor, surrounded by cabinets of butterflies, and long tables decked out with his tools, Nabokov found a professional satisfaction to rival the ecstasy of writing – another kind of sedentary work, but one dramatically counterpointed by long road trips into the wildernesses of America, hunting for rare species. 'From morning till night,' he wrote, 'I collect the rarest butterflies and flies for my museum.'[2] By the end of his time in America, Nabokov had established himself as one of the world's foremost authorities on the American (South and North) Polyommatinae butterflies – the blues. Drawing on the Museum of Comparative Zoology's collections and his own finds, Nabokov advanced uncommon methods for classifying butterflies (microscopic work examining genitalia and wing scales), and in doing so identified new species and subspecies of blues, and revised the Polyommatini tribe – substantial work that continues to impact the study of Lepidoptera today.[3]

My ambitions aren't quite as grand, but to me they feel substantial enough. I park on the side of a narrow road that leads to the chain ferry, tugging cars from the wild heathland of Studland across the mouth of Poole Harbour to the ostentatious homes of financiers and ex-footballers in Sandbanks. It's getting hotter. Too hot. I cross the road, drawn towards a narrow portal in the exotic-seeming trees that crowd the edge. I enter.

I find myself on alien terrain. Scramble of heather, furze and fern. Eight-foot-high thickets of gorse. It is a quenched, prickly landscape, flat, exposed. I follow a sand-scattered trail that runs a foot-wide seam through the abrasive carpet-life, but it tapers off into nothingness; another is swallowed by voracious thicket. It has already been a day of several hours' hard hiking in thirty-plus-degree heat and I am dehydrated and hungry. Most dispiriting of all, stranded on a barren planet, far from home, I can't see any sign of animal life.

Look closer, I hear Dad say. Rabbit droppings in the sand. Ants scurrying around my feet, off through the undergrowth. Unfathomable insects making crepitations. The ants are a good sign. The female Silver-studded Blue lays eggs near the nests of *Lasius* black ants (it has to be *Lasius* ants specifically, otherwise things do not end well). When the caterpillar hatches, it finds a taxi-transfer of ants waiting to perform a crossing of thresholds. The ants pick up the caterpillar and take it underground to the safety of their nest, where they tend to it, tapping it repeatedly with their antennae. The ants will even keep the caterpillar company during the day, when it comes out to feast on Common Bird's-foot-trefoil. When the caterpillar transforms into its pupal stage, the ants continue to assist, tapping away at the chrysalis like a whole entourage of hype men. When the butterfly at last emerges, its body is covered in a liquid that the ants go wild for, licking its thorax and head in an act of mutual benefit, running over it while it pumps and dries out its wings. The ants get a super-sized meal, and the butterfly is spared the deadly fungal infections caused by the sticky secretions and is simultaneously protected from wasps and flies.

I have moved from the cosmic vastness of the Lulworth hillsides to the quantum insect life of the heath. I try to embrace its otherness by leaving the trail, venturing into the entanglement of hostile flora which cuts and stabs, setting my legs on fire. As I walk through the scrub, crickets spark from my toes, tricking me into seeing tiny butterflies in my periphery. But there don't seem to be any here. Surrounded by banks and folds of sand, I'm not sure if I'm on heathland or dune, or if there is even a difference. Ahead of me is a small lake – an oasis in the desert – and beyond that the dunes and the mirage-like shimmer of the ocean. Behind me, on the other side of the road, is Studland and Godlingston Heath. Maybe I'm in neither heath nor dune, standing on the edge of the two, a liminal place of no fixed identity. I used to play in the dunes with my brother when we came to Studland Beach, anxious about the undetonated Second World War bombs buried there. What was within or beyond those dunes was far outside my comprehension, a disconcerting unknown that made me uneasy, wobbly around the edges. But now I am in that very beyond – probably no more than a mile from where we used to play, but the distance is folded against itself so that time and space lose their co-ordinates.

Searching for something you have never seen before is an odd experience. A kind of gentle estrangement. I have studied photos of the Silver-studded Blue and I am relying on two particular characteristics to help identify this elusive creature: the distinctive black outer ring of its wings' upper-sides, where the black tips of the veins spill ever so slightly over the margin, and the metallic flecks (the bits of bling from which it takes its name) set in the black spots on the underside of the hindwing. No doubt there are some pinned in Dad's collection, which I could have consulted in advance, like revising for an exam, but I didn't look. Part of the excitement is the very *firstness* of a first sighting, a singular event that can never be experienced again. Each new species takes on the lustre of a celebrity this way – someone you have read about and looked at photos of, who exists in a rarefied realm of not-quite-reality. I felt positively giddy when I saw my first Lulworth Skipper this morning, and I am excited about experiencing the same thing with the Silver-studded Blue.

But the difficulty is the process of attunement required to get to the sighting in the first place. Other than the Holly Blue and Common Blue that I have seen back home (once each), I have no point of comparison. I need to get my eye in somehow. I know from poring over *The Butterflies of Britain & Ireland* that the Silver-studded Blue lives for four or five days and rarely leaves a territory with a diameter of less than twenty metres in its lifetime. Although populations may be only one hundred metres apart, they are essentially isolated, subject to their own individual fortunes. So I need to find the right spots. The Silver-studded Blue tends to fly just a few centimetres above the ground, making turns when met by an obstacle (like sweaty humans with iPhones and back-packs). Jeremy Thomas, in my reference book, describes their flight as 'a slow, fluttering affair', which gives me hope.[4] Although the range of the species in the UK has decreased by four-fifths, it should be present in these particular dunes and heathland.

And yet nothing is coming my way. After tramping back and forth for half an hour, meeting with impassable walls of bush and tree, I start to wonder if I have made some miscal-culation. According to Thomas, the sun-loving Silver-studded Blue emerges from late June and its population peaks in mid-July. I should be skipping amongst swarms of them then. Maybe, I think, I have simply picked a patch without colonies. But this is Studland – if language has anything to do with it, it should be *the* land of this delicate blue and its glamorous studs.

The four-hour drive home is starting to hang over me. I want to get back before Kit goes to bed and find time to catch up with Dad on the phone. I decide to give a patch of gorse one last try on my way out. After a couple of minutes submerged in what feels like a phalanx of Lilliputian swords and knives, I see something. It's just a silvery flash, much smaller and more ethereal than anything I thought I was looking for. Now that I've got a sight of one I spot another. It lands on a tangle of purple and gold, and another flutters over it, sending it off again. The two split and I track one to more furze. It lands as I tiptoe towards it, but as soon as I go to crouch, it flies away. This time it lands on a small slope, and without thought I am gouging my way through the plants. I manage to lower myself within its aura, pressing my knees and elbows into the spiky surface of the heath. Its wings are closed, so I get a photo of the underside; then it opens, showing the bright crushed-velvet blue of the male Silver-studded Blue to the sun. I take another photo. Then I try my luck by putting my phone right up against it, but it has had enough of me. Off it goes.

I open my photos and pinch the image of the underside wing between thumb and forefinger (the same digits that Nabokov and collectors of old used for killing their catches by pinching the thorax) and spread it outwards, zooming in. But I cannot find the anticipated silver studs, the species' reflective jewellery, the treasure I want to take home to Dad. The Common Blue, Brown Argus, Chalkhill Blue and Adonis Blue all have very similar undersides to the Silver-studded Blue – a baroque collage of black dots and orange splodges set against white and beige – but what they *don't* have are the studs. Without them, how do I know I'm not simply looking at one of these more common blues? I check the photo of it with its wings open. The thick black outer ring of the upperside and the black tips of the veins going beyond the wing's margin are clear as day. Which leaves me puzzled – one side is surely the Silver-studded Blue, the other some other blue, like a puzzling hybrid creature sent to perplex me.

There's only one thing for it. I send both pictures to Dad.

Is this the SSB? No studs, but surely the upperside can't be anything else? X

While I wait for his reply I search through more images online, wound up by my own desperation, too obsessed with categorical knowing and completion, missing the whole point of being here.

Can't see the studs, but there's no doubt about that second picture. Well done xx

It's an unsatisfying conclusion. What if Dad is wrong? Can I trust his judgement? And what does it even matter?

22
What Is Man?

This is a moment Dad hoped would never come to pass. I walk into his bedroom from the adjoining bathroom having emptied his urine down the toilet. He's sat up in bed, topless, with his reading glasses on, preparing the paraphernalia that I have fetched for him.

'Thanks, son,' he says. 'Just lay it back in the bowl down there.'

He's opening some kind of sachet as he says this, out of which comes a wipe.

'Right, you're watching?'

'Yes,' I say.

He pulls the bedsheet down to his waist, revealing the stoma on the right of his stomach. It's a red-pink fleshy mound that balloons from his abdomen, made from a piece of his intestine, a bit like the rubber bladder that pokes through the split seam of a football, and it connects internally to his urinary system. It's porous, so it continually weeps urine into a bag that he attaches over it.

He starts rubbing around the edges with the wipe.

'This is just to get rid of the adhesive from the bag and to keep it generally clean.'

'Right,' I say. 'Does it hurt?'

'No.'

He looks good today – colour in his cheeks, hair combed. But it's important for me to learn how to do this. As he gets sicker, he will be unable to do it himself. I watch as he applies the new bag, carefully pressing any air out from the seal. He talks me through each step in his usual methodical way.

'Got it?'

'Who knows?' I say.

'I remember having to clean your granddad when he was in the hospice,' he says, pulling a T-shirt on. 'Sponge baths, shaving, cutting nails. You think you'll never be able to do it, but you can.'

He is trying to reassure me, but I think he's also telling me that it's harder for the bathed than it is for the bather – to be exposed, vulnerable, dependent. This is all such a radical challenge to his sense of manhood.

'Now let me look at those photos,' he says, shirt back on, bedsheet over his stomach. I hand him my phone and retreat to the doorstep that leads down to the landing, where I sit, trying to maintain some semblance of social distancing.

'That's it alright,' he says, admiring my first ever Lulworth Skipper. 'You know, your granddad caught one once, when we were on holiday in Dorset, when I was a boy. He wasn't a collector at all, but he wanted to get one for Beryl, our neighbour, who was a serious collector. Anyhow, your granddad spent ages setting this Lulworth Skipper for him, a very delicate task. But Beryl declined the gift. Said it didn't count if he didn't catch it himself. Only wanted his own finds in his collection. Your granddad was furious. They didn't speak for a while.'

'What happened to the Skipper?'

'Went in the bin, I imagine. But I've got all of Beryl's butterflies now, in my collection downstairs. Bought them from his son after he passed.'

None of this surprises me. Granddad had a short fuse. The stories have become legendary. How, working on the building sites (a bricklayer his whole life, once he returned from fighting in the Second World War), he hit a man between the legs with a hammer. This man, so the tale goes, was doing some kind of unimaginable party trick with his penis, and Granddad took issue with it. He didn't hit him, as such; more a donk, but right on target. The other guy was a notorious hard case, which only adds to the drama. Supposedly he chased Granddad around the site, until Granddad jammed his head in the door of one of the new houses and gave him a pasting.

It's not the only story involving Granddad and violence.

'Did you love Granddad?' I ask.

I'm surprised by the directness of my own question. I've never really doubted Dad's love for his dad, but I've always thought it complicated. He has been open with me about Granddad's shortcomings – his selfishness, his bloody-mindedness, his hardness, his short temper – but in some way he idolised him, especially his strength, his meticulousness, his fearlessness. Maybe, living the father–son cliché, he just wanted his approval.

'Very much,' says Dad, taking my question at face value. 'All I ever wanted was to be with him. I'm not sure he felt the same way. Well, that's not true. I went everywhere with him – the woods, the fields, shooting, fishing, just generally being outdoors and seeing what we could find. But these were the things *he* wanted to do. I was allowed along for the ride. It was only later in life that he saw me as a companion, rather than a shadow.'

Whenever I hear details about Dad's childhood, it feels like we grew up a couple of centuries apart: living outdoors with a total lack of anything I would consider a source of entertainment, eating 'hasty dick' for pudding (flour mixed with some milk and a sprinkle of sugar on top), using old towels for nappies, as well as the outdoor toilet, sharing bathwater in order of seniority (naturally, Granddad first, being the eldest), playing with the pet ferret (when it died Dad buried it in the garden and then dug it back up in a fit of emotion; the skull is still downstairs in his study), getting caned by teachers at school. Then there was the horrendous bullying he withstood before an athletic transformation in his early teens meant he lost the weight that had made him a target and also meant he could take care of himself. In his first year at grammar school, a group of sixth formers terrorised him – they hung him from coat hooks, flushed his head down the toilet, waited for him at the bus stop, pushed him around, called him Maggot Masters. One of the ringleaders was from the same village as Dad. When Dad told Granddad what was going on, instead of talking to the school or doing anything Dad or I would recognise as taking care of his son, Granddad ordered him to go to this older boy's house, alone, and sort it out.

'Can you imagine? The lad was seventeen, eighteen years old. I was almost in tears, shaking like a leaf, when his mum answered the door.'

No, I can't imagine Dad ever parenting me that way. (For what it's worth, the mother dragged her son outside and gave him a hiding in front of Dad.)

'He was selfish, but in other ways he'd do anything for you,' says Dad. 'Every day for a year he turned up to help build this house.'

He goes quiet. I can't tell if he's thinking or starting to tire.

'You worked on the building sites for a bit, didn't you?'

I've been asking Dad lots of questions like this of late, as if I need to make sure I have everything straight before the details disappear with him. He tells me how he wanted to be a vet (just imagine how much more terrible taxidermy we'd have in the house . . .) but was ill-advised on what subjects to take at school; how he commenced training as a surveyor instead but couldn't hack it, not only because he struggled with the studying but also because Mum and her parents had moved away to Suffolk; how he quit and went to work on the building sites like his dad (better money, he is quick to point out, plus the physical exercise, which he appreciated) while scouring the job listings in the newspaper every day. Even as he recounts all of this to me, I can sense a residual stress and anxiety: the pressure to provide, to amount to something, to be a success. Men put roofs over heads, clothes on backs, food on tables – that is his code. He had to be the breadwinner, and he had to have more than his parents had. These were non-negotiables.

Eventually he got a job as a sales rep for an agricultural company – a job he found he was good at, driving around the country and chatting with farmers, which set him up to start his own company. He reminds me how we had nothing when he quit to start a business in the 1980s, when I was a newborn and my brother was three; how he gave himself a year to break even, otherwise he'd go back to the job listings. Through sacrifice and hard work, Mum and Dad made a go of it. It took years before they saw any financial rewards, reluctant to employ anyone else, unwilling to take risks to expand, but eventually they were able to derive a comfortable middle-class existence from it. The dream?

'Yes. And being your own boss means you can get out to the woods when you want to see some butterflies.'

It seems like a nightmare now. Looking down the side of his bed I see a stack of files and folders. Dad is desperate to sell the business before he dies – once he's gone, there'll be no one to run it. The stress is killing him, like it might beat the cancer to the job. He takes calls from his lawyer and financial adviser when he can't even sit up; he listens to instructions he cannot understand and asks me to help him with online forms and digital signatures.

'We'll never get close to what it's worth,' he says ruefully.

Is this, we're both wondering in different ways, what it all amounts to?

I leave Dad to rest. I pinch his binoculars on the way out and go down to the bottom of the garden to watch the two Wych Elms for White-letter Hairstreaks.

I remember on my sixteenth birthday, Dad reproduced some of Rudyard Kipling's 'If—' in my birthday card, the poem that begins, 'If you can keep your head when all about you / Are losing theirs and blaming it on you' and ends, 'you'll be a Man, my son!'[1] – the implication of the poem being that if you can be a person of honour and integrity, then you will be a man.

Like most kids, my dad was the only evidence I had to go on when figuring out what it meant to be a man. And it all seemed to correspond with most of what I saw on TV and in the movies, so I accepted Dad as the paragon of masculinity. Masculinity was physical strength and size, it was being a provider, it was practical know-how, it was knowing what to do with one's hands (how to give a firm handshake or use the ball of your hand to manoeuvre the steering wheel when reversing), it was taking no nonsense, it was being in control of all situations, it was competitiveness, it was knowing what to do with an injured animal, it was knowing he could overpower me easily if he wanted to. It was also the brace of pheasants hanging from the rafters in the garage, the plucking of feathers at the utility sink, the pimpled skin slit open with a knife, the organs torn out with bare hands, the acrid smell of blood and guts (pheasant, rabbit, fish) wrapped in newspaper. It was something that made you feel confused and a bit sick. It was a lesson you didn't really want.

Mum was our protection from these things. While she, like my father, subscribed to a fairly rigid schema of masculine and feminine, being the woman of the house also meant being the buffer against the harsher aspects of masculinity and a man's upbringing. She would play the peacemaker whenever Dad and I got into it, trying to diffuse escalating situations, inserting herself between us to prevent physical confrontations, just begging us to back down. Dad was the enforcer, Mum was the comforter. Dad was also the breadwinner, Mum the nurturer.

Growing up, I never saw what an alternative model might look like. The conventions of masculinity were, I now think, something that added up to a problematic omnipotence. I remember holding the almost subconscious feeling that I owed the most gratitude to Dad, that he was somehow more responsible than anyone or anything for the good in our life, that we (including Mum) were the fortunate beneficiaries of his prowess. He would never say these things himself, but they are encoded in the assumptions of the patriarchal dynamic, and that was the dynamic of *our* home, where things divided along old-fashioned gendered lines.

But while Carli and I have consciously resisted the traditional configuration of our childhood homes (her parents followed a similar predictable template to mine), I can't pretend that many of the things I'm most proud of Dad for aren't precisely the things we associate with masculine, patriarchal codes. I always liked knowing that he could handle himself. I cherished the way he made us feel safe, protected, invulnerable; the way he seemed to know something about everything; the way it seemed like nothing was beyond him. So many of these qualities are of course nothing more than the naive illusions of the child willing them to be the case, or maybe they are the qualities that the child is conditioned to think of as reality, all part of our cultural programming. Often they are merely the deceptive aura of the very privileges afforded the man in the first place. But it's not like I would want my children to think the opposite things about me. You see, that's precisely how masculinity works.

Maybe masculinity is the thing that always makes you feel like you'll never quite come up to the mark. Kipling's criteria for being a man are certainly lofty – 'If you can bear to hear the truth you've spoken / Twisted by knaves to make a trap for fools, / Or watch the things you gave your life to, broken, / And stoop and build 'em up with worn-out tools', etc.[2] Maybe Kipling's point is that being a man is nigh on impossible. The thing is, Dad always *was* the man of integrity. He had a moral goodness that surpassed the superficial qualities I associated with his manliness. What exactly I mean by anything as woolly as 'moral goodness' is hard to say now, but I always felt it. It has something to do with love and care. But none of this has any bearing on being a man, of course, just as the virtues described in Kipling's poem are not the exclusive possession of men. If only I could see a White-letter Hairstreak, I think, maybe *then* I would be a man. Just another of the many things that Dad can do that seems to be beyond me.

The White-letter Hairstreak is one of the hardest British butterflies to observe. Its foodplant is the elm, an endangered tree, and it rarely comes down from the canopy. I have admired the striking white W etched on its underwing in Richard Lewington's illustrations in *The Butterflies of Britain & Ireland* – but it's no good to me as an identifier when the butterfly is the size of my thumbnail and hiding thirty-plus feet in the air. If it is up there at all, that is, of which I am doubtful. I need Dad out here to show me *how* to look.

By the late 1970s, thirty million elms, a huge proportion of the native population, had died in the UK after the arrival in the late 1960s of Dutch elm disease, a lethal fungus spread by beetles which pick up its spores and transport them to healthy elms, there to engrave the bark with the disease. Once the spores get into the tree's root systems, the capillaries constrict and the tree can no longer circulate and process water, causing it to die of thirst. The nadir of the British elm was in 1976, one of the hottest years on record, a year of tremendous drought and the year my parents got married.

Each year I teach *Howards End* by E. M. Forster (Woolf's pale blue butterfly) to my students, a book where a Wych Elm leans over the titular house, marking and overriding the boundary between garden and meadow and, therefore, the world outside the domestic sphere. 'It was a comrade,' writes Forster,

> *bending over the house, strength and adventure in its roots, but in its utmost fingers tenderness, and the girth, that a dozen men could not have spanned, became in the end evanescent, till pale bud clusters seemed to float in the air. It was a comrade. House and tree transcended any simile of sex [. . .] to compare either to man, to woman, always dwarfed the vision.*[3]

Evanescent but impervious to the efforts of even a dozen men, Forster's Wych Elm reminds me of Woolf's ideal form (incidentally, Woolf's ashes were buried beneath an elm), which she too calls evanescent, but also tough. The Wych Elm is an important symbol in the pale blue butterfly's novel, a novel that challenges patriarchal forms of legacy and inheritance. It is something solid and rooted, yet something that evades our grasp, slips binaries and fixed categories, and escapes the prison of symbolism. Staring up at the two Wych Elms in the garden, unable to find the thing I'm looking for, I wonder if it might reveal other things I never knew I was after.

What if I told you, Dad, that man is a cultural construction? I can't imagine we'd get far. We would mix our terms – you'd be talking about biology and sex, I'd be talking about society and gender – until we'd butt heads like two stubborn, competitive, know-it-all men.

Let me turn, instead, to one of the writers who has meant most to me over the years: Angela Carter. I don't think you would like Carter. Not because of her views on gender (though you would find them puzzling at first), nor anything to do with her politics (socialist, feminist, about which I'd imagine you'd have questions), but because of her ornate, flamboyant, densely literary style – the very thing that pulled me in when a beloved schoolteacher gifted me a copy of her 1984 novel, *Nights at the Circus*, as a congratulatory prize for getting into university. I've been reading her, writing on her and teaching her to my students ever since. But I don't think I've mentioned her to you before.

'Imagine having to be macho,' said Carter in a 1979 interview: 'I can't think of anything more terrible' – a quote that immediately gets male readers onside.[4] Carter loathed patriarchy, not men, and if femininity was a cultural construction, then so was masculinity. Both, according to Carter, are terrible constrictions. Much of her later thinking on gender developed during a brief period in Japan at the start of the 1970s.[5] Not only did she manage to escape an unhappy marriage by being there, she also 'learnt what it is to be a woman and became radicalised'.[6] In Japan she felt profoundly untethered by the discovery of her own otherness – to the Japanese men she encountered she was, in her mind at least, 'a bit like a phoenix or a unicorn', and she became 'very conscious . . . of being a European, being white & coming from a part of the world whose history is almost over'.[7] (The othering works both ways; there is more than a whiff of orientalism to her letters and diary entries from that time and how she eroticises otherness.) In Japan, Carter began exploring the uneven and distorting power dynamics of gender relations – she said that during her time there she 'found [herself] in the front line of the battle [of the sexes]' – and applied a social anthropologist's eye to the sleazier aspects of downtown Tokyo.[8] Carter had a memorable encounter in a mirrored 'love hotel' and even spent a week working in a hostess bar, sitting on the laps of salarymen while feeding them and fending off their advances ('under the table, a continuous groping goes on', 'a hostess can hardly call her breasts her own for the duration of the hostilities').[9] 'This is a heartbreaking country for a feminist,' she wrote in a letter.[10] And what was the name of the hostess bar? 'Butterfly'. 'It is hard to say which sex is most exploited by the system,' she says, but 'the hostess, poor butterfly, is selling her youth and time and energy at a very cheap rate.'[11]

Butterflies are rare creatures in Carter's work, though they do appear at moments where identity is shown to be unstable. Was Carter's time in the Butterfly hostess bar pupating in the back of her mind when she turned to butterflies as a way of symbolising a metamorphic masculinity in her final book, *Wise Children* (1991)? One of the wittiest and punchiest literary takedowns of patriarchy, *Wise Children* archly interrogates fatherhood and masculinity. One of its most memorable characters is Peregrine Hazard, or Uncle Perry, who flitters in and out of the narrative like an exotic nymphalid, an alternative father figure to Dora and Nora, the twins at its centre. Perry, by no means a morally virtuous or particularly enlightened man – he is an explosion of male ego, but also a glimpse of how it might be put back together differently – is a character blessed with the affection of his author. In her working notes for the book, Carter calls him 'the king of topsy turvy' and 'the lord of misrule' – morally ambivalent terms, perhaps, though for Carter these are values to be championed (she once described her own father, though a 'law-and-order man', as someone 'helplessly tuned in to misrule').[12] Perry is certainly the antithesis of the twins' biological father, Melchior, the great Shakespearean actor of his age. Melchior is vain, feckless and absent, too obsessed with status and legacy, utterly dependent on and deluded by patriarchal privilege. Melchior, unlike Perry, is the embodiment of rigid masculinity.

'Mother,' says Dora, the narrator, 'is always a mother, since a mother is a biological fact, whilst a father is a movable feast.'[13] I think Carter is comparatively fond of Perry in *Wise Children* for his ability to shapeshift and move with the feast. 'You spent your childhood on the road,' recalls Dora, 'here today, gone tomorrow; you grew up a restless man. You loved change. And fornication. And trouble. And, funnily enough, towards the end, you loved butterflies. Peregrine Hazard, lost among the butterflies, lost in the jungle, vanished away as neatly and completely as if you had become the object of one of those conjuring tricks you were so fond of.'[14]

In the novel's riotous conclusion, Perry turns up at Melchior's one-hundredth birthday wreathed in exotic butterflies. He is one hundred that day too (Melchior and Perry are also twins; it runs in the family), and he is now a lepidopterist (the latest profession in a colourful career that Dora describes thus: 'adventurer, magician, seducer, explorer, scriptwriter, rich man, poor man'),[15] equipped with the caterpillars of newly discovered species, one for each member of his family. The party ends when Uncle Perry, at one hundred years of age, and Dora, seventy-five, "fuck the house down" in an act of consensual geriatric incest (quite a concept to get your head around, that).[16] It is implied that this might not be the first time. More troublingly, it is implied that the first time was when Dora was in her early teens. The novel provides no overt judgement on this, no moral commentary. Indeed, for its duration, Perry is simply adored and championed by Nora and by the implied author too. Perhaps this itself is meant to tell us something about the insidious and often invisible influence of patriarchy, such that I wonder if the butterflies – symbols in this scene of both nature *and* illusion – are there precisely to alert us to the social fictions that have been passed off as natural and that regulate our lives.

In her 1972 novel, *The Infernal Desire Machines of Doctor Hoffman*, written during her stay in Japan, Carter writes: 'A sage of Ancient China, the learned Chuang Tzu, dreamed he was a butterfly. When he woke up, he was hard put to it to tell whether a man had dreamed he was a butterfly or a butterfly was still dreaming he was a man.'[17] Perhaps most men are busy dreaming they are men, when they would be better off dreaming they are butterflies. We do like to dream up our fathers, that's for sure. As Dora says of her father: 'I sometimes wonder if we haven't been making him up all along. If he isn't just a collection of our hopes and dreams and wishful thinking in the afternoons. Something to set our lives by, like the old clock in the hall.'[18] All fathers are *that*, in a sense.

Nabokov liked to refer to Tzu too. At the start of a sequence of lectures that he gave to his American students on literary metamorphoses (Kafka's *The Metamorphosis*, Stevenson's *The Strange Case of Dr Jekyll and Mr Hyde*, Gogol's 'The Overcoat'), he used to say: 'There was a Chinese philosopher who all his life pondered the problem whether he was a Chinese philosopher dreaming that he was a butterfly or a butterfly dreaming that she was a philosopher.'[19] Later in the lecture, having described a butterfly's pained metamorphosis in wonderfully Nabokovian detail, he would add: 'You have noticed that the caterpillar is a he, the pupa an it, and the butterfly a she. You will ask – what is the feeling of hatching? Oh, no doubt, there is a rush of panic to the head, a thrill of breathlessness and strange sensation.'[20] Nabokov's gendering of the different stages of the butterfly's life cycle may simply be butterflying parlance. But just as the butterfly's metamorphosis, from larva to pupa to imago, is overwhelming – skin tight, body itching, breath sucked away – it might also be discomforting for men to split, burst and shed the armoury of patriarchy. As it is for the butterfly, though, the change is necessary and vital.

23
Mum

I come from the garden, through the back door, into the kitchen.

'Any luck?' asks Mum, sitting at the kitchen table with a magazine.

'No,' I say, folding Dad's binoculars and putting them away. 'I've looked quite a few times now. To be honest, I find it hard to believe there'd be any there.'

'What are they, again?'

'White-letter Hairstreaks.'

Mum raises her eyebrows.

'From what I've read, they are very scarce. It seems unlikely that they'd be hanging around at the end of someone's garden.'

'Well, your dad would know.'

'I guess.'

On a couple of occasions, looking for the White-letter Hairstreaks, I have lowered the binoculars to find Mum has appeared at my side. She gazes up at the tree, but I don't think she is particularly looking for butterflies, just wanting to escape the house, just looking for some company. Mum showed even less interest in Dad's naturalist passions than Matt and me when we were growing up, but then she *has* read *Wise Children* (at my recommendation, though I don't think she was much taken by it). When I was studying English at university, Mum started buying Penguin Classics and reading about new publications in the newspaper, making an effort to keep abreast of this sphere her son was being irresistibly drawn to. I also think Mum quite liked being able to tell Dad that he read trash and that he was clueless when it came to 'culture'. It wasn't mean-spirited or anything – it's just that books were an area where she felt like she had the upper hand, Dad being a man who rarely let you feel like you had that. It gave her something over the man who dominated everything else. I could mention things to Mum – what I was reading, what I was working on – that I wouldn't mention to him.

Even when I was a teenager, Mum was the one I would play music to, watch films with, tell about my reading. She would indulge every new passion and fad. But we don't talk about these things anymore. I sit in Dad's chair – the special one with arms and a cushion tied to it, the patriarch's chair – and look across at her. She is drained, exhausted. Living with someone with a terminal condition is like living through a strange anticipatory grief, in mourning for someone who is still there. You can feel Dad throughout the house, in its pained silence, like an absent presence, while upstairs, in the room above us, he is shedding his recognisable forms. Mum talks more and more frequently about how big and strong he used to be, because such reminders are more and more necessary. He was my rock, she says, my strength. This chair, I think, feels too big for me.

She feels that caring for Dad is getting beyond her. The daily unpredictability, the profound tiredness, the guilt that comes from arguing with a dying man when things get tense – all of this is made worse, if possible, by the pandemic. Mum feels desolate, cut off from the outside world and the support it might normally have offered. This compounds her awful responsibility, left to make consequential evaluations and decisions by herself – should she be ringing the consultant, should Dad be going into hospital, should the paramedics be coming out? She speaks to the ward nurses at the Churchill Hospital on the phone, reporting new symptoms to them, convincing herself that she is being a nuisance, scared something is going to be missed. All the while, the pandemic and the lockdown are developing in her a fear of the outside world. I want to tell Mum that she is doing remarkable things, but any words I think up feel flat. Everything she has ever known is changing. She's losing her life's companion, contemplating what she has already told herself will be a future spent alone. She is also losing the person who took care of everything for her.

It is the latter, selfishly, that terrifies me. Mum and Dad have been together since they were fifteen, post Dad's athletic transformation (things would have started even earlier if Dad had had his way, smitten with Mum from the moment they met at the start of grammar school), so it's hardly surprising that they are dependent on one another. But the division of labour, once my brother and I were on the scene, was very rigid: Dad worked, while Mum did everything else. Or, another way of putting it, Mum looked after the kids, while Dad did everything else. I feel a bit overwhelmed by the intimation that I need to fill the monumental gap that

Dad will leave in Mum's life – a gap that is already forming, its gravitational force increasing by the minute – and knowing that I will never succeed. How can I ever be *him*?

When he has the energy, Dad is talking me through all the stuff he thinks someone needs to know, which means the stuff that *I* need to know because Mum says it's beyond her and because my brother is on the other side of the world: car and home insurance policies, savings and investments, when the alarm service and the boiler service are due, leaks and breaks that need attending to, when the hedges in the field need cutting and who needs to be contacted to do them, the details of the veterinary specialist I need to speak to about Poppy's failing eyes, the arrangements for the business, what days the bins go out, etc. I make notes and read through them when I'm at home, like I'm studying to become Dad, marvelling at how complicated a life can be made to seem. Sometimes I think it suited Mum to let Dad take care of all these things, acting like they were men's work, and it makes me angry; other times I think he designed it to be that way, wanted it that way, because it gave him all the power, which makes me even angrier. Of course, the truth is more complicated. I think Mum was happy for Dad to be in charge, and I think he was happy to have the authority, but deep down they both must have resented the consequences – Mum powerless, Dad overwhelmed with stress.

Angela Carter's feminism would make no more sense, would have no more appeal, to Mum than it would to Dad. Basically, my parents signed up for all the binaries – masculine/feminine, breadwinner/housewife . . . As I got older, I began to see how terrible a constriction they were for both parties, but especially for Mum. I don't think Mum and Dad ever saw it that way, so who am I to judge? But moving forward, helping Mum fill some of the gap left by Dad, can I play a part in breaking these limits down? Or will I simply conserve them by controlling all the things Dad once controlled, grabbing all the power for myself? I don't know. But I do know that Mum is more capable than she tells herself. These last few months seem to have convinced her that she cannot do *anything*, when in fact she is smart and perceptive and insightful. I want to say these things to her.

But my real problem with the conservative power structures of our family, more than the alienation and imbalances they perpetuate, is they require that *I* now become the man. It's a self-fulfilling prophecy. I *want* to come up to Dad's mark; I *want* to fill his shoes. Some of this comes from a place of purity and goodness, but some of it is simple vanity. It would bother me if others thought I wasn't taking care of my mum like Dad did, if friends, relatives, neighbours said I wasn't being the strong man that she needs. (Clichés of language, I remind myself, are useful indicators of clichéd ideology.) But what Mum really needs is her son, and already I am letting her down. We rarely have normal conversations anymore. Everything is about the cancer, of course, or jobs that need doing around the house. I find myself snapping all the time, my patience thinner than it used to be, my affection harder to show. It hurts Mum; it hurts me too. In my parents' eyes, I have always been the baby, which means Mum used to know she could come to me for warmth. But the more I find myself standing in for Dad, the more difficult it is somehow to access or convey that warmth.

We look at each other across the table once more. She is frightened – of being alone, of illness, of everything. I want to tell her that she'll never be alone, because she will always have me, for what I'm worth, and that I need her just as much. I'm shattered, ready to scream and cry and punch some walls, when really I just want to tell Mum that I love her.

'Well, I better be on my way.'

24
Chalkhills and Adonises

The next Friday Dad arranges an alternative lift to the hospital for his chemotherapy and gives me the day off. As if from guilt, or just a desire to be near him, I follow him to Oxfordshire in search of blues and hairstreaks, keeping within thirty minutes' distance from the Oxford Cancer and Haematology Centre at all times.

My first destination is Watlington Hill, a 235-metre-high hill in the east of Oxfordshire, looking out across the Oxford Vale and the Chiltern Escarpment. This is prime blue territory, with its south-facing chalkland slopes providing the ideal environment for species of the Polyommatini tribe – the tribe to which Nabokov dedicated his scientific career. Today I hope to see two particular species for the first time: the Chalkhill Blue and the Adonis Blue. (The butterfly Nabokov captured above the village of Moulinet in 1938, which he believed to be a new species and named *Lysandra cormion* when he arrived in the US, was proven in 1989 to be a cross between the Chalkhill Blue (*Lysandra coridon*) and *Meleageria daphnis*.)

One species of blue that demanded Nabokov's attention was *Lycaeides argyrognomon sublivens*, which drew him to Telluride, Colorado, in 1951 in search of its previously undiscovered female. Nabokov had first described the male in 1949 on 'the strength of nine males in the Museum of Comparative Zoology, Harvard', but the female had never been recorded.[1] This presented Nabokov with an irresistible challenge. Taking off in the family Oldsmobile with Véra at the wheel, Nabokov searched for other rare butterflies along the journey, as he did every summer on their epic road trips, clocking over two hundred thousand miles during their twenty years in America. But dramatic weather made the challenge greater. 'Owing to rains and floods, especially noticeable in Kansas,' he recalled, 'most of the drive from New York State to Colorado was entomologically uneventful.'[2] Fortunately, Nabokov took with him 'copious notes'[3] relating to his latest novel – one that had been pupating for many years, had even been glimpsed in other stories, but was finally coming into focus. Despite the trip being blighted by thunderstorms and floods, Nabokov collected details (the smells of motels, the obscure poetry of town names, the texture and moods of great American skies) for this most troubling novel, whose unfinished draft he had already attempted to burn twice. He worked on it from the back seat while Véra (who had saved the novel from the flames) heroically negotiated the elements.

Weather is not a problem today. At least not for the butterflies. For me it is already far too hot. I never seem to be well prepared for these butterflying trips – ill-equipped on the technology front, a clutter of poorly processed information on the research front, and hopeless on the practical front. Fortunately, things start off in the shade, a short walk through woodland that wraps around the base of the slope, a perfect spot for Speckled Wood butterflies, who like dappled sunlight, but I'm soon ejected into the basin between two opposing hills. Butterflies and their habitats are becoming slightly more legible to me now. On one side I see my first Small Heath, as well as lots of whites and some Brimstones and Small Tortoiseshells, all busy amongst an entanglement of green plant life (not so legible) on flatland. On my other side, rearing up, is the sun-baked slope of Watlington Hill. It rises with its short-cropped turf and pockets of small trees and downland flora (mostly scorched, the colours all burnt away), reminding me of the Teletubbies landscape that Kit likes to observe. I sip some water from my flask – it's luke-warm and tastes like plastic – and rue not bringing a hat or extra lotion (my eyes are now stinging from rivulets of the lotion that I applied before I left the house).

Nabokov succumbed to what he called 'a kind of sun-stroke' not long after returning from his Colorado trip, which triggered a 'brilliant but sterile turmoil of thoughts and fancies'.[4] Amongst these thoughts and fancies, perhaps, was his turbulent novel in progress, born of bad weather and filled with bad weather of its own – a novel where a whisper is 'hot thunder', an argument is a 'squall', windshield wipers cannot clear tears that mix with drizzle, and, Humbert Humbert, one of the most notorious anti-heroes in all of twentieth-century literature, loses his mother to a bolt of lightning on a ridge above Moulinet. The narrator doesn't linger: 'My very photogenic mother died in a freak accident (picnic, lightning).'[5] The weather, when Vladimir and Véra arrived in Telluride, Colorado, was not propitious. However, the constant to and fro between rain and sunshine generated a striking rainbow every evening that straddled the town – the town Nabokov described as a 'damp, unfrequented, but very spectacular cul-de-sac [. . .] at the end of two converging roads, one from Placerville, the other from Dolores'.[6] (Close readers will recognise the latter as the actual name of Nabokov's most famous fictional creation.) Véra and Vladimir stayed in the only motel in the vicinity, Valley View Court, at an altitude of nine thousand feet. From there Nabokov would climb steep trails, often accompanied by Véra, to at least twelve thousand feet, in pursuit of his blue butterfly, *sublivens*.

Nabokov took refuge from the daily electric storms in an abandoned roadside house, where he found old magazines to occupy him. Each day, when the sun eventually gained ascendancy, he was presented with the perfect habitat for the object of his desire: fine growths of flowering lupines and Green Gentians, in the turrets of which he watched Broad-tailed Hummingbirds and Striped Hawk-moths. *Lupinus parviflorus* turned out to be the foodplant of his butterfly, and it was owing to this that he finally discovered the female *sublivens*, one of the great highlights of a long butterflying career. After the trip he was able to deposit ten females and twenty males in the Cornell University collections and eighteen males and six females in the Museum of Comparative Zoology at Harvard.

I, on the other hand, am not destined for success in my novice pursuits. Watlington Hill is scattered with blue butterflies, but they rarely settle for more than a second, so that the slope appears to be disintegrating before my eyes. It must be too hot – we're well into the thirties now – making the butterflies frisky, like sun-drunk revellers on a Club 18-30 holiday. I chase and turn repeatedly, overheating but unwilling to give up. You might think the close proximity of so many blues would make it easier to compare and differentiate the species – by size, colour, pattern, flight – but they just merge into an indiscriminate bewilderment. When they do land and allow a rushed inspection, they're so tatty and worn that I can't make out the identificatory details I'm looking for. It's like someone has been on the scene ahead of my arrival, tampering with the evidence. In particular, I'm looking to see if the black veins on the upperside of the wings extend beyond the border and continue to the very tip. This will tell me whether I'm looking at a Common Blue or an Adonis Blue. A seasoned butterflier will tell you that it should be obvious from the colour alone – the Adonis Blue is a vibrating electric blue, distinct from any of the other British blues – but until you've seen one for the first time, how do you know with any confidence? I think I have seen some Chalkhill Blues – again, they should be fairly distinct, being larger than the other blues you find here and of a more faded tone, with heavier black patterning, but nothing will land and open its wings for me.

One glimmer of satisfaction lifts me for a moment. My first Silver-spotted Skipper, chilling on a Hawthorn twig, wide-eyed, its underwing funky green with silver chequers dashed across it so that it looks a bit like a racing flag. I even get a quality picture, something I'll be able to show Dad. But the satisfaction is short-lived. These cheeky chaps don't stay still for long, especially in this weather.

I spend another thirty minutes cooking, tramping the same patch of hillside. I look up Watlington Hill towards its vanishing point, which feels somehow immediate, disappearing into the electric Adonis Blue sky. I am stranded on an abstract plane rotating in space, and Dad is somewhere out there, probably on his way back from the hospital, stuck in a hot car. I gather these remote points together, pull them through a loop and find myself elsewhere. An enchanted slope surrounded by wildflowers that I somehow recognise as violet lupines and tall Green Gentians. I also know the Humming-bird Hawk-moths and hummingbirds flying through the snow-scented silence of the sheer mountainside, looking down at the toy-like tin roofs and poplars of the cul-de-sac valley below, boring its way through the monstrous granite mountains.[7] A cold, fresh sun pierces the crisp veneer of the scene, electrifying the flowers and butterflies. Ahead of me is a heavyset man in shorts and sneakers, flat-capped, holding so much speculation in the folds of his marquisette butterfly net. He rests one foot on a large rock and looks down at the valley. The tinkling noises of an American town float up the mountain trail, carrying with them the unmistakable music of children playing in the streets.

'Wonderful,' he says, acknowledging the sweet sounds that are instantaneously forming the nerves and secret points, the subliminal co-ordinates, by means of which his dark master-work is being plotted.[8]

The very idea of a masterwork is a curiously masculine concept. The obsession with greatness, with hierarchy and legacy. It must be nice to have one though – a masterwork, that is.

My failure with the blues on Watlington Hill has spun me into a negative state of mind, and on the drive over to my next location all I can think about is my work and everything that is going wrong with it. Throughout the summer I have been drafting a novel, what I hope will be my second novel in print, though it's the third I have written since publishing my first. I am now a prolific author of unpublished contemporary fiction. The previous novel (unpublished novel number two) was rejected by every publisher I submitted it to. The only thing I'm relatively confident about in my writing life is that I won't get published again. That and the fact that I have to write.

I pull up at a gate off a single-track country road, opposite an isolated thatched cottage so small it looks more like a teapot than a house. I get out of the car and follow the sign's instruction to close the gate behind me, unnerved by the two horses wearing fly masks in the adjoining field as they pause their grass-chewing, scouring my arrival darkly. I drive twenty metres ahead and repeat the process for another gate. I enter a small, shaded patch and park.

Once part of the Royal Forest of Bernwood, Whitecross Green Wood sits on sixty-three hectares of land close to the M40, south of Bicester. I step onto a wide grassy ride bordered by broadleaved trees. I am on the lookout for tall Ashes and thickets of Blackthorn, hang-outs of the rare Brown Hairstreak. This butterfly is no longer present in our home county of Northamptonshire, whose border is less than twenty miles away. In fact, it is uncommon throughout the UK, where it once flourished, due to widespread hedgerow removal and flailing (more than half of English hedgerow has been destroyed since just the mid-twentieth century), which erase the caterpillar's habitat from the landscape. Even in its scarce strongholds, it is an elusive creature, spending most of its time high in the canopy of Ash trees, away from human fuss. It's the largest of the British hairstreaks, all small creatures, and has delicate tails and an underside of distinctive white squiggles, like the data of an electrocardiogram (but more flatlined than the alarming peaks of the White-letter's reading).

I scan the ride edges for Ash as I work the wood's grid system. I recall Dad describing the Ash's symmetrical pairs of leaflets with a single leaflet perpendicular to the rest at the tip – something he pointed out to me many times on our walks over the years. But somehow, in situ, the trees perplex me. What look like Ash leaves are attached to wrongly shaped trunks and wrongly textured bark. It feels like it should all come together so easily – Whitecross Green is more manicured than Fermyn; there are even signs describing the flora and fauna here – but the environment is mystifying. The sound of the motorway folds itself around the woods, the noise of car engines merging with the wind shushing through the leaves, begging for discretion, trying to keep the M40 a secret. Everything is behaving strangely. Falling leaves fool me for butterflies, some even floating upwards as if time is being reversed (a bit Roeg, that); a superabundance of damsels and dragonflies glint and glisten, all looking like possible butterflies until you get near; the patterns of dapple and shadow make everything ethereal and translucent, making the wood just a trick of the light.

I'm meant to be focusing on hairstreaks now, but I can't stop thinking about the blues – all those damn samey species that have given me the runaround this morning. Why was Nabokov so obsessed with them? It seems a strange combination at first – the plainness and smallness, the repetitiousness, of the blues, versus the excess and rich variegation of Nabokovian style. Surely Nabokov belongs to the Nymphalidae family of butterflies, which comprises the grandest of species, including the Purple Emperor? Nabokov is baroque, and we tend to think of the baroque as the gaudy and ostentatious, but it is really an aesthetic of subtle fold and fractive granularity. And this, I think, is what the blues meant to Nabokov, appealing to his principled commitment to detail, his intellectual distaste for the general, the crude, the clichéd. Maybe the blues suited his predisposition towards miniaturised, self-enclosed worlds; the subtle variation, the minute particularity; the melting and merging of shades and quirks. Nabokov was a fondler of details, an ardent champion of the precise and surprising. The more I think about it, the more I see him as a blue rather than a Purple Emperor.

After an hour of traipsing the woods, my spirits are dropping by the minute. A creeping pessimism begins to overtake me, taking the shine off the beautiful weather and precious solitude that was so able to thrill me at the start of my butterflying summer. Hairstreak morphs into hardstreak in my mind, like a mantra planted there to irritate me. But hairstreaks *are* hard for the novice. Their profile appeals almost exclusively to the specialist – elusive, small, plain and inconspicuous, dependent on limited habitats. I am still yet to see the alleged White-letter Hairstreak in my parents' garden, I was too late joining the butterfly season to see the Green Hairstreak or the Black Hairstreak, which can be found near my home, and the Brown Hairstreak is mocking me now, watching from the canopies of Ash trees, probably just waiting for me to leave. Only the Purple Hairstreak has proved a friend, and even that encounter, in Fermyn, was accidental.

Nabokov knew the emotional perils of butterflying much better than me. Failure is part of the process. In *Speak, Memory*, he describes failing to catch what appears to be a

White-letter Hairstreak, and when a journalist from *Sports Illustrated* came to write a feature about him and butterflies in 1959, they went on a couple of walks together, but Nabokov couldn't find the wood nymph named after him (*Cyllopsis pertepida dorothea*, also known as Nabokov's Wood Nymph), which he hoped to show off: 'Where is my wood nymph? It is heartbreaking work. [. . .] Wretched work.'[9] And in a poem called 'Butterflies', he memorably describes the anguish of failing to catch a Swallowtail.[10] I will never try to catch a butterfly, but I suspect I feel something similar every time I crouch to photograph one and it shoots off, as if it has sensed the arching of an eyebrow, an exhalation of breath. Trying to arrange another feature on his butterflying pursuits, this time for *Life* magazine, Nabokov warned the editor of 'the whims of weather and collector's luck' that might foil even their best-laid plans.[11] Nabokov knew the inevitable frustration and failure of pursuing butterflies; they only made the successes sweeter.

Literary failure, however, was inconceivable to Nabokov. Difficulty with publishers and editors was one thing, but he never doubted his own worth. His confidence seems to have been unshakable. Any spectrum with Nabokov on it should find me at the other end. The problem with my writing, I fear, is that it has become all style. I don't believe you can separate style from substance – they are one and the same thing – but that doesn't mean style is inherently valuable. My sentences are good, I think, I hope. But what do they add up to? I fear that my latest novel in progress lacks experience, human depth, authenticity. The more troubling thought I am grappling with is, how will I continue to justify the time and sacrifice that go into not publishing books? What will I be able to show my family for all the time I have spent at my computer instead of being with them? More immediately, how do I justify the time spent here today, not seeing butterflies? All I have done is swap one failure for another: the Adonis and Chalkhill Blues are my second and third novels, unseen and unread, and the Brown Hairstreak is on its way to becoming my equally distant and fanciful fourth novel, hiding in the canopy where no reader goes.

Walking back on myself, down the wide ride of Blackthorn and possible-Ashes and other broadleaved trees, I find that my eyes are welling up. I want Dad here with me, now. It's the kind of emotion that I could probably find the words for – ways of describing the physical sensations of it, the thoughts attached to it, etc. – but not the *feeling* of it, which requires the right form. True feeling fucks up wrong form, weak form. It finds it out. Woolf knew this. It's why she wanted a form that was at once evanescent and tough. When Woolf wrote about form in this way, she was writing about something similar to structures of feeling, where 'feeling' suggests something spontaneous and overflowing, while 'structure' suggests something solid and containing. But the two are not mutually exclusive. One might keep the other honest.

I have wasted a day, and, besides the Silver-spotted Skipper, I have almost nothing to cheer Dad up with after his miserable morning in the hospital, no doubt feeling travel-sick on his way home now. I know *he* won't see it like that – he will point out that I have been blessed with several precious hours with nature, that I have seen so many other treats, that it's not about outcomes or quotas. But I haven't been open enough to appreciate any of this, too fixed on a couple of species and my absurd checklist, as if nature can be reduced to a child's game. All I feel, as I head home, is wound up. I feel like a failure.

25

Gossamer-Winged

Behind my desk are Joni's records, my own additions, slotted into your collection. They include her most revered album, *Blue*, with her spectral face emerging from the deep-blue sleeve, like the faint vision of the butterfly as it presses against the carapace of the chrysalis.

Joni pours everything into that record – the breakdown of her marriage, the pain of several tumultuous love affairs, the separation from her daughter, the bruising experiences of fame and unwanted sainthood. *Blue* marks the emergence of a new structure of feeling. She says she was 'crying all the time' while working on the songs for *Blue*, and has described how she began seeing the world and herself differently;[1] *Blue* 'simultaneously appeared when my insights became keener, so I could see painfully – things about people I didn't want to know [. . .] And because everything was becoming transparent, I felt I must be transparent, and I cried [. . .] That's how I felt. Like my guts were on the outside.'[2] In another interview she says: 'At that period of my life, I had no personal defences. I felt like a cellophane wrapper on a pack of cigarettes. I felt like I had absolutely no secrets from the world, and I couldn't pretend in my life to be strong. Or to be happy.'[3]

Zadie Smith, in her essay about Joni, says we have to lower our defences to let the new and different in; we have to be open in order for our sensibility to change. For Joni, the defences had simply been demolished. Repeatedly, she describes her condition as one of exposure, and in this state of delicacy and insubstantiality, she had to find new forms of expression, new forms for being *in* vulnerability. The blues belong to the Lycaenidae family of butterflies, which are also known as the gossamer-winged butterflies. Joni is gossamer winged on that record – transparent, exposed, but bold in her pain, in her singularity, able to fly above it all.

While male artists obsess over style as a kind of signature, a copyright logo that announces and protects their personality, Joni never wanted to be fixed or constrained. She didn't want to be a specimen marvelled over in a grand museum of creation. That was a luxury for male egos. Joni wanted movement, shape-shift, metamorphosis. She *needed* it. The development of a personal form was an act of survival. As it was for male artists too, of course, like Joni's friends and peers Bob Dylan and Leonard Cohen. But Joni felt their expression of personality differed from hers. They could use personae, rhetoric, posturing – male privileges.

There is an earlier version of Dylan's 1975 album, *Blood on the Tracks* (which contains 'Tangled Up in Blue', a song that Dylan wrote after listening to Joni's *Blue* for a week straight), which displays a more vulnerable and exposed Dylan. Joni was given a bootleg, having heard from a friend that it's 'like a Joni Mitchell album'. She loved it (a touch egotistical, that). But Dylan then recut the album and, in Joni's telling, covered up all the vulnerability and subtlety. One night, Joni hosted a party with a glamorous crowd that included Dylan, as well as Robert De Niro, David Bowie and Robin Williams. In the background she played the original, unreleased *Blood on the Tracks*. Dylan asked to see her in the garden. 'Why didn't you put that out?' she asked him. 'Somebody stole the tape,' he said. Joni didn't believe him. 'He chickened out,' she would say later. '[The original] was more honest. [. . .] He took the vulnerability out of it, and in the process he took the depth out. The New York sessions [i.e. the bootlegged version] were touching. The Minnesota sessions [i.e. the released version] were not touching at all. He asserted himself again as a man.'[4]

Watch this. If you punch 'Joni Mitchell Bob Dylan Coyote' into YouTube,[5] you'll find a three-minute video, with a thumbnail of Joni mid-performance, eyes closed, wearing chunky gold earrings and a large black beret. There it is. It's a behind-the-scenes clip taken from Bob Dylan's infamous 1975 Rolling Thunder Revue tour – a tour that saw the likes of Joan Baez, Roger McGuinn and Allen Ginsberg join Dylan for a repertory-style vagabond bus tour of North America, playing shows, taking drugs, making love, described variously by its participants as a dream, hallucination and nightmare. Joni joined the action for just under a month. Battling flu and high on cocaine, she sat up on the bus writing new material that would appear on her sublime records of the mid- and late 1970s.

Already she has transcended her *Blue* period here. She has metamorphosed into something more esoteric, less obviously crowd-pleasing. I think of her albums of this era as her hairstreaks. (The hairstreaks are of the same family as the blues

– both gossamer-winged – but they seem more specialist to me; an aficionado's butterflies.) These albums include *The Hissing of Summer Lawns* (her Green Hairstreak with its green and grey cover), *Hejira* (her Purple Hairstreak, because it travels furthest) and *Don Juan's Reckless Daughter* (her enigmatic White-letter Hairstreak). They represent the emergence of yet another structure of feeling in her work, now informed by jazz and R&B as she collaborates with virtuosos like Jaco Pastorius, Herbie Hancock, Wayne Shorter and, ultimately, Charles Mingus.

In this video, the touring group are hanging out in Gordon Lightfoot's house when they start jamming on Joni's new tune, 'Coyote'. Speaking to camera, McGuinn of the Byrds introduces Joni and her song ('Joni wrote this song about this tour, and on this tour, and for this tour'; it was also about her on-tour affair with the actor and writer Sam Shepard, the coyote of the song's title) while Joni strums her open-tuned acoustic in a percussive fashion (a tuning which makes her guitar sound like we're coming at that most familiar of instruments from sideways on, askance and anew). Dylan joins in on his guitar and Joni starts modulating, with remarkable ease, between conversation and soulful harmony. This is her voice at its best, to my ear at least – ever so slightly deeper and huskier, but still with range and elasticity. I prefer this to the higher voice of her earlier albums – it's warmer and yet grittier at the same time, speaking of hard-won experience and too many cigarettes.

A few things I love about this performance: how at the start McGuinn is watching intently, hands in lap, and yet by the time the camera comes back round to him he has grabbed a guitar and joined in too; how the close-ups of Joni's strumming fingertips show their discoloration and the dirt beneath her nails (the talent and lifestyle feel unimaginably distant from today's Insta musicians); how the song fades out at the end with string-picking in an almost-dream state; how Joni is metamorphosing into a new form in front of our very eyes.

Above all, I love how her talent eclipses all those in her orbit, the only woman in a room of peacocking superstars. McGuinn looks enamoured, almost hypnotised, while I can't tell if Dylan looks bored, truculent, bemused, melancholic or just spaced out (he certainly looks beat), strumming to keep up as best he can, thinking it was all about being a Purple Emperor while a hairstreak flies off into a more rarefied dimension before his eyes.

IV

Wood White

26

Hinterland

I'm back at my desk, staring at the screen and the draft of my novel, when my phone pings.

I think I could manage a short walk in the woods if you've time. Long shot at seeing a 2nd brood Wood White. xx

I'm in the car, driving south, before I can save the document, log out from work email or re-arrange my afternoon meetings. I have longed for this moment all summer but had resigned myself to it never happening. I must get to Mum and Dad's before the miracle is dispelled.

I find Dad in the kitchen, sitting in his special chair. Mum stands with her back against the oven and glances me a look that is hard to read.

'Are you sure about this?' I say.

'Yes,' says Dad. 'It's a lovely day and if we're lucky the second brood of Wood Whites might be on the wing.'

He is looking well, relatively speaking, the best I have seen him since before the surgery. Maybe the chemotherapy is starting to take real effect. Still, I can't quite believe it.

Dad has mentioned Wood Whites to me several times this summer. A rare and endangered species of woodland butterfly, limited to three strongholds in the country – the Weald of West Sussex and Surrey, certain forests and woods in the West Country, and the clays of the East Midlands, especially in Northamptonshire. For all I can tell from the images in *The Butterflies of Britain & Ireland* it seems to be just another plain white butterfly like the ones you see everywhere. But for some reason it holds a special place in Dad's heart – maybe because it is so scarce, but I wonder if there is a deeper explanation than that.

'I don't think I'll be able to go far though.'

I look to Mum. Why isn't she saying anything?

'It's really hot,' I say, feeling guilty. 'We can just stay here and hang out if you like?'

Is it selfish that I want nothing more than to go butterflying with Dad? Ever since the woods have become places of such unexpected wonder and release for me, in a time of lockdown and impending loss, I have not once been outdoors with Dad beyond the garden or on our car journeys to the Churchill Hospital. I want to share the special pleasure of the woods with him – *his* pleasure – before it's too late.

'No,' he says. 'I want to do this. We'll be sensible.'

Mum's expression says there's nothing sensible about this at all. But then there is little sense in death either.

'Enjoy yourselves,' she says.

We drive to a small woodland three miles from home, less than two miles in the other direction from where Dad grew up, nestled amongst the fields and country lanes that are conduits for Dad to a hinterland of roaming, shooting, fishing, and riding his Triumph motorbike to the town where Mum grew up. It's the first time Dad has seen these roads – all a single car's width, potholed and winding – in months. They remind me of going to Grandma and Granddad's on Sundays, the red-brick council house where Dad grew up with the outdoor toilet and the spooky tunnel that joined their house to the neighbour's, the nicotine-stained wallpaper, and all those knick-knacks that spoke of a time long before my arrival. We used to call this journey the 'wood way', as opposed to going up the A5, the old Watling Street. Dad always let us choose the route and we'd always ask for the wood way. It seemed more magical, and, returning home, smelling of ashtrays, with a bladder full of tea and a stomach stretched tight by roast beef and sponge cake, there was a chance we might see some pheasant or deer. But now I'm the driver and Dad is the one looking out the window.

'You see those oaks there?' he says. 'That's a good spot for Purple Hairstreaks.'

How will I ever pick it out from the rest of the hedgerow when he is gone?

'You can remember it because it's right by this turn-off,' he says, reading my mind. 'Turn left here.'

We're coming at things from a different angle today, not the way I remember getting to these woods. It feels like we're at the back of them somehow, if such spatial terms can be used for something once so wild, now segmented and bordered.

'And you see that gate?'

There is a small pull-in where the sheer tree-face of the woods is signposted PRIVATE LAND. KEEP OUT.

'I've seen Purple Emperors come down to feed on the puddles there.'

The time for Emperors has passed, as has the peak for Purple Hairstreaks. We're out of time. Dad is telling me these things because he hopes I will continue to pursue butterflies beyond this freak summer, transferring the local knowledge he has acquired through years of patient trial and error and being-with, preparing me for a future without him.

The dense trees come to an end and Dad tells me to park on a grassy verge by the entrance to a footpath that hugs the edge of the woods. I get out and run to the other side, where Dad has already opened the door and is starting to swivel his way from the car.

'You okay?' I say, holding my hand out, like I am cupping an imaginary elbow, guiding him to ground.

'I've got it,' he says, wincing, but able to manoeuvre out. He stands straight, closes his eyes and takes a deep breath. 'Beautiful,' he says, free of his bedroom at last, the sun on his cheeks.

At the start of the footpath, by the corner of the woods, Dad pauses and looks up.

'That tree there is a bullace tree.'

'Bullace?'

'A type of plum.'

'Okay,' I say. We won't get far, I think, if he is going to name each individual tree.

'There are Black Hairstreaks in there in late June and July. Your granddad told me they were there, years and years ago. I must've searched for at least a dozen years before I finally saw one. Funnily enough, it was only after I saw my first Black

Hairstreak at Fermyn Woods, up your way, that I finally had any luck here. The very next day. Can you believe it?'

'How strange,' I say, feeling rueful once again that I didn't accompany him to Fermyn.

We start down the footpath. I've been here before, when I was seven or eight. Another ghost-place, more real in memory than actuality, at the centre of a three-mile radius of countryside in south Northamptonshire that I associate with Dad's childhood and Granddad's adulthood, as much as for anything I ever did there myself. Is it possible, I wonder, to feel someone else's memories as your own?

The Blackthorn, bramble and nettles that guard the edge of the wood are exploding with Red Admirals and Peacocks and Speckled Woods, as if coming out to greet Dad, heralding his return. Dad moves slowly. I almost trip over myself in my care not to rush him.

'You have to go slow and be attentive,' he says. 'Patience is a virtue.'

I think of Dad's twelve-year wait to see Black Hairstreaks here, a small part of a lifetime's commitment to the natural world, and feel ashamed of my desire to cram as many butterflies into one summer as possible, like the Augustus Gloop of butterflying. In *The Gift*, Nabokov writes:

> *How to describe the bliss of our walks with Father through the woods, the fields and the peat bogs, or the constant summer thought of him if he was away, the eternal dream of making some discovery and of meeting him with this discovery – How to describe the feeling I experienced when he showed me all the spots where in his own childhood he had caught this and that.*[1]

After thirty-plus years of outwardly resisting fatherly advice, while relying on it, cherishing it, I am entirely open to him.

'There are lots of whites about,' I say, optimistically.

'No Wood Whites yet,' he says, peering into the hedge. 'You can't mistake them. They are daintier than the other whites and their flight is distinctive – floppier, less vigorous. You won't see them much higher than a few feet in the air. They float around the edges, looking for trefoils and vetches. Once they land, they're easy to identify. They never rest with their wings open, and on the underside they don't have the markings of the other whites – it's just white and a bit of grey marbling . . . no black dots or fringes or anything like that.'

While he's saying this, I make a conscious effort to lower my gaze to four feet above ground . . . a new way of reading. I'm so used to looking for trophy butterflies up in the canopies. I am learning from Dad, but even in his disadvantaged state, I want to beat him. We've always been competitive like that – sometimes to the point of confrontation – and I would love nothing more than to spot the first Wood White of the day, rather than have one presented to me by him.

'I'm not sure if we'll have any luck today,' he says. I wonder if he is trying to hustle me, tricking me into taking my eye off the prize, when he knows exactly where to look, just like searching for Corfe Castle all those years ago. 'The first brood, which is the much bigger brood, has been and gone already. They're at their peak in June. The second brood is scarcer.'

I imagine Dad walking this very path with Granddad, when he was a doughy child, before he got to the grammar school and became a star rugby player, when Granddad had no qualms about sending him up trees to look inside nests. I picture Dad struggling to keep up with his dad, but then they metamorphose, Granddad into an older man, still barrel-chested, broad-shouldered and wild-haired; Dad into a tall, fit youngster, the dog running off in front, Granddad and Dad with cocked shotguns in the crooks of their arms. Rough shooting, they called it; 'poaching' as the gamekeepers and landowners would call it. Even now there are signs at the entry points to the wood at the side of the track: PRIVATE WOODLAND. NO ENTRY.

All of the woods around here were once part of the medieval hunting forest of Whittlewood, which covered four hundred hectares of south Northamptonshire. The particular parcel of it where we stand now is, for me, located in Dad's childhood imaginary, but its history is much deeper and knottier than that; and this sign, warning us not to enter, is an echo.[2] Over a thousand years ago the sprawling woodland was a great storehouse for survival – food for the belly, hides and pelts for the skin, material for building, fuel for fire – but following the Norman Conquest, William I designated it part of Whittlewood Forest. Villages were burnt, common land stolen, rights to farm and forage revoked, all to create a vast royal hunting playground for the king and his elect. The very word *forest*, from the Latin *foris*, meaning 'outside of', letting you know that it is outside of common law, falling under royal jurisdiction and strictures that protect the King's game, particularly deer and boar. Anyone who exploited it would be punished, by either mutilation or execution. Things relaxed a bit between the eleventh and eighteenth centuries: in 1739 two men from Potterspury, a village just a couple of miles from here, which was designated an 'In-town' by the 1299 Perambulation of Whittlewood and therefore subject to the loathed Forest Law, were found guilty of killing a deer in the forest. Rather than execution or mutilation, each was fined thirty pounds. Unable to pay (an exorbitant fee that few could afford), they were imprisoned in Northampton Gaol for one year. After their sentence was served, they were committed to be set on the pillory in town for one hour on market days.[3]

Granddad was a trespasser and a poacher, activities that by the mid-twentieth century didn't carry quite the same consequences they once had, though still emblematic of hundreds of years of vexed politics and inequities. A good deal of the stories about Granddad, a staunch believer in his right to roam, seem to involve fracas with irate gamekeepers. Like the one where he and Dad – just a young lad – are shooting in private woodland, no doubt around here somewhere, when they are confronted by the gamekeeper and *his* son. Granddad lays his gun on the ground, ties the dog up, rolls up his sleeves and declares that he will take the gamekeeper and 'my son will take yours'. As Dad puts it, he was 'just a fat boy of ten or eleven', while the gamekeeper's son was a 'strapping lad' in his early twenties. I always found it both shocking and comic, the image of Dad looking up at his dad in disbelief and then across at his Goliath-like opponent; and the overwhelming relief when the opposing tag team backed off, probably recognising the hardness in Granddad's eyes and the reputation that preceded him.

There's another story about Granddad cycling these very lanes when he sees the car of a different gamekeeper approaching. (Every other person in south Northants in the 1960s seems to have been a gamekeeper.) Promptly, he parks his bike against the hedge and waits in the middle of the road, blocking the way. When the gamekeeper comes to a stop and asks what he thinks he is doing, Granddad orders him to get out. 'We're going to settle this here and now.' I remember that exact line from how Dad told it. What exactly they were settling I don't know, but I like to think of Granddad as a Robin Hood hero of the working class, even if Dad describes him as a fundamentally selfish man. 'He was a character' is how I've heard some people put it, euphemistically.

'Nothing yet,' says Dad, as we continue down the path. 'I'm not sure how much further I can go, son. I don't want to get stuck too far from the car.'

'Of course,' I say, not at all ready for this to end.

'We'll have to head into the woods, I reckon.'

That's more like it. We turn off the path, past another NO ENTRY sign, and through a gap in the trees. It has a special aura, as though a transformative threshold has been crossed, and, sure enough, there in front of us is the most enchanting ride I have seen all summer. One last adventure.

My dad is not his dad. He has had permission to walk these woods for years, so that he can observe the butterflies. But Dad is conscious, I think, that he might be abusing his privilege by sneaking me in with him. He won't let that stop us. My being here restores him to the frisson of trespass that he shared so often with *his* father.

We enter a glade where columns of sunlight cast their search-beams through the colossal trees, scanning the thick entanglements of briar, vetch, trefoil and other wildflowers beyond my ken. A good rule of thumb when butterflying: look for any yellow or purple flowers.

'You okay?' I ask, feeling paternal.

'We shan't go far,' he says. 'Let's just go round to the bend there and then I'll have to turn back.'

When this woodland was part of the royal hunting forest, visiting noblemen granted temporary hunting rights would blow a horn to announce themselves so as not to be mistaken for poachers. I wonder how we will announce ourselves.

'If we do see any Wood Whites and you put a picture on your Instagram or anywhere, don't reveal the location,' he says.

'Why not?'

'Because the Wood White is an endangered species.'

Does he fear that unscrupulous collectors will come after it, creeping where they don't belong, damaging its habitat and sweeping it up in nets? Or is he just asking for discretion because he knows I shouldn't be here?

'There's another wood a couple of miles from here. I used to have permission from the owner to go butterflying there too. A different owner from these woods. But before I knew him, when I was in my twenties, I was there foraging with Granddad, and he confronted us. I was apologetic and happy to leave, but your Granddad started ranting. *I fought in the war for this country and I won't be told where I can and can't go.* I heard him say that many times over the years. He would literally shake with rage. It was quite frightening. He had a point, to be honest, but where does it end? Anyway, many years later I met the owner of the woods at various events and once he invited me to be his guest at a private shoot. I don't think he remembered that confrontation or who my dad was. But I felt obliged to remind him of it, like it would have been dishonest not to. He didn't care, but that's how it was.'

'Are you worried we'll get caught?'

He looks at me and smiles.

'Not in the slightest. You're with me.'

We walk a little way into the wood, but we don't see any Wood Whites. We do see a Silver-washed Fritillary, which is a great thrill for both of us. The Silver-washed represents the kind of butterfly that didn't exist before this summer, so it is a special moment. We also see a Red Admiral, which soars above us, and stencil-winged Commas. All these new mutual acquaintances of ours.

'I'm sorry, son,' says Dad. 'It's time to turn around.'

'Of course,' I say. 'Not a problem.'

But I don't want this moment to end. Not because we haven't seen a Wood White (though I think this disappoints Dad, who doesn't want to fail me in any way), but because I know we'll never do this again. I have left it all too late. Dad looks exhausted and forlorn. I wonder if he is saying goodbye to the wood and its precious jewels. Not just this wood, but the natural world altogether, and all the places he has been most at peace, most himself.

'There! See it?'

Yes, I do – a spectral white butterfly, dipping amongst the long grass and yellow flowers.

'For sure?' I say.

'Oh yes,' he says. 'No mistaking it.'

We follow it together, back the way we came, like it is escorting us out, returning Dad safely home. It lands and we move closer. I take a blurry picture. In flight, to my untrained eye, it is just another white butterfly, but up close I see it as a delicate creature, almost ghostly, a milky blend of white and off-whites and a slight canister-spray of grey. It is a gift from Dad, plush with particularity, a new way of reading.

'Look, another one!'

A second Wood White doing a floppy Kate Bush dance around the glade's edge, like a miraculous salutation to the preciousness of this moment. I fight back an involuntary giggle. We watch them flitter away, along the glade, and silently accept that it's time to let them go.

'I'm so glad we saw some,' he says as we walk out of the woods, back onto the footpath, trespassers no more thanks to some invisible boundary that no butterfly cares for. 'I so wanted to show you. Now you'll know what to look for in the future.'

Again I wonder why this butterfly means so much to him. Maybe it's the satisfaction of having something rare in your own back yard, a subtle exceptionality that means something to a man who has never left home or seen much of the world, walking the same paths his whole life. I also can't help reading a more recent significance in the Wood White, whose endangerment speaks to Dad's condition.

27
White Butterflies

'Were you scared of Granddad?' We're driving home, through Dad and Granddad's territory. 'I remember finding him a bit frightening when I was little.'

Dad smiles.

'You didn't seem very frightened,' he says. 'You've seen the home video where you're pummelling him in the arm for talking while you were trying to watch that Michael Jackson film you liked. You must've only been five.'

'Sounds like he deserved it.'

'He was my dad,' says my dad. 'I looked up to him. Probably idolised him. As I got older, I became more aware of his ways, our differences. But he was still my dad. I always loved him.'

'What do you mean by his ways?'

Dad watches the familiar fields roll by, reflecting across the window.

'He didn't seem to fit in anywhere, other than outdoors, ideally by himself or with me. It wasn't so much that he was a misfit, but I guess you could say he had no social airs or graces.'

'No doubt about that,' I say, remembering how argumentative he could be at family dinners, when you never knew whether his mood might suddenly switch from good humour to confrontation. I also remember how, at those meals, he'd start by sitting down and taking his chewing gum from his mouth (he was always chewing gum, the same piece I assumed) and sticking it on the side of the table so that he could continue with it afterwards. (Dad pranked him once by replacing it with a bit of White Tack when he went to the toilet, which almost led to a punch-up.) And how, without fail, no matter the meal, he would have a stack of six buttered slices of Hovis wholemeal bread on a side plate, because his doctor had told him he could eat no more than that per day due to his type 2 diabetes. Granddad took it as a target, rather than a limit.

'I'd occasionally take him to invitational shoots and I would end up regretting it. Not really my cup of tea either to be honest, but I appreciated the shooting.'

'What would happen?'

'For a start, he wouldn't dress like everyone else, just in his old rough clothes.'

I remember the long green socks and red garters Dad used to wear when he went to those things and how mercilessly we gave him shit for it.

'And he'd get into arguments with people.'

'About what?'

'All sorts. Just disagreements. Sometimes he'd get into political arguments – he was all about the working man. Well, he was really all about himself, but he certainly disliked the toffs. Whereas I wanted to get on, move up in the world, Dad couldn't care less about all that.' (I'm reminded of how many times Dad has said to me, when having political discussions of our own: 'You don't half sound like your granddad.' I'm never sure if he means this admiringly or despairingly.)

'Now I think I respect him for it. But there's no getting around the fact that he was a difficult character. He'd get in people's faces. I don't mean in an aggressive way – though he did that too – more in an awkward way. He'd stop people when he was out on his walks and strike up conversations. But he'd make the other person feel uncomfortable, sort of not letting them go. I was so embarrassed. He was just odd sometimes. And he could look a bit funny.'

'Funny?'

'Red in the face . . . a bit wild. It's hard to describe.'

I realise I'm driving slowly – to extend the conversation, but also so Dad can take in his patch one more time.

'But he had been through an awful lot – things you and I can never imagine. He killed men in hand-to-hand combat in the war, out in the jungle; he nearly died of meningitis while he was in India and had an abscess on his brain; and don't forget his head injury – he was basically blown up in Burma. He was discharged after that. Do you remember how he'd let you rub the metal in his skull when you were kids?'

I thought there was an actual bomb in there and was convinced I could hear it ticking behind the scars – but he always seemed like someone on the verge of going off.

'He'd have blackouts and wake up in a field somewhere, unsure how he got there. And I'd hear him sometimes, in the night, screaming in his sleep.'

'Jesus,' I say.

'He was smart. Very capable – seemed like he could do anything he turned his mind to. He could have been so much more than he was. But then he didn't want to be any more. He was content, I suppose, in his own way.'

We are coming back into the village now, the fields and woods behind us.

'All he wanted, really, was to be outdoors with the dog, in nature where he was at peace. Or as at peace as someone who had been through what he'd been through ever could be.'

When we get home, Dad goes to bed. I convince myself it wasn't irresponsible to have gone to the woods. He's certainly adamant it was the best thing he could have hoped for. But he's exhausted.

In his study, in one of the desk drawers, there's a Manila envelope with some of Granddad's war records. I remember there being a letter in there, something Granddad sent back from India when he was convalescing, and I want to see it. I find it folded into a tiny square, the seams almost torn. The writing is wobbly, hard to read in places, and the address on the front looks like it has been written by a child. He describes how he longs to come home, how he misses his family, and how he yearns to be in the fields with the dog and his gun. (According to his postings record, he was stationed at Deolali transit camp either side of the date of the letter, which makes me wonder whether he was hospitalised at Deolali itself. The phrase 'gone doolally' derives from this notorious camp, where poor conditions, punishing heat and interminable stays (due to lack of transport out) often led to mental illness and suicide.)

After he left the hospital camp he was straight back in the jungle, fighting. That's when he suffered the head trauma, hit by shrapnel, and was discharged. He immediately threw away the medication the doctors had given him and got on with rebuilding his life, no longer a 'clerk' (his recorded profession on his military service book) but a bricklayer, a husband, and very soon a father of two. Granddad didn't talk much about the war, but a couple of stories made it down to me. The one I remember most vividly is how he fought alongside the Gurkhas, and how, once, in the dark of night, he felt a hand patting his leg – a Gurkha ascertaining from the shape of his boot whether he was British or Japanese. Your head would be off, he'd say, before you knew what was happening. Luckily, he had the right boots on.

Tucked inside his pocket Soldier's Service and Pay Book are some horrifying artefacts, like the instructions of surrender. Written in Japanese, they are to be shown to captured enemy soldiers. A separate translation is provided: 'You have fully done your duty as subjects and preserved your honor as warriors. I sincerely hope you will rely on the chivalry of our forces and instead of dying vainly – surrender to become brave warriors in rebuilding the New Japan. This is my strong advice.' Printed on the reverse are instructions for the captor: 'If the JAP does not observe the surrender conditions satisfactorily – shoot him.'

I also find a small black-and-white picture cut out of a magazine. It shows a gate opening onto a forest glade. He must have carried this generic pastoral image as a reminder of where he wanted to be. In his letter from Deolali, ailing in a sweat-soaked hospital bed ('the trouble is the terrific heat out here,' he writes), he was thinking about home and the freedom of *his* outdoors.

*

I wonder what butterflies Granddad might have seen in Burma and India. In *White Butterflies*, Colin McPhedran's harrowing account of his family's escape from Burma during the Second World War when he was just a boy, McPhedran describes following the brutal and often deadly refugee trail to India and coming across a corpse in the middle of the track. 'I shall never forget the sight of this body, even though I had already seen hundreds,' he writes.

> *It was covered in what appeared to be a white sheet. As we stepped carefully around it, our movement appeared to disturb the shroud. Then we saw a cloud of white butterflies rise up with a whirring, humming sound, exposing the bloated, shiny corpse of an Indian refugee. The body looked as if it had been smeared in oil and laid out in the midday sun. The butterflies must have been drawing on the juices secreted from the skin. When we had moved away, I looked back in amazement to see the cloud of white settling back on the corpse, a fitting veil for the deceased. It was a sight we were to encounter often after that.*[1]

Later, thinking he is about to die, McPhedran lies down in liquid mud and 'observe[d], or perhaps I dreamed, a cloud of white butterflies floating down towards me. It was a comforting vision and I was not afraid'.[2]

In 2019, an eighty-three-year-old man appeared in the local news in Oxford when he made his father's wartime collection of Burmese butterflies available.[3] Like my grandfather, his father had fought in Burma in the Second World War. The photographs of two glass cases in the *Oxford Mail*, filled with exotic species, are remarkable. How did his father catch and preserve these delicate creatures? How did they make it through the war, all the way to England, without damage? I have tried identifying some of the butterflies from the pictures: Tropical Fritillaries, Yellow Orange Tips, Plain Tigers, Common Sailors, some striking varieties of Swallowtail (possibly a Red Helen Swallowtail or a De Nicéville's Windmill). I may have some, if not all, of these wrong, but then Granddad wouldn't have been able to identify them either. What he would have given to see a common Brimstone in the fields of south Northants, or a Purple Emperor in the various remnants of Whittlewood Forest. I wonder if the sight of a Wood White would have brought back traumatic memories, like the veil of white dissolving around a corpse, or if it would have restored hope, just as the vision of white butterflies at the point of near-death could still comfort McPhedran, despite all he had seen.

28
Moth-Hunting

I'm not sure whether you would have heard of Virginia Woolf, Dad, but I'm certain you wouldn't have read her. Listen to this. Woolf is watching a moth trapped inside her home as it flies from one corner of the windowpane to another, trying to escape. 'It was useless,' she writes, 'to try to do anything. One could only watch the extraordinary efforts made by those tiny legs against an oncoming doom which could, had it chosen, have submerged an entire city, not merely a city, but masses of human beings; nothing, I knew, had any chance against death.'[1] This comes from an essay called 'The Death of the Moth', first published in 1942, the year after Woolf died. Woolf, it seems, is thinking about the war, but also her own depression. 'The Death of the Moth' was one of the last pieces she wrote before loading her overcoat pockets with stones and walking into the River Ouse, where she drowned.

I find myself thinking of Woolf and Granddad – about as unlikely a pairing as can be imagined. (You can bet Woolf would have been a ruthless snob about Granddad if they had met. The used chewing gum stuck to the tablecloth and the request for six buttered slices of wholemeal would not have gone over well at one of the Bloomsbury Set's dinner parties. By the same token, Granddad would have disdained the lot of them.) If the woods were a place of freedom for Granddad, where he rejected the status of trespasser, for Woolf they possessed an inherent foreboding. The woods marked psychological as well as physical forms of trespass. In an essay called 'Reading', Woolf recounts how she went moth-hunting with her siblings and cousins. In the day they would pin flannels soaked with rum and sugar to trees, and then return at night, equipped with lamps, nets and poison jars, to catch the disoriented moths battering frantically against the light or stuck to the tree, gorging, drunk. On one memorable descent into the dark centre of the woods they caught a prize treasure:

> *The scarlet underwing was already there, immobile as before, astride a vein of sweetness, drinking deep. Without waiting a second this time the poison pot was uncovered and adroitly manoeuvred so that as he sat there the moth was covered and escape cut off. There was a flash of scarlet within the glass. Then he composed himself with folded wings. He did not move again.*[2]

What happened next exerted a profound influence over Woolf's imagination:

> *Standing there with the moth safely in our hands, suddenly a volley of shot rang out, a hollow rattle of sound in the deep silence of the wood which had I know not what of mournful and ominous about it. It waned and spread through the forest: it died away, then another of those deep sighs arose. An enormous silence succeeded. "A tree," we said at last. A tree had fallen.*[3]

A tree falls and becomes the violence of gunfire. Woolf doesn't say it, but the children are not only in the inscrutable woods, they are also under the shadow-future of the First World War.

The episode of the falling tree forms something of a primal scene for Woolf, a haunting and uncanny moment, emerging from the darkness of her memory like a strange hairy moth, drawn to the light of her fiction. This is most overt in *Jacob's Room*, Woolf's third novel, published in 1922. Looking through the specimens in his butterfly collection, the eponymous Jacob, based in part on Thoby Stephen, Woolf's older brother and butterfly enthusiast, recalls the details of their capture: 'A whiff of rotten eggs had vanquished the pale clouded yellows'; 'The blues settled on little bones lying on the turf with the sun beating on them, and the painted ladies and the peacocks feasted upon bloody entrails dropped by a hawk.'[4] Even when remembered as living creatures, the butterflies are associated with death and decay, as if they were always destined for Jacob's boxes.

He looks at one of his moths, a specimen that has transmigrated from Woolf's own childhood to Jacob's story: 'The tree had fallen the night he caught it. There had been a volley of pistol-shots suddenly in the depths of the wood. And his mother had taken him for a burglar when he came home late.'[5] The 'volley of pistol-shots' that snaps the eerie quiet of the dark woods, signalling a passage from innocence to experience and guilt, prefigures the First World War, in which Jacob will die.

Masculinity and war are entangled in *Jacob's Room*, a novel that excoriates patriarchy for its oppression of women but also for the way it distorts men – not least the literal ways the male body is disfigured by war. Even in her biographical descriptions of moth-hunting, Woolf uses militaristic language and imagery, the children halting and advancing in obedience to their leader's orders, seeking the 'glory of the moment' as they 'proved [their] skill against the hostile and alien force' of the moth.[6] But Jacob too is a hostile and alien force, a moth-man who emerges pale 'out of the depths of darkness' into his mother's 'hot room, blinking at the light', having just returned late from the woods.[7] Despite his name being on the title page, Jacob remains other to us, a ghostly collage of half-remembered moments, brief glimpses, broken communications and other people's fragmented narratives. As a representative man, he eludes the novelist's net, which might just be the point.

'Something is always impelling one to hum vibrating,' writes Woolf in *Jacob's Room*, 'like the hawk moth, at the mouth of the cavern of mystery, endowing Jacob Flanders with all sorts of qualities he had not at all [. . .] what remains is mostly a matter of guess work. Yet over him we hang vibrating.'[8] At times Jacob is a butterfly, free and changeable, but he ends a moth, trapped in the glare of the novelist's and reader's lamp, though none the clearer to us. 'I am what I am, and intend to be it,' thinks Jacob in a moment of entitled self-fashioning, 'for which,' the narrator adds, filtering her commentary through Jacob's consciousness, 'there will be no form in the world unless Jacob makes one for himself'.[9] A thought that the woman artist knows as well as anyone.

Immediately after this, Jacob watches 'two white butterflies [circle] higher and higher' round an elm tree.[10] It is a curious self-contradiction of fate ('I am what I am') and free will ('and intend to be it'). Jacob must make his own form, like a rare aberration of a recognisable type. Instead, he is killed in the war. But even those who returned from war, like Granddad, could not count on the old forms, which no longer made sense.

29
Legacy

Dad wants to read an email to me. He is back in bed, not at all looking like a man who was able to walk in the woods just a few days ago. He asks me to pass him his phone and glasses, and shuffles up, into the pillow. He has sent an email to the owner of a large estate that borders the woodland where we saw the Wood Whites. Another man who has given Dad permission to access his land for many years, for which Dad is thanking him. The email, which he reads aloud, describes how he trained his spaniels in the woods there, and how, apparently, my brother and I caught our first trout in their lakes. (He doesn't mention that they were quite possibly our last too.)

'I have to tell you that my long fight with cancer is almost over and that barring a miracle, I am unlikely to walk in your lovely woods again.'

His voice is changing. Ever so slightly shakier, thinner somehow, higher than it used to be. Under his breath he makes that 'du-du-du-du-du-du' sound he makes when skipping a bit, while I try to ward off a burning sensation in my eyes.

'Probably the greatest pleasure I've had on the estate has been spending time in the cathedral-like woodlands, at peace and one with nature. I was hoping to spend more time recording butterflies as I eased back from the business but alas it's not to be. I wasn't sure whether to be pleased that I had spotted a Wood White last year, and that would suggest there are more that I hadn't seen, or be disappointed that it may have been one of the last to fly in the wood. The Wood White is a fast-declining butterfly that had a stronghold in the Whittlewood area, but is suffering from habitat loss amongst other things. I believe you could play a major (albeit private) part in its recovery, with perhaps just a few tweaks of ride management. I attach a link that you may find of interest.'

'What's the link?' I ask.

'A Butterfly Conservation report on supporting the Wood White.'[1]

'That's a good idea,' I say, humbled. He is thinking of a future world beyond himself. How many of us can truly say the same?

'What do you think?' he asks. He does this sometimes: reads me letters and emails, hoping I might apply some of that mysterious literary knowledge to his communications.

'Very moving,' I say. 'And worthwhile.'

Dad nods, satisfied.

'At the end of the email I describe my remaining shotguns to him, in case he's interested in buying any.'

That's more like it, I think. Ever the businessman. Again, I am struck by the realisation that he is not chasing profit, at least not for himself. He wants rid of them because he doesn't want to burden us after he is gone. He has taken my words to heart.

'I hope it makes a difference. The Wood White is such a vulnerable species, so easily overlooked. And unlike the other whites, it needs very particular conditions that require our co-operation.'

I think about the private ownership of estates and what Granddad might have had to say about it. For Dad the issue at stake in this email is conservation, not access (but then, of course, *he* has access). And if you can only have one of these things, conservation or access, then conservation surely is the right priority. But both should be possible. Granddad certainly wouldn't have let anybody stop him if he wanted to see the Wood White there.

I look around the room. It's disorienting to see the two-by-one-foot wooden box here, the one he used to keep by the bed when he shared a room with Mum. I always loved opening the padlock, trespassing into Dad's private life (the key was kept in it at all times; Dad is a man without secrets . . . at least I think he is) and looking at the odd assortment of stuff inside: a long black-and-white photo of his entire school cohort from 1970, which you'd have to unfurl and hold down at each end with books in order to scan the whole length in search of my parents; a hand-sized soft rabbit that Dad had held as a child; our school reports; some of Granddad's old watches; my great-grandfather's RAF medals from the First World War; and commemorative coins, including one given to Dad by his nana on his twenty-first birthday in 1975. On the other side of the bed are box files and folders containing the paperwork for the sale of the business. It strikes me how the fields, woodlands and meadows of Northamptonshire that have been Dad's habitat since he was a boy have been replaced by the corners of his bedroom, where no butterfly can dance or spiral. Instead of a promising entanglement of larval foodplants and nectar sources there is only paperwork and prescription medication, stacked in white paper bags like obscene school lunches.

The business has finally been sold, to Dad's relief. 'Gone for a pittance,' he says. 'A widow's sale.' I guess this means he thinks his situation has been taken advantage of, but I don't ask. It saddens me to hear how the deal was sealed: Dad outside the front of the house in his dressing gown, signing his life's work away on the bonnet of his car with Mum, and the lawyer who has swung by for the occasion. Dad couldn't travel any further, could barely get down the stairs that day. And besides, the lawyers aren't allowing clients into their offices because of COVID.

Selling his guns, selling the business – it's all one kind of legacy. Like, for instance, the butterfly collection that he mentions every now and then, wondering if I would like to have it. But the real legacy is not something that can be left in a will. It is the living butterflies, the as-yet-unseen butterflies, the butterflies of my future, that will be the true gift. The butterflies in his field that he has supported, the Wood Whites whose conservation he is advocating for in his email, the butterflies waiting for me in his old haunts. That is the real legacy. I don't think Dad would disagree. He is not a particularly materialistic man, and after twenty years of ill health, he knows better than me that you cannot put a monetary value on the things that really matter. Still, he wouldn't mind if Matt accepted the offer of his watch, or if I took the butterfly collection.

There is a new addition to Dad's bedside material. A plastic box filled with old photographs, some in albums, some in pharmacist's wallets, some loose.

'You've been going through these?' I ask, taking one of the albums out.

'Not yet,' he says. 'I thought I might though.'

I sit at the end of the bed and open it.

'That's one of your granddad's,' he says.

I flick through the heavy pages, the acetate crinkling, some of the photos shuffling loose, one hanging from its top right corner, shadowed in the other three corners by small cuticles of dried glue. The photo (Dad as a teenager, astride his first motorbike) clings on, trying not to fall into oblivion. I'm only a few pages in when I find some butterflies.

'What have you got?' Dad asks.

'A couple of Orange Tips, a Painted Lady and a Dark Green Fritillary.'

He doesn't ask to see. Doesn't need to check my answers anymore. I am learning.

The photo, when I find it, jolts me violently from casual reflections. On some level I always knew it was there, waiting for me, because I have seen it before. I had forgotten it though. I certainly did not associate it with the harmless pageant of holiday photos and butterflies in this album. The photograph is a black-and-white image of a decapitated head.

'Jesus Christ,' I say.

'What is it?' asks Dad.

I angle the page up at him. He sees the head of what appears to be a Japanese soldier on a table, eyes closed.

'Ah,' he says, sinking again.

'What's it doing *here*?'

'Your granddad brought it home from the war. How he got it I don't know. He certainly didn't take it, I know that much.'

'He wasn't responsible for . . . '

'God, no.'

'Why ever would he keep such a thing?'

'I have no idea.'

'Why haven't you got rid of it?'

'I don't know really. It's not my album.'

That doesn't seem a satisfactory answer, but I guess it speaks to the power Granddad still holds over him.

'It's horrid,' says Dad, looking off to the side, out the window. 'Put it away.'

He closes his eyes and grimaces. He is in pain. Feels sick.

'Sorry,' I say.

'There's a lot of things I can't explain,' he says, opening his eyes again.

'What do you mean?'

'So much about the nature of his experience.'

'It's all so fucked up,' I say, not my profoundest insight ever.

There's something else I've been wanting to ask. I want to clarify it before he is gone. I look him over, stuck in his bed exhausted, and wonder if it's the right time. Will there ever be a right time?

'What really happened when you confronted him?'

'Which occasion?' says Dad, like there are a few to choose from.

'The time, you know, you had a fight with him.'

Dad knows what I mean. He has never minded talking about it.

'I went over one weekend. I must've been in my early twenties. Your grandma had a black eye. So I had it out with him.'

'You hit him?'

'I told him he wasn't going to touch her ever again, and if he did he'd have to deal with me. He told me to mind my own business. It got physical. Then he disappeared outside and came back with a club hammer from the shed. If he wanted to hit me with it, what could I say? "If you're going to do it," I said, "just do it."'

'So what did he do?'

'He cried. He was shaking. He'd lost it.'

'What did Grandma say?'

'She had begged me not to say or do anything. She told me she'd fallen. Looking back, I was probably making things worse for her.'

'Were there other times? Did you ever witness him being violent with her?'

'I never saw him hit her. And that was the only time I saw evidence of anything. But he was a rough person. He man-handled all of us.'

Dad closes his eyes again, waning.

'I think I need to rest for a bit, sunshine.'

'Of course,' I say.

I squeeze his foot at the end of the bed, grab his binoculars from the windowsill and leave the room.

I point the binoculars at the first of the two Wych Elms at the end of Mum and Dad's garden, searching for White-letter Hairstreaks that I still haven't managed to see. I don't know where to look, where to train the lenses. I should have sought some tips from Dad before I left his room.

I thought butterflies were my escape, but standing here, my eyes going in one direction, my mind in another, I can't stop thinking about our conversation. I think of Dad in the living room in January, in front of the telly, before he had been given the terminal diagnosis, one sleep away from the surgery to remove his cancerous kidney. How he told me about picking up Granddad when *he* was dying, and dancing with him around the nursing home. I think of just a few weeks ago, out in the orchard, when he described how he would look up to the sky whenever he saw anything interesting in nature and discuss it with his dad, like they could still share it, together in spirit. I think about Dad as a boy, trailing Granddad everywhere, pursuing the same interests.

But the person I'm really thinking about is Grandma. Mum mentioned just the other day how whenever Dad and my auntie get together (something they have been doing in the garden when Dad has been up to it) and start reminiscing about the past, all they talk about is their father. Mum finds it curious, but very telling. They can't shut up about him, she says. They rarely talk about Grandma, or anyone else for that matter. And it's true: I've grown up hearing all these stories about Granddad but so little about Grandma.

What I can only feel as a vague intimation in that moment, there beneath the Wych Elm with Dad's binoculars pointed to the sky, trying to see the world like he sees it but blinded by the sun, is how *now*, writing this book almost three years later, now that Dad is gone, I don't know how to take Grandma's truth any further. Like the unseen White-letter

Hairstreak, would I even know it if I saw it? I've got nothing to go on, and I'm failing her.

Separated as I am now from that lost and confused son trying to see all the butterflies he can in one summer, as if it will somehow defer his father's death or miraculously transform his condition, I am troubled by the thought that I am merely repeating the cycle. All these stories of fathers and sons, the problematic inheritance passed down from Granddad to Dad to me and now to my two boys (Joss, our second, arrived in 2022). By writing a book on my dad and his dad and myself, am I simply mythologising the patriarchal line further? I think of Mum (who lived more of that exhausting summer with Dad than anyone else), I think of Carli and Grandma, and then, always quick with the excuses, desperately remind myself that *this* story is meant to be about a father–son relationship. But still it feels like a failing.

'My name is Brown,' writes Woolf at the start of one of her most famous essays, 'Character in Fiction'. 'Catch me if you can.'[2] The Brown she writes of is not a Meadow Brown or Wall Brown or Hedge Brown or any other species from the Satyrinae subfamily. No, this Brown is a diminutive, elderly woman on a train carriage, speaking with a sinister man who seems to be exerting a disagreeable power over her. *My name is Brown. Catch me if you can.* These are the words Woolf imagines the woman saying to her when she jumps hurriedly onto the train from Richmond to Waterloo in 1924 and finds herself sitting with Mrs Brown and Mr Smith (for so she calls them), disrupting their tête-à-tête.

If Woolf enjoyed catching butterflies and moths as a youngster, as an adult she was committed to catching humans.

My name is Brown. Catch me if you can. But instead of using camphor for the job, Woolf used fiction. As Mrs Brown and Mr Smith turn to small talk, trying to conceal the true nature of their conversation from Woolf, Woolf employs her novelist's intuition and speculates that, before she boarded, Mr Smith was plotting the downfall of Mrs Brown's son, using a painful episode from her past life to manipulate her, perhaps coercing her into signing some property over to him. However, Mrs Brown ends their false small talk by rather unexpectedly saying: 'Can you tell me if an oak tree dies when the leaves have been eaten for two years in succession by caterpillars?' Mr Smith, wrong-footed, bores on about plagues of insects and 'what fruit farmers do every year in Kent'. Then Mrs Brown takes out a handkerchief and begins to cry.[3]

'Myriads of irrelevant and incongruous ideas crowd into one's head on such occasions,' thinks Woolf.

> *One sees the person, one sees Mrs Brown, in the centre of all sorts of different scenes. I thought of her in a seaside house, among queer ornaments: sea-urchins, models of ships in glass cases. Her husband's medals were on the mantelpiece. She popped in and out of the room, perching on the edges of chairs, picking meals out of saucers, indulging in long, silent stares. The caterpillars and the oak trees seemed to imply all that.*[4]

But why *do* the caterpillars and oak trees imply all that? Because, like the oak tree, Mrs Brown's life has been ravaged by loss? Because the oak tree and the caterpillars promise regeneration, transformation, possibility? Or simply because Mrs Brown is a bit like a butterfly, perching on chairs, basking in Woolf's imagination, and then flitting away, in and out of the room, just like Forster does in her memory of him as a pale blue butterfly? Before Woolf can enclose Mrs Brown in the folds of her novelist's net, she is gone:

> *I had no time to explain why I felt it somewhat tragic, heroic, yet with a dash of the flighty, and fantastic, before the train stopped, and I watched her disappear, carrying her bag, into the vast blazing station. She looked very small, very tenacious; at once very frail and very heroic. And I have never seen her again, and I shall never know what became of her.*[5]

Flighty, small, tenacious . . . a Gatekeeper, perhaps, rather than a Meadow Brown or Wall Brown, but either way a mystery to Woolf. If the impossibility of ever really knowing another person is a fundamental proposition of Woolf's writing, then her form – evanescent on the surface, but clamped together with bolts of iron – makes her characters seem uncannily real.

Instead of an oak tree I am staring up at a Wych Elm, thinking of Grandma and Granddad and Dad, unsure what exactly it all implies. All I see is an absence of White-letter Hairstreaks – nothing more than a ghost species for all I can tell, its distinguishing white W on the underwing forming the 'very initial of woe', to quote a line from *Lolita*.[6] And I don't know how to feel about Dad's fight with his dad, except pity for everyone involved. In fact, all I can feel, beyond my sadness for Grandma, who I can no longer speak to about her experiences, in some senses full of life to me and yet somehow absent of it, as Mrs Brown is to Woolf – all I can feel is a stupid fucking pride that Dad stood up to his dad like that.

30

Style is Substance

Piecing together all these different stories that you shared with me in those final months, about Granddad and your relationship with him (most of which, to be fair, I had heard before), makes me wonder how you became the father you did. So much of your parenting style must have been informed by *your* parents, and yet your relationship with them sounds so different from ours. You were devoted to Matt and me. Not that your parents weren't devoted to you. But there is an evolution in style.

Matt and I shared a special companionship with both you and Mum. We were very fortunate. The idea that children were to be seen and not heard seemed like something from a different century to us. There were subtle differences between the two of you though. Mum would get into whatever Matt and I were into – she must have been the only mum at school drop-off playing hip hop and hard rock in her car, and the only mum who had opinions on Michael Jordan and Kobe Bryant. You were less open, in the sense that you knew what you liked and anything else was a hard sell. Wherever we entered into your existing interests and tastes, you were overjoyed; you could find contemporary R&B artists introduced by us in the six-disc changer in your car (D'Angelo, Maxwell, Joe); and you and I spent inordinate amounts of time following and discussing the Northampton Saints rugby team, going to every home game together right up towards the end of your life. But you were unwaveringly supportive of and committed to my other interests. You came to all of my football matches (a sport you low-key despised), and when I was a teenager, you drove me up and down the country to my basketball games even though you had no interest in the sport and the mileage was substantial (and, unlike me, you could clearly see that I wasn't destined for a lucrative career in the NBA). You also attended all the gigs I did with my little punk band of schoolmates, even though we sounded *nothing* like Marvin Gaye or Stevie Wonder or the Temptations. I know you shared a tremendous amount with your father too, but it sounds like you had to fit in with what *he* wanted. He helped you plenty – he practically built the house, with you as lackey – and he was there for you in a loose sense, but he didn't support you in the way you have supported me.

One thing is for sure: you would not have sent me to an older bully's house to 'sort things out'. You were fiercely protective, always. You would, however, have encouraged me to take care of myself. Don't let anyone push you around, you would have said. Be a man, you would have been thinking. I remember the boxing lessons and random tips for self-defence – hit him (whoever this imaginary assailant was) in the throat; or, even better, slide your fingers through his hair, yank his head down and smash him in the face with your knee . . . (I can't help but feel sorry for this fictional bully who has suffered unimaginable violence from my never-tested skills as a martial artist.)

I can sense Granddad in lots of the things we did together and the lessons you taught me. Especially when you'd say things like 'these boys don't even know they're born', usually in response to spoiling us yourself with presents, or when (at roughly three-month intervals) you'd go on a rant about how we needed to help around the house more, or when you would fixate on minor things like how I didn't fold my school trousers properly, as if there was something profoundly moral at stake. These lessons were part of a general toughening up that I think, for you, was an important element of the father–son relationship: teaching us to be men. My hunch is that you were actually correcting yourself as much as you were correcting us, as if these flashpoints came from a sudden self-consciousness about your own softness as a father, relative to your granite-hard father.

But I always knew that nothing was more important to you than caring for us. That's one of the most disorienting things about you not being here, no longer taking up the metaphysical station between me and death. For all your unspoken desire to be a good man, what you really wanted to be was a good *parent*. It hurts that I can't say this to you in person, like I should have done more often when I had the chance, but you were absolutely *that*.

31

I Hug You

We left Nabokov on a hillside in Telluride, Colorado, looking down on a small mining town enfolded in a valley while the distant melodies of child's play drift around him. 'I stood listening to that musical vibration from my lofty slope,' writes Nabokov, 'to those flashes of separate cries with a kind of demure murmur for background, and then I knew that the hopelessly poignant thing was not Lolita's absence from my side, but the absence of her voice from that concord.'[1] Nabokov's words, yes, but here spoken by his demonic creation, Humbert Humbert.

That moment on the hillside in Telluride, when Nabokov discovered the female *Lycaeides argyrognomon sublivens*, buried its way into the conclusion of the book that would make him one of the most infamous and successful writers in all modern literature. In the closing phases of *Lolita*, Humbert Humbert looks down on a similar town and, like Nabokov, hears children playing. In this moment, Humbert tries to convince us of his remorse, as if he is now a butterfly who has escaped the dark solipsism of his cocoon. Whether we believe him is another matter. Humbert is a master dissembler and manipulator, with a fancy prose style to boot, and the consequence of his twisted manhood is the repeated rape and systematic destruction of a young girl, Lolita.

Nabokov never lets us forget Humbert's obsession with manliness. Humbert describes himself as 'a great big handsome hunk of movieland manhood' with 'clean-cut jaw, muscular hand, deep sonorous voice, broad shoulder'.[2] 'I do not know,' says Humbert, 'if in these tragic notes I have sufficiently stressed the peculiar "sending" effect that the writer's good looks – pseudo-Celtic, attractively simian, boyishly manly – had on women of every age and environment.'[3] But Humbert's masculinity isn't all Hollywood cliché brawn and dashingness. His is also an 'orchideous masculinity', where an exotic dandyism (Humbert is a butterfly dandy whose old-world culture and aesthetic are reframed as effeminate in his new American context) complicates dichotomous notions of the masculine and the feminine.[4] Humbert can lurch from 'shedding torrents of tears', modelling himself as a sensitive 'merman', to boasting about how he would twist his first wife's 'brittle wrist' in order to manipulate her.[5] (His next wife, Lolita's mother, calls Humbert 'her ruler and her god'.[6]) Humbert, then, presents himself to us, insidiously, as a wounded masculinity in need of pity. This should be enough to make us sceptical about much of the current reactive conversation about the 'male condition' as a kind of victimisation.

And yet, for all the darkly parodic tone of much of *Lolita*, Nabokov was clearly attracted to a romanticised, Hollywood manliness himself. Humbert describes himself as 'writer and explorer',[7] which encapsulates Nabokov's ideal, recalling his father whose physicality, as portrayed in his memoir, isn't too far from some of Humbert's self-aggrandisements and is mirrored in *The Gift*, where the narrator valorises his father's 'live masculinity, inflexibility and independence, the chill and the warmth of his personality, his power over everything that he undertook'.[8] Manliness and fatherhood are intertwined in Nabokov's work, as are tenderness and parenthood. But as Robert Roper persuasively puts it, Humbert's 'fathering of Lolita is the dark negation of this'.[9]

Nabokov called *Lolita* 'a painful birth, a difficult baby', and this most heralded of novels came out of an intense period of parental concern for his beloved son, Dmitri.[10] At the same time as writing *Lolita*, Nabokov was also working on a story of devoted parenthood, the antithesis of Humbert Humbert's abhorrent parenting of Lolita. 'Lance' is the quite singular tale of two parents waiting for their space-explorer son to return from a dangerous expedition to outer space. It is a story of courage and intrepid adventure, implicitly identified as masculine traits, but also a story of parental love and concern, informed by the anxiety Vladimir and Véra felt about their son's passion for mountaineering and peril more generally. Immediately after netting his *sublivens* specimens in Telluride, Vladimir and Véra dropped Dmitri at the Petzoldt–Exum mountaineering school in the Tetons, on their way north-west for more butterflying and more bad-weather work on *Lolita*. (Actually, Dmitri dropped himself there, racing his parents through the Rocky Mountains with maverick style, like Juan Manuel Fangio on a bender, taking tight corners above monumental falls.) Nabokov's biographer Brian Boyd tells us that 'Nabokov felt constantly alarmed at this time', as did Véra, fearing for their son's safety as he pursued his daring hobbies without restraint.[11] But Nabokov understood the vulnerability of children and of the parent–child bond.

We might like to think we can protect our loved ones, but it is a fiction.[12]

'Lance' and *Lolita* are the culmination (one the negative image of the other) of a sequence of writings that have the dread of losing a child at their core.[13] These include 'Christmas', an early story in which a mourning father looks through the butterfly collection of his dead son; Nabokov's second novel in English, *Bend Sinister*, in which the protagonist sees the 'morpho-blue sky' (an allusion to the Blue Morpho butterfly) in a painting while officials in a dystopic Ministry of Justice apologise for killing his son;[14] and *Pale Fire*, the novel which most directly alludes to the assassination of Nabokov's father, where the poet John Shade watches white butterflies fly around the tree where his dead daughter's swing once hung. Repeatedly, when Nabokov thinks of fathers and their sons (a rare daughter in Shade's case), butterflies seem to appear.

Nowhere is this more affecting than in the conclusion of Nabokov's autobiography, *Speak, Memory*. Before describing how he and Véra led their six-year-old son down to the boat in the French harbour that would take them away from the Nazis and the outbreak of war, Nabokov recalls walking with Dmitri in a public garden in Paris, where he notices a young girl walking a 'slightly crippled' butterfly by a piece of thread tied around its body.[15] Nabokov attempts to divert his son's attention, not necessarily, as he points out, because of the suffering of the butterfly (he has killed countless insects himself), but because of its symbolism. He doesn't spell out what that symbolism is, but he does acknowledge, to Véra, that 'you and I did our best to encompass with vigilant tenderness the trustful tenderness of our child' in a world of 'hoodlums'.[16]

And they must protect him from much worse than that: the scene in the Paris public garden is immediately preceded by a recollection of seeing Hitler's ubiquitous image in Berlin, with his son, before they escaped Germany for France.

Nabokov's work is filled with high-literary moments where the tenderness and concern a parent feels for a vulnerable child charges the writing, making the clichéd masculinity of rigid gender roles look silly. And yet it is the simple lines with which Nabokov signs off his letters to his son, shorn of design and embellishment, when his defences are down, that move me most: 'Your father embraces you, my dearest,' he writes; 'I hug you, I'm proud of you, be well, my beloved.'[17]

32
Waking Dad

When my phone rings on a late-August evening, I fear the worst. Ever since I stopped leaving my phone on silent at night in case of emergencies, the 'Marimba' of the iPhone's default ringtone is capable of drilling a direct hole to the pit of my stomach. The screen lights up: *MUM AND DAD HOME*. Dad doesn't call from the home phone anymore, so it must be Mum. I answer with trepidation.

She has called an ambulance, but she's unsure if it was the right thing to do. Dad's temperature has been rising all day, and on his way to the toilet he collapsed. He hasn't hurt himself and was able to get back into bed, but now his temperature is soaring. He looks an almost bluish shade of red, she says. They've been told that if his temperature goes above forty degrees, it could indicate sepsis. But Dad is adamant he doesn't want to go to hospital. He is anxious about COVID, has heard all the worrying stories of overfilled hospitals, no beds, interminable waits. The ultimate fear is that he will never return home, and that with the current restrictions on visitors in the General he will not see us again. It's just a temperature, he said to her. He is asleep now and doesn't know that she has called 999. He's going to be so upset and angry, she says.

'But I didn't know what else to do. There's nothing I can do for him.'

'You've done the right thing,' I say. 'I'm on my way.'

Forty minutes later I am letting myself in.

'He's still fast asleep,' says Mum. She looks exhausted. 'They'll be here any minute now.' She also looks frightened. I hug her and tell her not to worry, but they are empty words.

As I climb the stairs the headlights of the ambulance pour in through the front of the house, spotlighting me on the landing. I feel a protective urge to get to Dad before they do, but I pause at the threshold to his room, a small wooden step. The door is open, the curtains closed, the room dimly lit by the landing. I feel like a child again, as if there is something forbidden about what I am about to do. I remember how I would call Mum from my bed in the early hours if I was feeling ill or frightened. My room was on the other side of their bedroom wall, so I'd start quietly, just repeating her name at ten-second intervals, getting incrementally louder until I'd hear a lamp-switch click and the creak of Mum getting out of bed.

I shouldn't be intruding at night, waking my parents. But old codes must be broken, roles have been swapped. Dad needs my protection, not just from his illness, but from the intruding outside world, which I can hear in muffled voices coming up the stairs. I go into his room and step towards the dark mass that is his bed in the centre, his form within barely visible.

In a poem called 'To a Butterfly', William Wordsworth

writes of a butterfly he is watching 'self-poised' on a yellow flower: 'I know not if you sleep, or feed'.[1] For a moment I am unable to tell if Dad sleeps or *sleeps*, bringing me back to those early nights of my son's life when, experiencing vertiginous cliché, I would watch Kit in his cot and wonder whether he was alive or dead. Dad looks peaceful, a shame to wake him, but there is no time. I gently squeeze his foot through the duvet, nervously stirring him.

'Dad,' I whisper, my voice no longer quite my own, almost my child's voice instead, calling from the darkness of its room in an alternative world where there is no Mum to call.

'Dad, it's me.'

He wakes instantly.

'Ben?'

He sounds confused, surprised.

'What are you doing here?'

I swallow hard.

'Dad, there are some paramedics here to see you.'

'No!' he says in a plangent, despairing voice that haunts me still, inflected with disappointment, distress and helplessness. 'What has she done?'

'It's the right thing,' I say. Before I can complete the thought, two paramedics are bustling in and I am turning on his bedside lamp.

The rest happens in a daze. I stand at the back of the room listening to the conversation, watching them take Dad's observations (pulse, blood pressure, temperature, who knows what else). Dad doesn't disclose his frustration to the paramedics; he knows they're only doing their job. They instantly warm to him though, making friendly banter. Mum chips in. She is relieved to have people in the house taking care of her husband, easing the burden, reassuring her with expertise. These have been long days and weeks, all alone with a dying man who is getting beyond her help, beyond all of us. The paramedics decide they will take him to the hospital, just as a precaution. Mum starts packing an overnight bag for him. Dad is able to walk himself down the stairs and out the house.

Mum looks at me and begins to cry as we watch Dad getting into the ambulance. I put my arm around her and she rests her head on my shoulder. I know what she's thinking. It's the same thing she was thinking when I rushed him to the Churchill in Oxford just a few weeks ago. Is this *the* goodbye?

'He'll be back,' I say.

It could very well be goodbye though. She doesn't need me to tell her this, so I don't. The ambulance reverses down the drive, its lights receding, leaving us stranded in the quiet night, just the rustling of trees, like the two Wych Elms looming at the end of the garden, brooding in darkness, sheltering secret life.

33

Who's Afraid of Tony Soprano?

Let me read some more Woolf to you, Dad:

> *'Do you remember the lake?' she said, in an abrupt voice, under the pressure of an emotion which caught her heart, made the muscles of her throat stiff, and contracted her lips in a spasm as she said 'lake'. For she was a child, throwing bread to the ducks, between her parents, and at the same time a grown woman coming to her parents who stood by the lake, holding her life in her arms which, as she neared them, grew larger and larger in her arms, until it became a whole life, a complete life, which she put down by them and said, 'This is what I have made of it! This!' And what had she made of it? What, indeed?*[1]

That is from *Mrs Dalloway*, published in 1925, the first work of modernist literature I ever read, eighteen years of age in the summer of 2005, before I started university. It couldn't have meant to me then what it means to me now, back when the idea of losing a parent was as fanciful as falling in love and becoming a father, as unlikely as a pandemic that puts the world into lockdown. But now I read it through the knowledge of your death and it moves me immensely. The best books grow with you, that's why I keep coming back to Woolf.

The idea of being able to hold an entire life in your arms, and then giving it back to the people who gave it to you, like you're returning a gift, is an overwhelming thought. True gifts, according to the scholar Lewis Hyde, are meant to be passed on, and in the act somehow enlarged.[2] Maybe this book is an attempt to carry my life and your life in my arms, to embrace them together, forever inseparable, even in death, and to present them to you so that you can tell me their worth. But it's never a whole life, a complete life. It is speculative and contingent, equally defined by what isn't there as by what is, by its multitude of absences, by the painful fact that I'll never really give it to you. I picture you too, carrying your life in your arms and offering it to *your* parents, asking them to see their lives in yours, to make it whole, to make it complete, and I wonder what they would make of it.

There is an episode of *The Sopranos* where Tony Soprano, the mob boss who is the centre of the show, buys a holiday home on the Jersey Shore. It is the fulfilment of a family dream, and in Tony's mind an opportunity to keep that family together now that his two children are flying the nest. But it descends into nightmare when Carmela, Tony's wife, discovers the latest in a long history of marital infidelities.

There are Woolfian undertones to the episode: the foreboding presence of the water and all it might symbolise (water is everywhere in Woolf's fiction, from the opening of *Jacob's Room* to the symbolically saturated *The Waves*, and it is the element in which her life ended); the presence of a holiday home as a concentration of family history recalling Woolf's *To the Lighthouse*; and Woolf's polemical 'A Room of One's Own', in which she famously argues that 'a woman must have money and a room of her own if she is to write fiction', getting an ironic twist when Tony is thrown out of the family home and has to drive down to the coast in the middle of the night to sleep on the floor in the empty, unheated holiday home.[3] I'm not sure that these are conscious allusions – the estate agent who shows them around is called Virginia Lupo, 'lupo' being Italian for wolf, but I think the allusion there is to Edward Albee's play of marital turmoil, *Who's Afraid of Virginia Woolf?*, rather than Woolf herself.[4] This is what I love about art though – its ability to converse and connect, even without intention.

Looking out across the water while his families (including his Mafia family) fall apart all around him, Tony must be reflecting on the meaning of his life. After a lifetime of betrayal and crime, his children growing up, his wife's pain, what can he hold in his arms to offer to another? And what is its worth?

We used to watch *The Sopranos* together. One of those televisual experiences that unite a family. We all loved it. It's absurd, looking back, how we used to eat our ritual Sunday tea (the components of which never changed) in front of the telly, nibbling Mum's mince turnover with a cup of tea while Italian American mobsters committed brutal acts of violence. I wasn't conscious of this then, as a young teenager, but *The Sopranos* is one of the most penetrating explorations of masculinity, and it's a show that, like Woolf's writing, continues to grow with me.

There is one episode, 'Calling All Cars', which starts with a dream. Tony is riding in the back of his dead father's Cadillac. But it is Carmela, his wife, not his father, who is driving. For once, Tony is the passenger. (Later in the episode, recounting the dream to his therapist, Tony says, 'If my father were alive he wouldn't have stood for [a woman driving for] two fucking seconds.') Alongside Carmela, in the passenger seat, is Ralph Cifaretto, an ex-associate of Tony's, who Tony, it just so happens, murdered. The rest of the car is filled out by a revolving cast of women that Tony has hurt and abused over the years. But the thing that strikes me most about the dream is the bulbous green caterpillar on the back of Ralph's bald head, directly in front of Tony where he can't avoid it. It squirms over Ralph's scalp, and when the camera cuts away and then cuts back, it has metamorphosed into a butterfly.

The dream is both awkward and obscure. Held in a car rather than one's arms, it seems to be asking a similar question to Woolf and Clarissa Dalloway: what is life? Is the butterfly a symbol of change (indeed, *can* Tony change, or is he too far gone?); or does it represent fate, the butterfly's metamorphosis being a fixed outcome, predestined, such that the butterfly is only ever a false image of possibility? Which brings me back to Clarissa Dalloway standing between her parents, by the lake, feeding the ducks, wondering what she has made of her life. '"This is what I have made of it! This!" And what had she made of it? What, indeed?' It seems to me there is another question nestled inside these questions. Not only what has she made of her life, but what has her life been made of?

Tony, too, is a philosophical feeder of ducks. Like many a murderous sociopath before him, he has a soft spot for animals, most famously the ducks that visit the family swimming pool in the back yard. Tony tends to the ducks, even getting into the pool with them in his dressing gown so that he can feed them, and he is heartbroken when they leave. The family pool plays an important role in *The Sopranos* on several occasions. Perhaps nowhere more so than in 'The Second Coming', an episode in the final season, where Tony's son, AJ, now eighteen years old, finds his life has unravelled. He hasn't got the grades for university, he can't hold down a job and he can't escape the smothering shadow of his father. He has talked to psychiatrists, taken antidepressants, but being the son of a man like Tony takes its toll. Tony loves AJ, but he can't relate to him, while AJ feels like he'll never come up to the mark . . . basically that he'll never be Tony.

Tony is the man who has to be the man, can't speak about his feelings, can't show weakness. Yet he is attached to his children in all sorts of intense and conflicted ways. 'Blood is thicker than water' is a central tenet of his old-school Italian ethos. He would do anything to protect and care for his family; in fact, he often tells Carmela that everything he has ever done has only been to put food on the table and a roof over their heads. (That in itself would have some effect on you, wouldn't it? To think that Tony's terrible deeds were done *for you*?) And for AJ, Tony presents an impossible example. AJ is doomed to inadequacy. Being morally superior just doesn't cut it.

In the episode, on a cold, dreary autumnal day, we watch AJ attach a breeze block to his leg with a bit of rope, tie a plastic bag over his head and drop himself into the swimming pool – the same pool that offered refuge to Tony's ducks. Tony returns to the house in the middle of the day and notices the back door ajar. Inspecting this, he hears a noise from outside. He steps out and finds AJ flailing in the pool with the plastic bag pulled up so that he is wearing it like an oversized hat. As Tony nears, bemused at first, slightly irritated by how pathetic his son is, the awful nature of the situation dawns on him. AJ isn't messing around; he is in fact drowning. Tony runs and jumps into the pool, his suit jacket fanning out around him, and swims to his boy. Pulling AJ into his arms, he tears the bag off his head and tries to ferry him to the side, but AJ can't move. 'My leg,' AJ shrieks. 'It's stuck.' Tony goes under and shifts the breeze block and eventually is able to haul AJ out.

They lie in puddles by the pool's edge, beneath a portentous grey sky. At first we think Tony is going to revert to his default emotions – rage, violence – and, sure enough, he grabs AJ and begins shaking him. 'What's wrong with you?' he shouts. AJ wails, helpless, just a baby in his father's arms. Then Tony sits up and places AJ's head in his lap and begins petting his hair, weeping over him, begging him to stop crying: 'You're alright, baby; you're alright.' Tony looks gorilla-like, a larger and more powerful primate performing his most essential function: protecting his offspring. To my mind it's the most moving moment in all the show's eighty-six episodes. And in this tragic embrace, Tony holding his son's life in his arms, we are confronted with a symbol of their essential differences – Tony's largeness and physical strength, set against his son's smallness and helplessness. But whereas Tony usually towers, he now crumples, cowering over his baby. They are at last one in their shared vulnerability.

*

I see you now on Studland Beach, where you held me when I was a little boy, but you look like you did towards the end. I am a child, not quite throwing bread to the ducks, coming to you by the sea. But unlike Clarissa Dalloway in Woolf's novel, rather than holding my life in my arms to offer to you, it is you who holds my life in *your* arms, which, as I near, grows larger and larger, until you put me down and say, 'This is what I have made of it! This!' And what had you made of it? What, indeed?

V
Clouded Yellow

34

Unexpected Readings

I'm sitting at the end of Dad's bed, trying to figure out if he has changed since he returned from the hospital after a night and a day of observations by those who know what they are looking for. I cannot remember who initiated the topic, but Dad is discussing his final wishes. He tells me he wants to be cremated, and that he would like a church service, which I question, but without any great tenacity. When I was a child, Dad would say he was a Christian. There was a Bible on the bedside, a cross around his neck, and on occasion he prayed, but that was the extent of his religious conviction, so far as I could tell. It was more a vague moral principle, to say you believed, the upright thing to think. At least that's how I interpret it, though I accept it is pretty arrogant to judge another person's faith.

Either way, Dad lost his religion somewhere in the last fifteen years. I may have played a small part in this, staging heated arguments with him once I was at university and became pompously intolerant and (ironically) preachy about such things. (We had a habit of vehemently disagreeing about something and then coming out on the same side, the changing party never quite acknowledging the change, at least not directly.) More influential than my plagiarised lines of argument, no doubt, was his ill health around that time. His change of mind coincided with his toughest phase of chronic fatigue and, in 2012, his first cancer diagnosis.

Yet it doesn't surprise me to hear that he wants a service in the village church: both of his sons were christened there, he reminds me, my brother was married there, he watched us at numerous school services there, carrying candlelit oranges spiked with liquorice and jellybeans on cocktail sticks around the aisles or stacking tins of beans and sweetcorn by the altar while singing songs of harvest. It just seems the proper place. After all, Dad is a provincial boy. He has spent his entire life within four miles of the village in which he was born and is respectful of the area's ways and traditions. The village church is where you go at important times, whether to celebrate the incoming or commemorate the outgoing.

'There are a couple of things I'd like to be read out,' he says, passing me a book.

It is a slim volume of John Clare's poetry. I think I might have given it to him a few Christmases ago. Whether he requested some Clare or whether Clare was my suggestion, I can't remember, but I do recall that he expressed a desire to read some nature poetry, hoping I might fix him up. I look at the cover and feel a flutter of regret. I was always happy to buy him books, an easy deferral of articulation and communion, symbolic acts that might just about satisfy whatever Dad was longing for. Had he hoped for conversations that never materialised? Clare made sense though: arguably the greatest English nature poet, but more importantly for us *the* Northamptonshire poet, who immortalised the fields, meadows and woodland of our home county. But I never thought to ask Dad if he had actually read any of the books I bought him. Did I even want to know?

Now I am confronted by the painful evidence that he did indeed read them. A bookmark is slotted inside. I open to a short lyric: 'Love lives beyond . . . '. I read it quickly and find the experience oddly toilsome.

'You've been reading this?' I say, holding the book up.

'Yes. I've been reading quite a bit of poetry. Clare. Robert Frost.'

'Oh,' I say. 'I had no idea.'

It's a limited and limiting response. Why don't I ask him what he makes of Clare? Which poems he likes best? What they mean to him? Maybe it's because I don't want to confess that I haven't read much Clare myself, or maybe for reasons more challenging to outline.

'If someone could read the one that I've marked there at the funeral. And if you could read this one please.'

It strikes me straight away, before he has even handed me a second book – a small notebook from the side of his bed – that this time he has identified a specific reader. He wants *me* to read it.

'What's this?'

'Some poems I've been writing,' he says.

I am stunned. I leaf through the lined pages, humbled into silence by the careful pencil of Dad's secret poems.

'I had no idea,' I whisper, almost breathless. Why does this feel like heartbreak?

Each poem is titled and dated, the earliest from June 2019, when Dad was ill with the symptoms of his undiagnosed kidney cancer, the latest from March 2020, the same month he received his terminal diagnosis. He hasn't written anything since.

'You should have said.'

'I think I did,' he says, not in an accusing way, just trying to remember.

Maybe he did. I recognise one of the poems, called 'Butterflies', under which he has added a note: 'Written as an inscription for Ben in a Butterfly Book.' Yes, how had I not thought of it in this year of butterflies, written in pen on the title page of Jeremy Thomas's *The Butterflies of Britain & Ireland*, which I've been consulting all summer?

I take in all the other titles: 'The Hay Field', 'Falling Leaves', 'Autumn Gales', 'Emotions', 'Mum and Dad's Oak', 'Another's Wood', 'To Family' and 'To Jane'. And at the very end, a poem marked with a piece of card cut from a tissue box on which he has written: 'To be read at my funeral.' It's called 'For the Love of Life'. It starts 'I'm free at last, I'm free again / I'm free from suffering and pain / My spirit's free once more to roam / In places near and far from home. / Fields and meadows and breathing wood . . . '. I stop.

'I had no idea,' I say again. 'You could have shared these with me.'

'I would like to,' he says. 'I thought you might help me improve them.'

I feel an unsettling pressure in my chest. All these years teaching literature and creative writing at universities, while the person who would have most valued my thoughts was at home all along. Yes, we should have discussed these poems, read them aloud together, polished their imagery, tightened their rhythms, reflected on their meanings.

'Can I take this home with me?' I ask. 'Take some time to read it all?'

'Please do,' says Dad. 'I'd like to know what you think.'

I close the notebook, my thoughts zigzagging like a blue, darting like a skipper. Will we ever speak of them again?

'I'm running out of butterflies,' I say later. With the summer drawing to an end, high season for butterflies is over. Most of the species have completed their cycles, including the White-letter Hairstreak, which I never managed to see at the end of Mum and Dad's garden. But cycles start again, never really end, the new generation repeating the stages of the last. In Fermyn, the Purple Emperors are now minute eggs on half-shaded sallow leaves, or first-instar caterpillars eating their own eggs; the Lulworth Skippers on the Dorset hillsides are larvae spinning cocoons inside sheaths of Tor-grass; the Silver-studded Blues in the sand dunes are eggs too, and will stay in this form, clinging to the heather all winter until they hatch and enlist their support staff of ants; while the Wood Whites in our secret wood are already at the chrysalis phase, in which they will overwinter. But all I see is absence and death, ignorant of the hidden life.

'There are still opportunities,' says Dad, charitably.

He describes how, of the fifty-nine regular species we get in the UK, two are migratory butterflies – the Painted Lady and the Clouded Yellow – plus the Red Admiral, which is a migrant too, though it is considered a resident butterfly, and all three are still on the wing. He tells wondrous tales of transcontinental flights: how the Painted Lady journeys from North Africa, the Middle East and Central Asia to Europe, crossing oceans in fronts hundreds of kilometres wide that cast shadows below; how the Red Admiral comes from southern Europe and returns in the autumn; how every ten years or so we get 'Clouded Yellow years', when the Clouded Yellow arrives from North Africa and continental Europe in bumper numbers, like during the Second World War when the coast-watch mistook them for an attack of yellow poison gas.[1]

'Isn't nature amazing?' he says, when we both know it to be cruel. The migratory butterflies make me think of death, the ultimate border crossing. I keep the thought to myself.

'Have you seen a Painted Lady yet?' he asks.

'No, but I've been keeping an eye out especially.'

As autumn sets in and the butterflies wane, I feel intimations of a new bereftness, the coming mass of an absence I never knew existed before. There are only a couple of species still on the wing that I haven't seen – chief amongst them the Painted Lady and Clouded Yellow.

'Painted Lady numbers vary year on year,' says Dad. 'There should be some around though, even in a quiet summer.'

'I've seen several reports of them on the Butterfly Conservation website,' I say.

Dad nods.

'How about the Clouded Yellow?' He sent me a text about this particular butterfly a week or so ago (I'm losing sense of time), after seeing a number of sightings reported on the local Butterfly Conservation branch website. He's no longer checking for himself.

'Not so much,' I say. 'But there have been a couple more records.'

'Keep looking,' says Dad, his eyes heavy, shuffling his body. 'They like clover fields. Don't give up.'

35

Northamptonshire Poet

The man walks on, beyond hunger and fatigue. For four days he has walked without real food or drink (he eats grass for sustenance), carrying five books (also sustenance). He hobbles north, or what he hopes is north, his disintegrating shoes blighted by gravel, one sole almost gone completely; and at night he lies with his head pointing northwards (or what he hopes is northwards) so that he doesn't lose his way during his fitful, hallucinatory dreams. He spies inside homes and public houses, their windows portal-lit, cosier lives from which he is excluded. He spends one night sleeping in the porch of an isolated house near a wood. Walking in the dark he becomes disoriented, anxious that he might have circled back on himself like a senseless pair of compasses that think they are tracing a straight line. He continues, chasing the edge of the horizon. A cart approaches carrying a woman, man and boy. The woman jumps down, takes him by the hand and implores him to come on board. She must be drunk, he thinks, or mad. It is his wife, Patty, they tell him. He is home.[1]

*

I wonder what butterflies the poet John Clare saw on his legendary walk out of Essex, when he absconded from High Beech asylum near Epping Forest in July 1841, where he had lived for four years after being certified 'insane'. Clare hiked some eighty miles home to north-east Northamptonshire, hoping for a reunion with his first love and dream wife, Mary Joyce. But Mary had died three years earlier, and she had never been his wife.

Clare would have encountered most of the hedge and field butterflies we find in summer today, but in much greater abundance. Clare's was a time before large-scale habitat destruction and the invention of deadly pesticides. Scientists refer to 'shifting baseline syndrome', whereby we measure change against the perceived norm of our personal early experiences, so my sense of butterfly normality is different from even my dad's, let alone Clare's. Since as recently as the 1970s, 80% of British butterfly species have decreased in abundance or distribution, and the abundance of habitat specialists, like the hairstreaks, Wood Whites, Purple Emperors and many of the blues, has decreased by 27% and their distribution by 68%. One can only imagine the butterfly traffic of an 1840s summer.[2]

Would Clare have tramped past bramble-nectaring Brown Hairstreaks and beneath canopy-soaring White-letter Hairstreaks, or any of the other species that are endangered now? And what of the four extinct British butterflies? He quite possibly would have seen Large Tortoiseshells, a fluctuating species even then, but so common in its occasional bumper years (not least in Essex, the departure point for Clare's escape) that to see one would have caused very little excitement in the Victorian collector. Lepidopterists cannot put a precise time on the Large Tortoiseshell's extinction, but, due to climate change, Dutch elm disease and the impact of parasites, it had more or less disappeared by the mid-1950s, when Dad was born.

Clare may have seen some Black-veined Whites, though they only existed in isolated colonies. Their last stronghold was Kent, just south of Clare's departure point, and they were present across Essex, Hertfordshire and Northamptonshire, through which Clare's route ran. Its population peaked in July, when Clare was on foot, and it favoured hay meadows and the edges of woodland, which Clare was probably skirting. Of the four extinct species, Clare was least likely to see a Mazarine Blue – an uncommon butterfly in the mid-nineteenth century, living in scattered colonies, most abundant in Dorset. However, it is not impossible that some would have passed Clare by, on the wing in July, favouring heavy clay habitats, a common geology in Northamptonshire.

The fourth extinct species is one that Clare had a bond with. The Large Copper was already on the cusp of extinction – the last British record dates from 1864 on the Norfolk Broads – but Clare had admired it in the past at Swordy Well, an old heathland and quarry near Helpston, the village where he was born.[3] 'The Lament of Swordy Well', one of the most unforgettable poems of ecological protest in the English language, comes out of a particularly turbulent period of Clare's life. In 1832 he moved three miles north-east from Helpston, where he had lived his whole life, to the village of Northborough. But those three miles were a thousand in his heart. This is the central subject of his momentous poem, 'The Flitting', which begins:

Ive left my own old home of homes
Green fields and every pleasant place
The summer like a stranger comes
I pause and hardly know her face[4]

Clare had lost his essential landscape, first through the devastating and divisive acts of enclosure, whereby the English countryside was wrested from the commons and parcelled off as private property, and secondly through his move away from Helpston, such that the familiar plants and creatures, even his own 'corner chair', became radically unfamiliar. All is 'strange and new', he writes; everything feels 'itself from home'.[5] One meaning of the word 'flitting' is the removal from one's home, typically against one's wish or desire. But for Clare this doesn't just mean removal from a physical house, but removal from a habitat, from one's nature. The poems he wrote at this time – including 'The Lament of Swordy Well' – are marked by loss, alienation, endangerment and extinction.

Flitting also means transformation from one state of being to another. It evokes in my mind a butterfly, whose movement is of course a flitting – flittering and fluttering – and whose very condition is a flitting, programmed to fundamental change. But it is unnatural change that haunts Clare. As a child, he visited Swordy Well in search of its distinctive flora and fauna, not least the Large Copper. Years later he would return to this beloved habitat through an act of astonishing imaginative sympathy. For what makes 'The Lament of Swordy Well' so poignant is that it is written in the voice of Swordy Well itself. The land speaks to us directly, a vivid personifying thing, making its complaint, bearing witness to its own abuse. 'I used to bring the summers life / To many a butterflye' it says, including, one presumes, the Large Coppers that Clare saw there: 'But in oppressions iron strife / Dead tussocks bow and sigh'.[6] The butterflies 'may wir and come', but Swordy Well 'cannot keep em now'.[7]

It is a devastating poem that plays on inversions of giving and taking – what the land gives freely to the nature it supports, and what the parish takes from it – and renders shifting senses of value. Swordy Well is alienated from itself, much like Clare, whose essential landscape, and with it his essential self, was disfigured by enclosure and the segregations and inequities of private ownership. Nature is thus doubled in Clare's sensitive vision: it is both a living being and a spectral reality, a hinterland of phantoms and shadows and shades, where a tangible past is deformed by the unfeeling and greedy present.[8]

This is memorably conveyed in another poem, 'Shadows of Taste', which Clare wrote on the back of an electioneering handbill (as a poor rural labourer, Clare struggled to find paper).[9] Here, describing the alienation caused by the changing nature of his environment, Clare traces his own anguished striving for poetic form, which is a striving to understand and articulate himself:

> *From these old fashions stranger metres flow*
> *Half prose half verse that stagger as they go*
> *One line starts smooth and then for room perplext*
> *Elbows along and knocks against the next.*[10]

This is an important story in Clare's self-conception as poet: the search for form in a life whose stability depended on home and its recognisable natural forms. 'But take these several beings from their homes,' he says of the butterflies, birds and flowers that were his friends and allies,

> *Each beauteous thing a withered thought becomes*
> *Association fades and like a dream*
> *They are but shadows of the things they seem*
> *Torn from their homes and happiness they stand*
> *The poor dull captives of a foreign land.*[11]

Clare's compassion for other creatures is folded into his sense of bereavement of the nature that has shaped and sustained him.

'Shadows of Taste' champions the person who sees particularity; the person who therefore values, over any kind of superficial or material value, the sentience of all living creatures. The person 'of taste' respects these creatures as their own peculiar, singular beings, and, like Clare,

> *loves not flowers because they shed perfumes*
> *Or butterflyes alone for painted plumes*
> *Or birds for singing although sweet it be*
> *But he doth love the wild and meadow lea*
> *There hath the flower its dwelling place and there*
> *The butterflye goes dancing through the air.*[12]

This is the Clare I value, whose poetry comes from a place both intimately familiar to and eerily estranged from my life. Clare is the gift, and he certainly had the gift. He was so much: the great nature poet, the late Romantic poet, the peasant poet, the Northamptonshire poet. And from now on, Dad, he is the poet you have returned to me.

36
Time Passes

Carli, Kit and I go for a late-August walk along Pitsford Reservoir in central Northamptonshire. I try to be in the moment, pushing Kit's pram, the wheels digging and swivelling in the gravel track. I don't tell Carli that I suggested this location because it was the last place Dad sighted a Clouded Yellow a couple of years back. I also don't tell her that the Clouded Yellow and Painted Lady are the only two species still on the wing in the county that I haven't seen yet.

But I can't see *any* butterflies. Kit doesn't care, staring up at me with Carli's wide brown eyes, beneath his decadent long lashes. Carli doesn't notice either, routinely stepping in front of the pram, walking backwards, adjusting Kit's blanket. The seasons are changing and with them my hope of seeing more butterflies. I'm quiet, a bit despondent, a little tetchy. I know I need to get out of my own head and be a more present husband and father, but I can't stop wondering what it is I've been doing this summer. The company of Carli and Kit on this undercover butterfly hunt brings into sharp focus how all those transformative experiences with Purple Emperors and Silver-washed Fritillaries and White Admirals have been experienced alone.

I look down on the top of Kit's head and wonder how *he* sees it all.

The next day, changeable weather at Twywell Hills and Dales, five minutes from home, clouds moving across the sky, rubbing out the sun. All I have seen so far is a solitary Comma, its scalloped outline looking melancholy. I try to lift myself by imagining next year's butterflying, when I'll be prepared for the Dingy Skippers and Grizzled Skippers and Green Hairstreaks that I missed on the scrubby banks here this spring. But will I know what to look for without Dad? And who will I share my sightings with?

A large butterfly charges past me, late for our meeting. I see it settle on the hard dirt track, taking advantage of a momentary gap in the clouds. A Painted Lady, at last. I take a photograph and imagine its passage across the ocean to see me. I send a picture to Dad. The Painted Lady flies off, a few more miles left to go yet. I wait for Dad's usual prompt response, but nothing arrives.

I enter Fermyn Woods. The place I have returned to most persistently all summer. The oak where I saw my first Purple Emperor, the wide grassy ride where I saw my first Silver-washed Fritillary, the intersection of two paths where I saw my first White Admiral, the grass beneath a shelter of opposing oaks where I saw my first Purple Hairstreak. But what had seemed a place of excess and volume at the start of the summer, noisy with unknowability, has fallen silent. All I see on my four-mile walk is one Peacock, one Speckled Wood and a couple of whites, dispersed ruins of the past.

The forest expels me onto a softly undulating plain of harvested fields, wind turbines far in the distance and parcels of further woodland. I take a diagonal towards Lady Wood and Souther Wood, which had bustled with Purple Emperor fanatics just a month ago. I reach the edge of the field and find myself on a dirt path running horizontally across an opening in the hedgerow. Framed within this gap, about two miles off, is an incomplete house, like something dropped out of cosmic time. It is a grand Tudor manor without roof, doors or windows. The abandoned fantasy of a man who died before it could be completed.[1] How have I not noticed it before? I stare across the distance, unsettled by this fragment of meaning whose incompletion I am unable to fill.

37

Homeless at Home

The young GP whom we have not met before is cramped between Dad's bedside and the wall, reading the thermometer. We must open the window, he says, remove some layers. It is jarring to see other adults in Dad's bedroom, to see him submitting to someone else's authority in his own home. Dad looks flushed. This morning he was felled by a sudden sharp crippling pain in his lower back. Mum found him on the bathroom floor. Through a combination of dragging (Dad is twice Mum's size) and shuffling, they got him back into bed. He was in tears, says Mum, when I arrive too late and hug her.

The doctor prescribes liquid morphine and I am dispatched to a distant Tesco, the nearest pharmacy open on a Sunday, to collect it. I navigate the shiny aisles of toiletries meant for ordinary lives where hair products and smelling nice still matter, unaccustomed to other people after five months of lockdowns and social distancing, glad for the mask on my face, which is obscuring at least some of my emotions. While I wait for the pharmacist to prepare the drug that I associate with the end of things, I shuffle quick thoughts about what this might mean, where we are headed. At home I show Mum how to use the syringe. Dad sleeps.

I speak to my brother on video call from Japan. He has been agonising all summer over when the right time to fly over will be. He is faced with prohibitive travel restrictions that will separate him from his wife and young daughter, as well as his work, for an impracticable amount of weeks, so we all know the likely outcome without ever quite articulating it. We discuss the cruel realities of losing a loved one during a pandemic. Dad lies on his back while Mum holds the phone in front of his face. He tells Matt to stay in Japan. It is unrealistic, he says, and Matt's priority must be *his* family. Matt can't agree, at least not out loud. He insists he will fly over when the time is right, certainly before the end. But we all know timing that is impossible. He could get on a flight right now and still not make it.

After they finish their call, Dad tells me he had accepted he would never see Matt again back in January, when he said goodbye to him in the ICU ward after he had had his kidney removed, weeks before he had even been given the terminal diagnosis. Matt was saying one kind of goodbye, en route to Heathrow, while Dad was saying another.

Dad speaks to his oncologist on the phone. They have results from some recent investigations. The cancer has spread to his bones. It is in his ribs and his back. It is growing in his abdomen too. Time to change strategy. Dad will end chemotherapy immediately and begin immunotherapy and radiotherapy. While the particular immunotherapy he will undergo is relatively new and experimental, with little historical data to draw upon, the doctor believes there is a small chance its efficacy could be much greater than the chemo. Don't lose hope yet, he says. Sitting at the end of the bed while Dad relays this to me, I realise that I am watching him die.

The days begin to unfold. I empty Dad's piss down the toilet. I've done this a few times now and have figured a knack for draining it without any splashback or run-off. Naturally it plays with your sense of perspective, holding your father's bladder in one room while he is in another. Unable to sit up because of the pain in his back and the exhaustion, he can just about reattach the bag to himself without my help.

'I've not been able to wash for a couple of days,' he says.

Mum drops her head. Some things are now beyond her and she fears she is failing him.

'I could give you a bath?' I say.

Dad closes his eyes for a second – just enough time to agree parting terms with his pride and sense of natural order – and nods.

'Okay,' he says. 'I'm sorry.'

'I don't mind,' I say. 'It's just a bath.'

I prepare a bowl of warm soapy water in the en suite while Mum helps Dad undress.

'I'm sorry,' says Mum in tears, when I return with the spare washing-up bowl and a look on my face that says it's a shame not all things can go in the dishwasher. 'I just can't do it,' she says.

She stays with me though, wanting to assist in some way; maybe she can offer practical advice. It's the fraught act of touching that she cannot cope with anymore.

'Right,' I say, sitting by Dad with the bowl on the bedside

table. He is tucked under his bedsheet, like a patient awaiting his dreaded inspection.

He is teary, the look on his face one of anguished resignation. To an extent I know what I will see: a body much thinner and more atrophied than I associate with Dad; the shiny wound of his stoma; moles and freckles that I didn't know were there; his penis (something I haven't seen since I was a little boy, before I was in the business of making accurate memories). What I will see is his mortality.

'I'm not what I used to be,' he says, almost at a whisper. 'I'm sorry.'

'Come on,' I say. Dad closes his eyes as I pull back the sheet, and a tear rolls down his cheek.

That night, at home, I bath Kit. Most nights we bath together. Kit sits between my legs with his toys, using my legs and arms as bridges for his cars, driving them around the full circuit of my body. Something worrying has been happening recently though. I start sliding downwards and then jolt awake.

I'm exhausted, or more exhausted than usual. It's what Martin Amis distinguishes from local tiredness in his 1995 novel, *The Information.* A cosmic tiredness that cannot be alleviated by sleep. The increasing proximity of death warps and disfigures body and mind. Tonight, I wake after a couple of seconds to find Kit staring at me. He smiles and laughs at his silly dad for doing odd things. I say sorry, getting in some early apologies in what will be a lifetime of them. Kit chuckles again and a tractor brought back from my trip to Dorset takes my kneecap and descends into the foam and the junction of toes beneath.

Of course, I don't explain to Kit why I am so tired. He

knows nothing about Dad's situation beyond a few occasions when I have explained my ever more frequent absences by saying I am going to help Nana and Granddad because Granddad is a bit poorly. He hasn't seen Dad in at least a month. He has seen Mum a few times in that period, out in the garden and the field, keeping two metres distant (as if he knows what a metre is or why his grandparents don't touch him anymore), but he is not allowed inside their house. I've got some photos on my phone of the last time Dad was able to join us, the two of them sat on the garden bench together, at opposite ends, probably not quite the right distance, pulling similar smiles, though there is a sadness beneath Dad's that Kit would not understand. 'How am I supposed to not touch him?' you can hear Dad ruing on one of the live photos.

I get Kit to stand up and lather him in baby-bath. His skin is soft and smooth, impossibly unblemished. I wash him all over, cleaning all those pesky folds where the dirt gathers and hides. Will he remember this one day as he washes my dying body? Will he recall me as I once was?

I think of the three most recent generations of men in our family, in which I form the midpoint. If Kit is the caterpillar, then I am the chrysalis and Dad is the butterfly. Only Dad is one of those deteriorating butterflies, faded in colour and incomplete in wing. As for the sleepy chrysalis, I am in an ambiguous state. The chrysalis, dry and crinkled, is in some way the parent of the adult butterfly – its shell, its protection – more aged somehow than what comes next, so that it complicates the natural hierarchy. Who is the parent, and who is the child? That old cliché.

*

Clean and towelled off, Dad covers himself back up with the duvet, dressed in fresh pyjamas. I have never seen him so demoralised. If things aren't going to improve, he says, then what is the point in all this? He has lost faith in treatment and his doctor's carefully worded hope. Why prolong things? he asks rhetorically. I recall him making comments in the past about terminal conditions. If I ever get anything like that, he'd say, please put me out of my misery, like he'd be one of the rabbits out in the field with myxomatosis or a pheasant with a broken wing.

'Come on, let's just see what the new treatment brings.'

Easy for me to say. But I hate speaking such futile words. I can see where he is coming from. I would want it to end too.

'Just try to rest.'

38

A Change in Sensibility, in Four Parts

1.

3 a.m., about ten years ago. An unlit country lane, the darkness torn apart by my car's full beam. Carli and I, in our mid-twenties, driving home from a night out in Northampton town. Carli has been drinking, but I am designated driver, bleary-eyed and head-hammered from a few too many sober hours in the company of drunken others. The road winds and undulates. A barn owl launches from invisible hedgerow, a reflective beacon crossing our lights and disappearing again. We slow as we pass through a hamlet, everyone tucked up inside the thatched cottages, and regain speed when the road drops away from the houses, dipping and rising into a sudden bracing incline. We take a bend onto level ground, where I spot something just ahead in the middle of the road. I slow the car until we are almost upon it.

A rabbit. It is sat up in our lights, unmoving. There is no way around it, the road too narrow, so I flash and beep the horn, its piercing eyes sending the full beam back to me, turning observer into observed in some unspoken judgement of humankind. It won't budge.

'I'm not going to drive over the top of it,' I say, bringing the car to a halt, unbuckling my seatbelt.

'What are you doing?' says Carli. 'We can't just stop *here*.'

I climb out of the car. It's cold, the moon bright.

I find myself adopting a soft voice as I say, 'Hey, matey.' I walk closer and still it doesn't move, head and chest upright, fixed in the glare of the headlamps. Why isn't it running away? 'Are you okay?' I ask. 'What's the matter?'

I turn to the car and shrug. I take a step closer. The rabbit is in a strange pose, its top half erect, but its bottom half laid out flat behind it, like a starlet posing for a glamour shot in the 1950s. Or more like a hand puppet, I realise, its bottom half *literally* flat, hind legs crushed and twisted at an obtuse angle, run over by a car.

'You poor thing,' I say. I turn to Carli again and shake my head. She is sitting forward, her face almost against the windscreen.

I turn back to the rabbit. It makes me jump when it suddenly tries to move, dragging its mangled lower half across the road, only making it a couple of inches before giving up.

'Fuck,' I say, wondering what Dad would do.

I know what he would do. Tucked fingers under chin, foot on legs, neck break, instant sleep. He would see it as a moral failing, an act of wicked cruelty, to leave such a creature in distress when the outcome is inevitable.

But I am not my dad. I share his moral outlook, but not his capacity. I remember just a couple of years earlier, walking his dogs for him in the field, on my own, when Holly – an old and ailing springer spaniel, once a well-trained gundog, now basically senile – began charging a rabbit by the pond. Even from a little distance I could see that the rabbit wasn't going to move, eyes purple, swollen like rotten plums, congealed shut so that it was blind to the approaching threat. What did it think when it heard my voice darkly, blasting its sensorium with the too-late words 'NO, HOLLY, LEAVE!'? What did it feel when a split second later it was clasped in a warm wet mouth, held between teeth trained not to puncture? 'LEAVE! LEAVE!' I shouted, running towards Holly, Holly running towards me, tail erect, wagging for joy, the rabbit imprisoned between her jaws. Holly looked up, eyes filled with instinct, the rabbit's ravaged by myxomatosis. 'Leave, Holly,' I said, putting my hands beneath the struggling animal, ready to catch it, when really I should've been grabbing its body firmly, assertively. Holly relaxed her jaw, but I made a total fumble of it, unsettled by the sensation of its otherness in my hands, its quick contortions and foreign mass, convinced I could feel its heartbeat pulsating through my hands to the top of my skull. It sprung from me and weaved across the grass in blind loop-the-loops, Holly watching with her tongue flapping.

The rabbit stopped. I waited. And in that moment of indecision Holly caught it again. 'LEAVE!' I yelled, and this time Holly responded, dropping the rabbit, which ran to the pond, plunged into the cold water and began to drown. I found a broken branch and used it to pull the half-dead creature towards the bank, its lungs filling with water, terminally shocked. I had been indecisive, and because of me the rabbit had suffered more than it should have. I crushed its head into the mud until it stopped kicking.

*

The rabbit tries to drag itself across the road again and manages only an inch or two. I look to Carli in the car, her eyes wide, hand over mouth, unable to stifle alcohol-quickened emotions. I must be decisive this time, but I am botching the job, basically botching the task of being my dad. The rabbit is crippled, I tell myself, beyond healing. I can't take it to the vet's at 3 a.m. (they'd only put it down anyway). To take it home and try to nurse it would be foolish and possibly selfish. How would I even get it home? Put a wild rabbit in the boot and let it bash itself against the sides? Let its heart give out from terror? I couldn't exactly ask Carli to pin it down on the front seat . . . Each successive thought is more ridiculous than the last. Meanwhile, the rabbit tries dragging itself away one more time, but now it can't even begin.

I pick it up by its hind legs, conscious that I am distressing the very source of pain, and carry it to the verge. In the light of the moon, I pick out a tree. I swing the rabbit from far behind me and strike its skull against the trunk. A dull thwack, like a cricket ball being hit far off in the distance. The rabbit goes loose in my grip, unresisting. I strike it one more time to be sure and leave it in the ditch. When I get back into the car, Carli is in tears.

2.

In Dad's study I turn the key in the mahogany cabinet and open the double doors. Two columns of drawers, each about fifty centimetres wide and five centimetres high. I slide one out from the left side. It is glass-topped, lined with pure white foamboard, but empty. I slide out more, each as empty as the last. I feel disappointed rather than relieved.

I pull the top drawer from the right-hand side. A cornucopia of dead Nymphalidae, organised in vertical rows by species. Red Admirals, Painted Ladies, Small Tortoiseshells, Commas, Peacocks, White Admirals, all creatures I now know, friends and companions of a long, troubled summer. They lie motionless around the pins in their hearts. There is one species in here that I haven't seen before, but I recognise it from my reading: the Camberwell Beauty, called the Mourning Cloak in America, an infrequent visitor to these shores.

I'm unsure how to feel about their fixed poses, all fully spread, a couple specimens of each species pinned from behind so that you can see their underside. I identify the tiny white bit of punctuation on each hindwing of the Commas, short breaths for dead clauses. Up close the reverse of the Red Admirals' hindwings almost look like alligator skin, and the underwings of the Painted Ladies look like five-eyed owls, or an owl rapidly shaking its head so the eyes blur into multiples. A large black butterfly baffles me at first until I tilt the drawer slightly and catch the light at just the right angle to release the purple aura of the Emperor.

I begin pulling drawers at random, glancing, closing, pulling another, like a stunned onlooker who has just happened upon a massacre. Dozens and dozens of butterflies in each, all of the species I have seen this summer are accounted for, and some I haven't seen, including Clouded Yellows and White-letter Hairstreaks, which make me feel like a cheat. Some have labels pinned behind them detailing dates and locations. I gather that the majority come from a couple of antique collections – many are dated from the 1920s and 1930s, and some are from the collection of my grandparents' neighbour (the one who rejected Granddad's gift of a Lulworth Skipper). While I am confident Dad wouldn't have collected from the wild, certainly not any protected species (he is by nature a morally conscious, law-abiding sort), a small number, I assume, have been reared and then pinned by him.

Far more will have been released though, I tell myself, trying to assuage some inner unease. I can hear Dad's voice in my head, launching possible defences in response to imaginary critics: people kill spiders, flies and wasps all the time without batting an eye, so what can they say about an organised scientific collection? Do these people refuse to drive cars, because cars are devastating to insect life? – We make innumerable hit and runs on every journey. This reminds *me* of Nabokov, who gave the following advice to any hypothetical butterflier stopped by a park official in the US National Parks:

> *just point to the nearest series of parked cars. Let him count the number of butterflies that the radiators have collected while passing through the Forbidden Zone. Have him talk to these motorists, take their license numbers, compute how many cars pass daily through and how many 'bugs' they accumulate per day. [. . .] Tell him he has just destroyed a new species of mosquito on his cheek.*[1]

And if you're going to decry my collection, continues Dad in the echo chamber of my imagination, I hope you don't eat fruit and veg from the supermarket, because the chemicals used to cultivate those will have killed millions more caterpillars than you'll find butterflies in my collection. Through all my conservation work (getting emotional here), the creation and protection of habitats, the rearing and releasing of species, I have done far more than most could even dream of to protect wildlife. What have *you* ever done?

I have no leg to stand on. If I was to deduct the number of butterflies that Dad has pinned in his collection from the number he has reared and released or simply assisted through habitat conservation, the net gain would be dramatically greater than the number of butterflies *I* have ever benefited. Which is better, I ask myself: to kill a handful of insects for the purpose of a collection while supporting an abundance or to simply do nothing? Dad is by far a greater friend to butterflies than I. Yet still I imagine unclipping the glass covers from these drawers to let the butterflies fly free, only to be greeted by a dissonance of cries and screams.

I close the cabinet and turn the key.

3.

Vladimir Nabokov's Dream Diary.[2]

Somewhere in continental Europe. Vladimir descends from the cable car to a vast collecting ground of timberland. He is topless, wearing shorts and long socks – he still has his footballer's legs, an aloof goalie in his Cambridge days, but no longer the breasts that bounced as he hiked across the sprung rhythms of middle age.

The collecting ground is sensed rather than seen, a promise carried on the breeze, twitching a collector's finely tuned reflexes. But instead of a lush wilderness of nectar sources and larval foodplants, an uncanny hotel rears up from the clouds, like a great Clouded Yellow with symmetrical wings and lemon-yellow scales over its many balconied eyespots. Vladimir walks through the empty lobby in black and white, a Hitchcockian clip-clop of heel on cool marble, and out through the multi-paned doors on the other side, into lucid technicolour. He skips down the steps, which seem to go on forever, descending into different climes, until he finds himself on the marshy border of a lake, the hotel vanishing behind him in opaque thought. He walks amongst colourful bog flowers that vibrate, scintillant in the dappled light, his feet sinking in cushiony turf. The conditions are perfect, yet he cannot see a single butterfly. He looks down and instead of a net finds a huge spoon in his hand. How could I possibly have forgotten my net, he thinks, dreading its absence like the loss of a limb. How shall I catch anything with *this*?

Puzzling over the spoon, he notices a weird kind of letterbox to his right. It is noisy. A timpani of tapping and whirring. As he nears, his spoon poised in the air ready to catch or bat, the letterbox flings open and out flies a large fritillary, its chequered wings tumbling like dice until it lands in Vladimir's outstretched spoon. The creature is a surprising green – possibly a *valezina* form of the Silver-washed Fritillary, or some rare aberration of the Dark Green Fritillary, it's hard to say, its wings so oddly elongated, the green fused together with variegated brown. Balancing the spoon gently so as not to disturb this oddity into flight, Vladimir peers into the open letterbox and finds that it is packed with dead butterflies. Is his catch the only living butterfly in all this fertile land?

He eyes the exceptional butterfly on his spoon, watches it tremble, its wings closed, antennae twitching, returning his stare. Then in a rapid jump cut, ten seconds sliced from the record, Vladimir has the butterfly's thick, furry thorax between thumb and forefinger and is squeezing. It continues eyeing him, in conscious agony now, as its life is pinched from it. Vladimir has to look away, overcome by murderous guilt, yet he continues to throttle, eyes closed. He swears he can hear the butterfly let out a quiet gasp, tenacious of life, but helpless. In his back pocket he finds an old morocco case, red and zippered, in which he delicately encloses the specimen.

Just as he pulls the zip he is startled by a man seated next to him, to the left of the box of dead butterflies. He has a small microscope on his lap and is about to place a slide under it when he notices that Vladimir has seen him.

'I'm so sorry,' says Vladimir to the collector. 'I didn't realise.' He proffers the morocco case. 'Please, let me return this.'

The man palms it away and shrugs.

Vladimir stands embarrassed in the glare of the sun, looking about at the wildflowers like a child who knows he has done wrong, ashamed to make eye contact.

'I don't know how I'm supposed to catch anything with this anyway,' he says, waving the spoon. He puts it in his mouth and goes to bite down, unsure if it will be met by the clink of teeth or the quiet thud of naked gums.

4.

In the cabinet beneath the bookshelves, I find a stack of pocket diaries and a larger, leather-bound game diary (I think I remember watching you open this one Christmas when I was a little boy and asking if it was for keeping scores of all our board games, alarmed when you told me it was for noting down the birds that you shot). Even as a child I recoiled from these hobbies of yours. But why, or *how*, was that, when all I knew was what you told me? Maybe it was Mum's influence. They seemed unfeeling practices, and neither Mum nor I could square them with our deep sense of you and your sensitivities.

The rich musk of the canvas and leather satchel that you kept your cartridges and ear defenders in, the tang of the dog whistle hung by the back door, the large tweed coat which only a giant could fill hanging in the utility room, the wellies in the garage which could swallow my own whole; the eternally cold weather of outdoor pursuits, the memories of stinging ears and throbbing cheeks, the cling of rain, the clutch of mud; the fetid pong of wet spaniels in the dog box in the back of the car. These impressions became less obtrusive as I got older and your activity decreased. But they were imprinted on my consciousness by then, the sensations of an unlikely masculinity that I simultaneously longed to possess but also wanted to challenge and reject; the spectres of a manhood I could never quite imagine myself growing into.

Was all the killing and collecting contradictory of your love for animals and the care you showed them; contradictory of your intolerance of suffering and cruelty; contradictory of your conservational efforts? Can I square these things? Would you even want me to? Love, surely, is accepting someone fully as they are, without the need to resolve their contradictions. I wonder if you even see these things as contradictions though. For BB, rural sports and pastimes were part of his intimacy with nature, bringing him closer to the creatures he loved.[3]As you tell me, it was just the norm for a rural kid in the 1950s and 1960s to shoot and fish and pilfer eggs and collect butterflies – an easy cop-out, I always thought. And this explanation only made me feel a muddled belatedness – not because I too wanted to experience the ghost-times of your childhood, but because I felt a troubling disconnect between what I was and what you were, as if I had come too late to truly be you. These disjunctions of time, culture and sensibility seemed to problematise something I felt to be so self-evidently true: that you and I are one and the same.

But maybe *you* were slightly belated too. I can see how for the generations before you, like BB's pre-war generation, rural sports and a caring intimacy with nature were not antithetical impulses, but two sides of the same coin; a vexed kind of being-with. But we live within shifting structures of feeling, where new sensibilities are continually emerging at odds with the norm. Maybe, by the time I came of consciousness, you were just slightly out of date.

As I matured, I realised I couldn't sit there as a meat eater and chastise you for the death of animals. But to kill as a pastime, when I knew I couldn't harm or kill an animal without feeling cut up about it? Too soft, you might say; too much of a hypocrite. To be clear, I certainly don't claim any kind of moral superiority. But I guess I also feel, well, just a bit confused.

I turn back to your shooting diary. The next entry is dated early 2014:

> *I have decided that I shall no longer shoot driven game on a 'reared' shoot. I no longer can justify the shooting of reared birds and the wounding that goes with it. Commercial shoots have lowered the life of the birds to be worth nothing but money and too little care is taken to ensure the bird's suffering is kept to a minimum. Many of the guns have little respect for their quarry*

and often do not even pick the dead birds up or give directions to the pickers-up where wounded birds should be looked for. I now find I am falling out with fellow guns over such issues rather than enjoying the day. At the moment I intend continuing a few walked up days, shooting over dogs and returning to my roots of 'rough shooting'. A very big decision made, but one I am very comfortable with at the moment.

FOOTNOTE: Following much soul searching, I have decided not to shoot any live game at all – not even walked up. I have also retired my judging qualification for Field Trials. I may shoot corvids etc. to control the songbird damage that they cause. Otherwise I shall just shoot clays.

I reread that date: 2014. Just under two years after your first bout with cancer. Would it be too contrived for me to say that this changed your perspective on life? To identify the extreme pressure under which selves change? You were the same person then as you always had been, as you are now. Maybe, though, a new structure of feeling had formed unbidden, part of the continual flux of sensibility, all these conflicting values vying with one another, but still essentially *you.*

39

Dark Vanessa

I put on my trainers and run through the small north-east Northamptonshire town where I live, past the Londis and the Co-op and the Premier and the Tesco, past the Victorian junior school, the playing field, the 230-year-old obelisk, three nail salons, two fish and chip shops, a Chinese and an Indian, an MOT garage and estate agent, following the pavement along the busy road out of town. The 30-mile-per-hour sign changes to the national speed limit. Something catches my eye on the edge of the pavement, up against the grass verge that drops to a litter-strewn ditch and skeletal hedgerow. I put myself in reverse and close in on a dark object, pausing the timer on my watch and the music on my iPhone. A pristine Red Admiral, wings fully open, presenting all its vivid colours – deep orange bands and white jewels set against black velvet – to an uncaring world of hurtling lorries and cars. I kneel down, the hot breath of the traffic upon me, and delicately touch a wing. Dead. A butterfly that travels continents, has especial significance in Nabokov's writing where it is adorned with metaphysics and lyricism, a cameo in paintings by Brueghel and Bosschaert, dead on the side of a Midlands A-road, opposite a caravan outlet, beside a castle of McDonald's cups and a sea of bubble wrap.

Breathing heavy, slick with sweat, I take an extreme close-up. I feel an urge to pick it up and take it home with me. But what would I do with it? Start my own collection made entirely of found corpses? No butterflies harmed in the making, at least not by my hands. But death is too much on my mind, on everyone's minds, in this summer of body counts and infection statistics. I run from the butterfly faster than I approached it, fleeing this *memento mori*.

No butterfly means more in Nabokov's art than the Red Admiral – or the Red Admirable, its old-fashioned name, which he insisted on using.[1] The crippled butterfly pulled on a thread by a promenading girl in a 1930s Parisian garden, as recalled in *Speak, Memory*, is a Red Admiral, symbolic of the cruel, fascist century that Nabokov cannot shield his young son from. It is the omen of tragedy and farce in his second novel, *King, Queen, Knave*, when it lands by a wealthy man whose wife is about to embark on a fatal love affair with his nephew. And it is the talismanic creature of Nabokov's greatest work, the peerless *Pale Fire*.

I wonder if the Red Admiral – *Vanessa atalanta* – was important to Nabokov precisely because of its migrant status, a kind of voluntary exile covering vast distances in search of more hospitable environments. Applying his years of experience butterflying in Europe, Nabokov was an important figure in identifying migrant butterflies in North America.[2] He knew an exile when he saw one. It is apt to find the Red Admiral materialising at the most significant co-ordinates of *Pale Fire*, a story of multiple transformative, and often painful, border crossings. It is there, coded in wordplay, as an omen of the impending suicide of the protagonist's daughter; and it is there distracting the same protagonist, John Shade, before he is murdered (a murder that recalls the death of Nabokov's father).[3] This is how Charles Kinbote, Shade's demonic double, glosses it in his commentary:

> *One minute before [Shade's] death [. . .] a Red Admirable [. . .] came dizzily whirling around us like a colored flame. [. . .] One's eyes could not follow the rapid butterfly in the sunbeams as it flashed and vanished, and flashed again, with an almost frightening imitation of conscious play which now culminated in its settling upon the delighted friend's sleeve.*[4]

The Red Admiral is an omen, then, sent to alert Shade to his mortality, a beautiful *memento mori*.

When asked why he liked the Red Admiral so much, Nabokov replied:

> *Its coloring is quite splendid and I liked it very much in my youth. Great numbers of them migrated from Africa to Northern Russia, where it was called 'The Butterfly of Doom' because it was especially abundant in 1881, the year Tsar Alexander II was assassinated, and the markings on the underside of its two hind wings seem to read '1881'.*[5]

But it is more than an omen. It is the epitome of what all butterflies meant to Nabokov: love. Earlier in *Pale Fire*, in the narrative poem that makes up the novel's first phase, the Red Admiral stands for Shade's beloved wife, and by the end of the poem it is the reincarnation of their dead daughter, tugging at Shade's sleeve moments before his own apparent death.[6] If the Red Admiral is the loved one in elevated form, then it is also Dmitri and Véra, just as it is Nabokov's father making his longed-for return; just as every butterfly I see from now on will in some sense be you.

40

Taking Stock

Dad is barely able to prop himself up in bed when I show him the picture I have just taken of a Small Copper in the field.

'Beautiful, aren't they?' he says. 'Delicate little things.'

They are. A diminutive butterfly, the wings a variegated orange with leopardish black dots, and tiny tails pointing out from the hindwings.

'There's still life to be found out there, eh?'

'It's slim pickings,' I say. Butterflies are scarce now, compared to the height of the summer when I was voraciously searching for life. The predictable phases of each species' cycle, set against the unknowability of Dad's cycle, should place things in perspective somehow. But they don't. He has been put on an odd footing with time, at once living to a projected schedule (the ever-nearing terminal date occupying months, then weeks, then days) and to fraught guesswork. His oncologist has to be a professional evader when it comes to the question of time, inured to patients and their families who want exact timetables for unpredictable phenomena. Dad is resigned to his doctor's necessary vagueness, but it frustrates him. Sometimes he takes the doctor to be saying there is the possibility of months of relative comfort, should the immunotherapy and radiotherapy (which he has undergone in the last week during a brief stay in the Churchill Hospital) have a positive effect; other times he infers that he is dealing more in weeks and days. One thing that has stuck with him is the doctor's advice that he get all his affairs in order, ASAP.

'Still no Clouded Yellows?' he asks before shifting an inch or two down in the bed, face pointed to the ceiling. There's something a bit Red-Admiral-like about him – the fringe of white hair, the crimson bar across each cheekbone of his flushed face, the black T-shirt he wears in bed. He once had something like the muscular power of the Red Admiral, but that's gone. He is more like the frayed and faded Red Admiral I photographed in my garden at the start of the summer, when I first started taking pictures.

I open a note I've been keeping on my phone. It's a list of all the species I've seen. I add the Small Copper to it. That takes me to thirty-three for the year. A modest number, but not bad considering I started late in the season and from a position of total ignorance. I read them out to Dad, and he makes affirmative noises.

'Silver-spotted Skipper, Large Skipper, Small Skipper, Essex Skipper, Lulworth Skipper, White Admiral, Purple Emperor, Painted Lady, Small Tortoiseshell, Red Admiral, Peacock, Comma, Dark Green Fritillary, Silver-washed Fritillary, Wood White, Green-veined White, Orange Tip, Small White, Brimstone, Large White, Speckled Wood, Gatekeeper, Marbled White, Meadow Brown, Small Heath, Ringlet, Purple Hairstreak, Silver-studded Blue, Common Blue, Brown Argus, Chalkhill Blue, Holly Blue, Small Copper. Possibly an Adonis Blue, but I'm not counting it.'

'A list anyone would be proud of,' says Dad, ready for sleep, as if the list and the thought of accumulating it have exhausted him.

My list represents the merging of our sensibilities and how far we have come to meet in the middle. Something to hold on to. And yet what I really see are its omissions and limitations, the lost opportunities, the wasted years; absences that I will have to fill when Dad is gone, no longer here to guide me or share in it. Though I had semi-seriously said I would see as many species as possible this summer, I gave up on any kind of completion early on. With a small child at home, pandemic restrictions to contend with, an ill father to support and a busy job, I have been restricted to small windows of time and, mostly, the species of the local area. But then I've always been quick with excuses.

'I'll get more next year,' I say.

'Yes,' says Dad. 'You'll know what you're about then. And you'll be prepared for the Dingy and Grizzled Skippers around your way, and the Green Hairstreak . . . ' He stops. There are more to mention, but he is in discomfort and drifting sleepwards. He takes a laboured breath in order to say, 'Think of me when you see a butterfly.'

I want to tell him I wish he would be there for it, but I can't somehow.

'You might add one more yet,' he says, surprising me with another burst of energy. 'Clouded Yellows will still be about.'

'I've given up on that one,' I say. 'Feels like I've been keeping an eye out forever.'

'Ah, yes, well.' He closes his eyes again. The words are physically onerous now. He takes another pained gulp. 'They'll be sparse around here. You can't really go looking for them. Just have to be present. Don't give up yet.'

I scroll through the list again, dwelling on the names that are attached to particularly memorable first sightings – the Silver-washed Fritillary that took me by surprise and led me deeper into the woods; the Purple Emperor on its feast of dog poo at Fermyn, surrounded by a merry band of oglers; most of all, the Wood White that summoned Dad out of the house and back into his natural environment one last time.

When I look up from my phone, he is fast asleep.

Over the next couple of days Dad slips deeper into a liminal state. He is still alert and talkative in moments, but sleep can pull him under unexpectedly, sometimes only seconds after a conversation, or in the time it takes me to check my phone for a distraction.

'So much for that radiotherapy,' he says, convinced it came too late. His temperature is soaring, the discomfort is acute. He cannot get out of bed, doesn't want to eat, even drinking is a battle.

The decision to call for an ambulance, unlike on previous occasions, is uncontested. I stand at the back of the room, watching the paramedics take his readings while he connects with them, still able to charm and empathise. It is decided that he must go into hospital. His temperature is too high – it could be the cancer causing this, it could be an infection, it could even be both – and so he needs close attention. Dad accepts the verdict without question.

On this occasion he is unable to walk down the stairs by himself. The staircase is too narrow and angular for a stretcher, and to pick him up and carry him would be dangerous. Even having lost so much weight, Dad must still be at least twelve stone, and the configuration of the staircase, with a low overhang from the room above and a door at the bottom, makes it practically impossible. The eventual strategy settled upon is to support him to the stairs, and from there he will slide down on his haunches while the paramedics form a human carriage around him.

Looking back, I can't even say how many people were in the room at this point. I feel like there were at least three, maybe four paramedics. But how many paramedics fit in an ambulance? Did they send for backup to help with the stairs? Did two arrive in a smaller vehicle first and then call for a full-sized ambulance once they knew Dad needed to go into the hospital? I don't know. What remains clear in my memory is what Dad said next, once the tactics had been decided and the paramedics were finalising who was going to take what position. I was standing out of the way, opposite his bed, when he said it.

'Please don't take offence,' he says to the paramedics; then, looking directly at me, 'But I want my son to carry me.'

The paramedics turn to look at me, like they're weighing me up – smaller, untrained, inexperienced.

'I trust him.'

'Of course,' says a paramedic. 'We can all do it together.'

They make way for me to get next to Dad. Mum puts a dressing gown on him and we pivot him to the side of the bed. Everything is done slowly from here. One of the paramedics helps me lift Dad to his feet, his arms around us, negotiate the narrow alley between bed and wardrobe, and lower him down the step from the bedroom onto the landing. Every pound of Dad's weight upon me is the weight of all our memories and similarities and intimacies, the mass of the love between us. Dad looks into my eyes. I see pain, love, tears, but mostly I see fear. Not about the end, I think, but the very immediate task of getting out the house. 'It's going to be okay,' I say, but I am a three-year-old again in *his* arms on Studland Beach, grateful for the strength of his shoulders, the thickness of his neck, the smell of his aftershave, the shine of his necklace, just a small boy enfolded by his father. 'I've got you, Dad.' He closes his eyes and nods.

We pause several times as we cross the landing, other bodies in front and behind – Mum with the hospital bag, paramedics with cargo, but also phantom selves: the baby crawling on hands and knees; the child charging back and forth, jumping down the two steps at the landing's mid-point, hiding in the alcove beside the spare room to leap out at people; Dad with his handheld camcorder filming two pyjama-clad boys dragging bags of Christmas presents to their parents' bedroom; a moody teenager trudging forwards on school mornings, returning in the opposite direction as a university undergraduate with a term's worth of unwashed laundry in bin bags . . . Is this the last time Dad will walk this corridor? Is he saying goodbye to it all in his heart?

We reach the top of the stairs, where we all need a pause – Dad to gather his strength, the paramedics to assess the descent.

'I have to sit down,' says Dad, and we lower him onto the top step. I put my hand on his shoulder and he places his on top, looks up at me, a small comforting smile, patting my hand and then squeezing. Mum goes ahead and props the door open at the foot of the steps; she is followed by one paramedic trying to get out of the way and another who stops a few steps down from Dad and looks up at us. Walled in on both sides, the staircase ricochets with suggestions and tentative instructions. I try to block them out, making space for a private moment with Dad. I kneel behind him, put a hand amongst his hair – thinned slightly, but still going strong – and kiss the top of his head.

I hook my hands under Dad's armpits and feel his full weight as he shuffles down the first couple of steps. 'Have you got me?' he asks.

'I've got you,' I say.

'You're not going to fall, I promise,' says the paramedic in front.

Dad takes deep breaths, steeling himself.

'Again,' he says, and I lift slightly to give him momentum. He shunts forward, a couple more steps.

We pause again. I sit on the step above him, my legs enclosing him. It's an undignified way to leave the house he half built, shuffling down the stairs on his backside, in a dressing gown. But he is going out under his own steam, and that matters. All I see are strength and courage, values Dad rates highly.

At the bottom of the staircase, we help him straighten up and guide him to the front door. It must have taken at least thirty minutes to get from bed to ambulance. The sunlight hits his cheeks for the first time in days. Once he is strapped onto the stretcher in the back of the van I go inside and kiss him, hug him, tell him to keep giving us updates if he can. I tell him that I love him. Mum shares a longer goodbye and joins me in front of the house, helpless, subtracted. One of the paramedics confirms what we already know – we are not permitted to come into the hospital due to COVID restrictions. We thank her for what they have done. She gives us a sympathetic look.

The rear doors of the ambulance close and Dad vanishes. I hold Mum tight as the ambulance rolls down the drive, feeling the vibrations of her sobbing against me.

41

Shadows of Taste

We lose Dad to the hospital. I call his phone but there is no answer; I send messages and none come back. I convince myself that Dad would never allow this to happen if our positions were reversed. He simply wouldn't accept Mum and me being left to fend for ourselves, our contact broken; he would somehow defeat all the obstacles, including COVID restrictions, to be by our sides. At least that's what the child in me believes. But the idea that you can protect the ones you love is an illusion. That's why we keep each other close, tell each other we won't let anything bad happen, that we'll always be there, that we are safe. These are the fictions we live by. The feeling behind them is so strong that they take on the force of truth, but the pillow in the middle of the night, when the terrible information makes its repeated arrivals, knows better.

I look in on Kit. It's gone 9 p.m. and he is asleep inside the cage of his cot. If my protection was absolute, he wouldn't need those bars. I lean over and plant a secret kiss on his forehead and wonder if it creates a subtle kink in the texture of his dream (an exotic butterfly lands on his forehead and tells him a secret), or whether it triggers some monumental adjustment (the beat of the butterfly's wings that stirs the hideous monster from its cave), but his eyelids don't even flicker as he lies flat on his back with his arms above his head, frozen mid-celebration.

Downstairs I try Dad's phone one more time. He picks up. I have to turn the volume to full, this colossus now an almost inaudible voice in my ear. He tells me he has been left by himself in a side room, hasn't had any food or drink besides a yoghurt since he arrived almost ten hours ago, hasn't even been able to take his medication, which is overdue.

'I'll sort this, Dad,' I say, a muddle of anger and fear.

I select different numbers from the switchboard, trying to locate Dad in this obscure complex that has swallowed him whole. I imagine phones ringing on unstaffed desks on sterile wards, reverberating off whitewash and linoleum, echoing in the empty corridors of the hospital in *The Godfather* where Michael Corleone goes to visit his wounded father and finds that his security has vacated the building. By the next morning Dad has been given a bed on a busy ward. I continue making calls – to Dad, to the hospital – hoping to understand what is going on: where he is exactly, what's being done for him, what the doctor's assessment is, what the plan moving forward will be. But I cannot get hold of anyone. I leave voice messages on Dad's phone, send text messages, pace the house, wondering if I will ever see him again.

I try to distract myself by reading your poems. I hope they might overcome the physical distance, bring our minds together. I follow you into forbidden territory in a poem called 'Another's Wood', which starts:

Into another's wood I stepped
From the lane where verge and trees met.
The smell of rotting leaves was strong
As through the undergrowth I crept.

This border-crossing also signals a trespass into poetic form. There is a sense throughout these poems that the form somehow isn't yours. Your approach is cautious, done in secret, though I suspect you always had this reader in mind, just as I had pursued the Purple Emperor in Fermyn Woods at the start of the summer without telling you, hoping for some degree of success before disclosing what I had done. I felt a frisson of trespass then, like I was sneaking into your territory, just as I realise you have tiptoed into mine. The poem ends:

Into another's wood I've been
By human eye, I was unseen.
I step back on the rural lane
That runs beside this ancient green.

All of the stanzas are four lines in length and follow an AABA rhyme scheme (I remember you asking me whether poetry should always rhyme, now I know why!), yet in this particular stanza you have allowed a half-rhyme to creep into the non-rhyming line. Was that intentional? It suggests a state of semi-fitting, so that the lane has an almost-affinity with the woods, while being somehow fundamentally different, never fully rhyming. It suggests to me that the lane, the place of human eyes, isn't quite where you belong; that you fit best in the wood and the ancient green.

In 'For the Love of Life', the poem you want me to read at your funeral, you describe being with butterflies, but also with flowers, birds and beasts. I like the final two lines, where you write: 'The pleasure they would always bring / Will make once more, my heart to sing.' The archaic syntax here (you don't simply say 'will make my heart sing once more', hunting for the required rhyme) is probably, I think, what you expect of poetry. But I like it – how it halts time for a moment, to then allow the surprising continuation of life, in some kind of afterlife where you are free in nature once again. It makes the heart follow against the flow of time and makes me think of another writer from whom I think you have derived some of your pastoral perspective: Hardy, whose body was buried in Westminster Abbey, and whose heart was buried in his native Dorset.

One poem in here was written for me: 'Butterflies', which you inscribed in my copy of *The Butterflies of Britain & Ireland*. 'The pursuit and tales for sharing,' you write, 'will never leave the mind.' I'm struck by the relationship you elicit between butterflying and storytelling, but also between butterflies, stories and gifts. They are to be *shared*, so that the sense of trespassing into one another's interests falls away and instead we mutually belong.

I know you'd want me to be honest with you. I admire your poems, but I think you are too consciously on your best behaviour with poetic form, a little too respectful, possibly feeling inferior to it, though you shouldn't. You are over-committed to rhyming, which leads to forced and laboured language – let the rhythm and the feeling dictate; likewise, don't be so inhibited by metrical patterns. Find your freedom in form. And watch out for cliché. When you use recycled language or imagery, you're telling me how someone else saw it, when what I want is how *you* see it.

And yet your poems move me immensely. None more so than 'Falling Leaves', a poem for children, which you have dedicated to your grandchildren:

Mr Wind puffs out his cheeks
What fun he has in store.
If the leaves don't fall off
He'll blow and blow some more.
He loves to see leaves in flight
Or tumbling across the ground.
He blows and blows harder still
To make an awful sound.
So let's join in with his fun
We'll dive and leap and shout.
We must catch a falling leaf
Before October's out.

Here it is in print, for them to read whenever they want, a gift from their grandfather, the published poet.

42

The Anxiety of Influence, in Three Parts

1.

Reading your poetry, I wonder about your influences. I can see traces of the nature poets you had been reading, certainly Hardy and Clare. The pastoral perspective, the natural imagery, the quiet lyricism, the melancholic tone. But influence isn't always so clear or legible.

Take Prince (my Purple Emperor) and Joni (my blue, my hairstreak). They don't seem to bear any relation to one another – the poetic and deeply personal folk singer and the playful crotch-thrusting pop-funk extrovert – and yet Prince considered Joni to be one of his greatest influences.[1] The influence isn't obvious in the music itself, but Prince certainly dropped lots of clues. In the liner notes to his 1980 album, *Dirty Mind*, when he was still in the developmental pupal phase (or pupil phase, processing all those strong teachers – James Brown, Little Richard, Rufus and Chaka Khan), he thanks Joni in a list that starts with God and ends with 'Joni and U'. She's on the sleeve of his next album too, 1981's

Controversy, Joni in big letters. And then he sings of her on 'The Ballad of Dorothy Parker' from his greatest album, *Sign o' the Times* (full-blown imago stuff, this), where Joni's 'Help Me' is Dorothy's favourite song.

Prince dropped clues directly to Joni herself. She would later recall receiving letters from him when he was an unknown: 'Prince used to write me fan mail with all of the U's and hearts that way that he writes. And the office took it as mail from the lunatic fringe and just tossed it.'[2] And there he was, when she played his home town in the early 1970s: 'I remember seeing him sitting in the front row when he was very young. He must have been about fifteen. He was in an aisle seat and he had unusually big eyes. He watched the whole show with his collar up, looking side to side. You couldn't miss him – he was a little Prince-ling.'[3] But as Prince blew up and became friends with Joni (a charm of success, befriending your heroes), Joni was puzzled by his claims that she was one of his most important influences. 'I couldn't hear it,' she said. 'There was a harmonic passage in one of the songs that really interested me, and I said to him, "Oh, you know, where's that coming from?" Because it sounded fresh to me, you know, and he said, "You."'[4]

But when two sensibilities meet, themselves matrixes of the pluralistic sensibilities of others, something new is created. Prince wanted to collaborate with Joni. 'He implied that something would happen between our two musics,' she recalls. 'Something that he had never done before [. . .] I asked him to explain it, but he said he could not put it into words.'[5] So Joni told Prince to build her a track and send it over. What he gave Joni, the great artist of subtle, lyrical, confessional poetry, was a ditty of repetitive erotic synth pop called 'Emotional Pump'.[6]

2.

Raymond Williams recognised the seeming contradictoriness of his own concept, the 'structure of feeling'. Feeling suggests something elusive and amorphous, while structure suggests something certain and fixed. One speaks to the emotions, the other to something systematic or mechanical. 'As firm and definite as "structure" suggests,' he says, grappling with the term, 'it operates in the most delicate and least tangible parts of our activity.'[7] Which makes me think of Woolf's ideal form, 'the colour burning on a framework of steel; the light of a butterfly's wing lying upon the arches of a cathedral'.[8] Like Nabokov's description of the butterfly's metamorphosis ('There comes for every caterpillar a difficult moment when he begins to feel pervaded by an odd sense of discomfort. It is a tight feeling – here about the neck and elsewhere, and then an unbearable itch'),[9] the emergence of a new structure of feeling might entail confusion, contradiction, rupture. The old form must be burst open, no longer adequate to the new experience. I think of Angela Carter's evolution into a baroque form, an excessive style that can keep moving without being evasive, that can be simultaneously flamboyant and hard-headed, as a way of understanding 'how that social fiction of my "femininity" was created, by means outside my control, and palmed off on me as the real thing';[10] I think of John Clare, the barely educated poet, generating his own syntax of thought, his own grammar and rhythm of feeling, in order to capture vanishing things; I think of Nabokov and his gifts of style that might embellish reality while making it somehow truer, more particular.

Zadie Smith, in her essay on Joni, writes about the multiplicity of selves we all comprise: 'The girl who hated Joni,' she writes, 'and the woman who loves her seem to me similarly divorced from each other, two people who happen to have shared the same body.'[11] But they also share the same essay. It is in this literary form, which is a folding of possibilities, shot through with Smith's personal sensibility, that she can be these different selves all at once, just as your poems, Dad, give you negative capability (to use Keats's phrase for how the poet can inhabit more than one truth, can live in contraries). There you can be trespasser and belonger, constrained and free, past and present, sick and healthy. In your poems, Dad, like Smith in her essay, you can trace transformation, you can demonstrate the very constructedness of identity, all while being coherently and singularly yourself. Because the self is process. It is a structure of feeling.

I think back, now, to that time you finished reading the book version of my PhD thesis and asked me what I meant by 'the ethical value of literature'. I had no answer for you then, nothing that synthesised our different terms for thinking about the world and could therefore mean something to both of us. Maybe this book is one way, an indirect way, of answering your question. I just needed the butterflies – all of which is to say I needed *you* – to articulate it.

3.

In a rehearsal session at his home studio in 1983, Prince recorded a one-minute jam on Joni's 'A Case of You' – just

Prince, a piano and a microphone. Until the lyrics come in, you'd be unlikely to recognise it as Joni's song, here transformed into soulful R&B chord progressions and occasional flourishes. A few years later, Prince played the tune, without words, on Joni's piano in her Malibu home. Joni said: 'Oh wow! That's really pretty. What song are you playing?'[12]

The month prior to that rehearsal session, Prince performed Joni's song (refashioned into 'A Case of U') for the first time live. 3 August 1983, First Avenue, Minneapolis. A show imprinted in Prince lore as the concert where he recorded the versions of 'I Would Die 4 U', 'Baby I'm A Star' and 'Purple Rain' that would end up on his classic album, *Purple Rain* – the album where Prince metamorphises into *Prince*, the emergent imago, the inimitable Purple Emperor. Joni is there, in some way, in the material that is most recognisably *him*.

The rehearsal session where Prince plays 'A Case of U' was posthumously released in 2018 as *Piano & A Microphone 1983*. The recording ends with a six-minute improvisation called 'Why the Butterflies'. It is clearly incomplete, fragmentary, the sketch of a feeling. The music is just a series of jaunty repetitions of a few piano chords, refining now and then into a sequence, with Prince ad-libbing over the top in a raw, tremulous, exploratory voice, a true artist attempting to understand a barely articulable feeling. Repeatedly, he asks his mama where his father is, and then forms a question out of the song's title – a question I have been asking, in a different sense, ever since the summer of 2020.

The very particular shift in my own sensibility, from butterfly-ignorer to butterfly-obsessive, brings me circling back to my relationship with you, Dad. In the past, seeking to understand our relationship and, more specifically, your influence on me, I went looking for the big clues – the lessons you had taught me, the experiences we shared, our comparative parenting styles, etc. But I should have been more attentive to the nuances: the impulses, restraints, tones. But for that I needed a new form. Which is to say, I needed the butterflies, those ultimate form seekers.

43

Strange Meeting

I text Dad and call, but he rarely answers. When we do talk his voice is frail, his conversation less lucid. It is hard to piece together his situation. There are tests (urine, blood), observations, interminable waits for doctors' rounds, conflicting reports from nurses. Has he got pneumonia, is it a urinary infection, is it all just the cancer taking its final toll?

Dad entered Northampton General Hospital thirty years to the week that BB died there, two nature lovers confined to a habitat of sterility. (BB, unlike Dad, was allowed visitors.) But, when I picture Dad there, it is John Clare who companions him. He lies just a stone's throw from where Clare spent the last twenty-three years of his life as a patient in 'Northampton General Lunatic Asylum' (now St Andrew's Hospital).[1] Clare was classified as a fifth class patient, which meant he was allowed to walk into town alone, where he could be found with his notebook, sitting in one of the porticos of All Saints Church (the same portico I would drunkenly pass as an eighteen-year-old on my way from the Goose to Revolution on Bridge Street), happy to sell some lines of poetry for ale or tobacco. Despite the 'freedom' to wander from the asylum grounds, the asylum years were the final imprisonment in a life of enclosures. Like the butterflies and flowers taken from their familiar habitats that become 'but shadows of the things they seem [. . .] poor dull captives of a foreign land' ('Shadows of Taste'),[2] so was Clare in Northampton Asylum. 'I very much want to get back,' wrote Clare in a letter, 'and see after the garden and hunt in the Woods for yellow hyacinths, Polyanthuses and blue Primroses as usual.'[3]

In 'For the Love of Life', the last poem in *his* notebook, Dad writes: 'In footsteps where before I stood / As man and boy, in awe I stared.' But as his poem apprehends, he will not re-inhabit those footsteps until he is 'free at last . . . free again', which is to say released by death, the ultimate flitting. I picture Dad in his unhomely enclosure, isolated from those familiar places that are his essential environment: the woods where we saw the Wood White, the field behind the house where the Marbled Whites and Gatekeepers and Small and Large Skippers relish the habitat he has cultivated. I wonder if he is still able to think of nature, if he imagines seeing a late Small Copper or a chance Clouded Yellow. If only I could be with him and tell him more of the things I have seen this summer, maybe, I think, it would help.

But I can't even get near him. In my place I imagine a strange meeting with a permitted visitor, a portly man with rubicund cheeks, thick mutton chops, wild eyebrows like caterpillars squirming over his eyelids, and a beak-like nose; a patient who has the right to roam between buildings. He crosses the ward in smart Victorian dress – tailcoat, waistcoat, long cravat, high boots – like he has stepped straight out of his own portrait with a grimace on his face, the self-consumer of his woes. Here he is bewildered by a living sea of waking dreams: hand-sanitisers for wildflowers, chirping monitors for birds, drip stands for trees, computer screens for reflecting streams. This modern world, for which he has no natural history, is disturbing, with its lunatic voices coming from tablets, people with buds in their ears talking to themselves, all strange, no, *stranger* than the rest.[4]

Eventually he finds a man flat on his back on an overfull ward, staring up at the ceiling, simmering with cancer; a man who I struggle to envision now, his image fading from my grasp. If you see him, tell him I miss him.

44

Voice

I receive a voicemail from Dad. *Ben, I'm ringing to bring you up to date. Bye.* Nothing else – no endearments like he would normally use, the words laboured, his voice distant and frail. When I call back, he doesn't answer.

I think about how he danced with his father in the hospice, not long before Granddad died, and how earlier this year, sick in bed, he would listen to Luther Vandross's 'Dance with My Father' and remember that precious moment. He told me he'd like to do the same with me one day. I fear that the opportunity has already been and gone.

Having played that five-second voicemail at least a dozen times, I go to my study and pick a Luther record from Dad's old collection. (From as far back as I can remember we were on first-name terms with Luther in our house.) It's *The Best of Luther Vandross: The Best of Love*, one of those premature greatest hits collections, released in 1989, just eight years after Luther's debut solo album (itself preceded by a decade as the most overqualified backing singer for the likes of David Bowie and Roberta Flack), so it doesn't include all the hits that I remember, but most of them are here: 'Never Too

Much', 'Stop to Love', 'Give Me the Reason', 'Any Love', 'I Really Didn't Mean It' and 'So Amazing' (my first dance with Carli).

Luther's voice is prominent in my childhood soundtrack, his records played over and again by both my parents in the house and the car, so that his voice is, for me, the feel of a period, the speak of memory. It's not the specific songs or albums that are able to move me almost to the point of tears, nor is it the words. It's the voice *in itself.* The texture, the tone, the timbre. It's the voice that somehow enfolds for me, and now unfolds, the feeling of being a child. Luther was often referred to as 'The Velvet Voice', and velvet seems about the right textile. One could go for silk, but that would suggest a smoothness that lacks the purchase of Luther's voice, which is at once luxurious but also woven thick with (to steal one of Nabokov's favourite words) *quiddity.* 'Breezy' is another word used, which I think has something to do with the ease of Luther's voice – the way he traverses his full tenor's range from speaker-booming depths to light rarefied heights without betraying any of the effort. Luther's great idol and friend, Dionne Warwick, put it well when she said that his voice was 'smooth to the touch, easy to feel, wonderful to look at'. Language has a way of capturing things that are beyond the frame like that – Luther's voice is almost synaesthetic in Warwick's description, something to be touched, felt, even seen. 'When I heard Luther's voice,' she said, 'I heard peace. It made me feel good.'[1]

When I was young, I struggled with my voice. An inability to refrain from shouting meant that Mum would be reduced to tears as she pleaded with me to quieten down, and in the end I developed nodules on my vocal cords from all the strain. It's the kind of ailment reserved for hard-rock singers towards the end of a long, gruelling world tour. I succumbed to it by the age of three. By my sixth birthday I had twice had surgery to remove the lumps, and in home videos of my earliest Christmases and birthdays I sound like a jazz singer who has spent too much time in smoky clubs, nursing a glass of bourbon. I remember getting into Mum's car to go home after the second surgery and finding Luther's latest album, on cassette, in the central tray. I can still see the gold and purple cover of *Power of Love*, associated now with pangs of relief and a longing for home.

It's the *feel* of Luther's voice that I carry with me, rather than the details of individual songs. This applies to the books and writers I love too. It only takes a day for me to completely forget the specifics of a book – the plot, the characters, even their names. What stays with me instead is a unique feeling of *being-with*. It's difficult to describe, but I'm sure all readers have experienced it: that peculiar sense of intimacy with what we might call a voice. It's somehow both private and social at the same time, the way a voice can seem so individual to the writer and their personality, and yet also communal in its ability to connect, its magical ability to speak to us.

I save Dad's voicemail to my files. I will keep it forever, so that I can play it when I need to hear him. And now I can add the voice of his poems to my private polyphony too, another way for us to communicate. I close my eyes and imagine him holding Granddad, swaying gently, his mouth close to his ear, telling him, despite it all, that he loves him.

I'm still at my desk. Carli thinks I'm working. But that's been hard to do of late. It's much easier to spend time flicking from one app to the next on my phone.

On a whim I search 'Luther Vandross butterflies' on the internet. Did you know Luther sang on a fairly obscure track called 'Hot Butterfly' by Gregg Diamond and Bionic Boogie in 1978? I had no idea! I've been listening to it on repeat. The wordplay isn't exactly subtle, but it's a catchy tune with a classic late-1970s disco-funk vibe. I've also discovered that Chaka Khan covered it on her 1980 album, *Naughty*, opting for the more entomologically technical title 'Papillon'. I think I might actually prefer her version. It's less disco, more soul, which suits both of our tastes better.

I can't find any videos of Luther singing 'Hot Butterfly' on YouTube. Instead, I am watching clips of live performances, one after another, just like you sat listening to him sing 'Dance with My Father' on your iPad. For example, Luther singing 'Man in the Mirror' at a tribute concert to Michael Jackson in 2001, along with Usher and the supremely forgettable 1990s US boy band 98 Degrees.[2] Usher and 98 Degrees handle the first half of the song, building to a peak in the middle when, to great cheers from the crowd, Luther strolls onto stage, dressed all in black – long black leather coat, black sunglasses and a large crucifix medallion – like an R&B undertaker come to bury lesser talents. Then there's a 1987 performance at the Soul Train Music Awards of 'That's What Friends Are For' with Dionne Warwick, Whitney Houston and Stevie Wonder.[3] This performance is notable for how the four legends engage in a friendly round of one-upmanship – an ironically gendered term given that, for my money, Whitney just about takes the prize on this occasion.

But the video I have been watching on repeat for the last thirty minutes is Luther's rendition of 'A House Is Not a Home' at the NAACP Image Awards in 1987.[4] It is a loving tribute to Warwick, who originally recorded the Burt Bacharach and Hal David number in 1964. Warwick is in attendance and the camera cuts back and forth between Luther on stage in black tie and Warwick in the audience, sometimes splitting the screen between the two. Luther is on fire here. He shows off the whole range, gliding from stage-shaking bass to the highest altitudes of his tenor, throwing in unpredictable embellishments so that it is impossible to sing along accurately (if such a feat wasn't already made impossible by virtue of not being Luther Vandross). It's astounding, almost beyond description. It reminds me how aesthetic experience, in its most intense form, seems to increase one's sense of possibility while simultaneously shrinking it, because it is singular, an unrepeatable encounter.

I play the voicemail again. You used to have a special telephone voice, depending on who you were speaking to. You'd always answer the house phone by saying the last three digits of our number instead of the conventional 'hello', as if you had just been transferred by a 1940s switchboard operator, and you would pronounce words more carefully, your normally extended Northamptonshire vowels self-consciously contracted. (It wasn't until I got to university that I realised we even had accents. Made self-conscious about my own voice, for which I got teased, I turned my embarrassment on you by picking up on your even stronger accent all the time.) Once my voice broke, your friends would mistake us for one another on the phone, often going straight into conversation before I could correct them (didn't they notice that I had said 'hello' like a regular person)? Maybe we do sound similar, I don't know.

It's uncanny how voices stay with us. How we can recall

a voice in our head, so that someone long gone or absent is oddly present. Maybe that's why to overhear something is still to hear it, whereas to overlook something (at least in its primary sense) is not to see it at all. For all the immateriality of a remembered voice, it is pregnant with presence. But then acts of the imagination are real as acts of imagination. Like aesthetic experience, they press on us in genuine ways – they move us, they haunt us, they change us. Like your voice on this voicemail will do for me, and now your poetic voice, and the voice in my head advising me on everything else, continuously overheard.

I fear losing your voice. But then we've been overhearing each other my whole life.

45

Visitation

After nine days in the General Hospital, Dad is moved three miles across town to a hospice. Now we are permitted to see him, which indicates the severity of his condition. There are still restrictions though: only two designated people allowed, one at a time. Even this is subject to change, we are warned, depending on the public health situation.

I find Dad in a room of four beds, which he has to himself. I see him, a disembodied head and shoulders above some sheets, before he sees me. The physical transformation in just the few days since I helped him down the stairs and into the ambulance, is shocking. His face is gaunt, silver-washed, staring off vacantly to the side. I wonder if he sees anything there, or whether the movie of his sixty-six years is playing invisibly in the air to an audience of one. I swallow back an immediate compulsion to cry. He doesn't notice my approach, not until I come round the side of the bed, stepping out of the movie, such that he must wonder whether I am even really there. I take his hand and squeeze gently, no spectre this, his flesh and blood.

'Hey, Dad.'

I pull down my mask so that he might know me. But he is more with it than I expected. I have to lean close to understand what he says. I speak words of comfort and try my best to talk in our normal, everyday terms. I notice blood stains on his fingers. Nosebleeds, he whispers. I wet some paper towels at the sink and request nail clippers from a nurse at reception. I wipe the blood away and cut his nails, which are longer than he would have ever allowed. They can only find me some kitchen scissors, so the result is jagged, but it's an improvement. I attempt spoon-feeding him some leftover jelly that I find on his bedside tray, but he doesn't fancy it. Pineapple, he tells me, he longs for pineapple.

A nurse pulls me aside. They are still trying to ascertain whether the sudden deterioration is due to infection or whether it is the cancer. They have started him on a new course of antibiotics and taken more tests. We should know the outcome of those in the next twenty-four hours. If it is the cancer that is precipitating the rapid decline, he does not have long left. They are adjusting the morphine accordingly. He will not suffer, she assures me. I get her to agree that next time Mum and I can come in together.

I spend more time with Dad, waiting for someone to tell me to go. When he has the energy he can converse, still pretty sharp, all things considered. He is emphatic about one thing: it's time for all this to end.

As the sun sets, I dash out to the mini Tesco across the road. They don't have any pineapple, but I find pineapple juice. I ask the nurses if they can freeze it into ice cubes for him. Of course, they say. Bless you. It's all inadequate though. I stand back at the door and look at Dad cocooned in his strange bed. I imagine picking him up, holding him close in my arms, and dancing across the room, in and out of the beds and trays, the closest we'll ever come to it.

I kiss him on the cheek and tell him I'll be back tomorrow.

The next day, Mum and I visit Dad together. If the first time I saw him in the hospice he was one of those disintegrating butterflies at the end of its cycle, half a wing missing, the edges torn and frayed, today he has almost regressed back into a chrysalis, and it seems as though the caterpillar and egg phases will vanish in a breath, hurtling towards the void of non-being. But just this morning, before we visited, for a brief moment in his rapid reverse time-travel, Dad became the lucid imago once again. It was a phone call (*he* rang *me*!), and he sounded almost like his old self, telling me where to find a water meter buried in the garden, a detail of some outstanding business that is characteristically on his mind. A most banal conversation – Dad discussing water supplies and stopcocks, the classic pedantry of our domestic life – and I shall cherish it forever.

But now he is struggling to locate his self, let alone the water meter. He acknowledges us, talks a little, but mostly communicates by nods and pained expressions, before falling asleep, slipping from the warm hands that determinedly keep hold of his, here on the physical plane.

I take Mum home and hang around for the afternoon. I return Dad's notebook of poems to the desk in his study. I sit in his chair and reread a couple, thinking about how these last works so nearly went unshared and unread. Perhaps I would have always found them. I look around the room and realise with trepidation that Mum and I are going to have to sort through all these drawers and cabinets and files one day.

*

When Nabokov and Véra began their residence at the Montreux Palace Hotel in Switzerland in 1961, a maid emptied Nabokov's butterfly-decorated wastebasket, losing to history a series of valuable Nabokoviana, as retrospectively inventoried by Dmitri: 'A thick batch of U.S. roadmaps on which my father had meticulously marked the roads and towns that he and my mother had traversed. Chance comments of his were recorded there, as well as names of butterflies and their habitats.'[1] Things to be kept are lost, just as things to be binned are kept. Nabokov instructed that his final novel, the draft of *The Original of Laura*, was not to be published if left incomplete, yet Dmitri fathered it to publication in 2009. The son must make his own decisions in the end.

What will be done with Dad's personal effects? I look at the taxidermy on the walls, the locked door to the gun cabinet, the shelves of natural history and BB books. Much of the contents of this room are still not for me. Knowing Mum, the vast majority will stay in situ, frozen at a time when everything made sense, how she wants it. But what about the butterfly collection? Despite my conflicted feelings about it, my sharp distaste for the idea of killing and collecting living creatures, I find I want it near me. I turn the key and slide a drawer out at random. A sequence of Clouded Yellows dated from the 1930s. I feel a pang of regret and longing. Might I see one yet? Something urgent to report to Dad, one last boost of life?

I find myself talking to Dad. At first out loud – 'Do you reckon I'll see a Clouded Yellow this year?' – and then internally, where the one-way conversation loses its shape, the edges loosening, the content melting into something more like stream of consciousness. It's not the first time I've spoken to Dad like this, riding the telepathic channel between father and son, but the complexion is different today, as if this is how it will always be from now on. The terrifying part is that I struggle to hear his voice answering.

Nabokov talked to his parents after they were gone. In the summer of 1976, during an extended period of delirium caused by a urinary infection, he continued working on his *Laura*, reading it aloud to 'a small dream audience in a walled garden' that 'consisted of peacocks, pigeons, my long dead parents, two cypresses, several young nurses crouching around, and a family doctor so old as to be almost invisible'.[2] I wonder if Dad is conversing with his own dream audience in the hospice right now, pointing out an unexpected Clouded Yellow to his mum and dad in the field, or maybe reading his poems to them. I wonder if one day I'll have something to read aloud to him.

Once his parents moved into the Montreux Palace Hotel, Dmitri talked with his father of exploring the foothills to the Mont Blanc massif, visible from the bedroom window. It would be an opportunity to look for butterflies and to view Montreux from a new vantage. But the expedition kept getting deferred, first because of work and travel, then ill health. At the age of seventy-six, in July 1975, butterflying at an altitude of 1,900 metres, Nabokov fell down a steep slope and lost his net in the fall. When trying to recover the net from a fir tree, where it had become lodged, he fell again. He waved to the cable car that passed overhead and up the hill, only for those on board to assume the laughing man was fine, until they passed him again in the other direction. Two and a half hours after his fall he was rescued on a stretcher.

Nabokov was soon back on the hunt, but the fall triggered a sequence of ill health, culminating in a severe bronchial congestion that would bring a most singular life to an end on 2 July 1977. 'During our penultimate farewell,' Dmitri later recalled,

> *after I had kissed his still-warm forehead – as I had for years when saying goodnight or goodbye – tears suddenly welled in Father's eyes. I asked him why. He replied that a certain butterfly was already on the wing; and his eyes told me he no longer hoped that he would live to pursue it again. Nor would he ever visit that enchanted mountain valley on the far side of the lake. But perhaps, in Father's memory, I shall.*[3]

*

I find more Clouded Yellows in the cabinet. The less common Pale Clouded Yellow and the Berger's Clouded Yellow, and some that I assume are rare aberrations. We should be admiring these vivid creatures in life, chasing them across the wildflowered slope of Ballard Down in Dorset, overlooking the caravan site where we used to stay, the smell of barbecues drifting up on the breeze, the rumour of the ocean just around the bend of the hill.

I return the drawers to the cabinet and go to check on Mum.

Mum asks if I can bring some logs in from the garage. Now isn't the time to query the necessity of burning a fire in early autumn, the kind of heated argument Dad and I knew how to conduct so well. Loading logs into the wheelbarrow in the damp and musty garage, I'm struck not only by the fact that the summer has ended, but that Mum will need me to do many of the things that Dad used to do for the two of them. Here I am, setting her up for a long autumn and winter alone without him; and an even longer winter than that, trying to fill his place.

Shifting the logs, I am startled by a flash of colour amongst the crumb of soil and bark. I stop and pinch the dead jewel carefully between thumb and forefinger. The near-perfect wing of a once-hibernating Small Tortoiseshell. I admire the repeated blushes of lilac along the delicate edge, like multiple painted nails, and I am struck by the realisation that most of the butterflies I see now are dead ones.

A couple of hours later, just as I get home from Mum's, the call arrives from the hospice. It's time to come in.

46
The Flitting

As soon as I see Dad from across the room in the dim early-evening light, I can tell that the change in just the few hours since we left him has been extreme. His head is tilted to the side, towards the windows, his chin pressed against his shoulder, his line of sight not much above where the ground meets the wall. As I walk around the side of the bed, my legs unsteady, my heart fluttering, I am struck by the deserted focus of his cold, hard stare, and how his face seems to be crumpling into itself, tugged under by the slow motions of his chest. He doesn't breathe like my dad anymore, as if the soul has been taken out of him, replaced by apparatus that doesn't quite work the same. For the first time in my life, he doesn't look at me when I say hello, doesn't quicken to my attention, doesn't rise to the occasion of being Dad.

'Hi Dad,' I say again, holding his limp hand. 'It's me, Ben. I'm here now. I won't leave you. I promise.'

I bury my face into my shoulder, keeping hold of him, my body shaking. Can he tell that I am crying? Does he even know I am here? He looks haunted, almost angered, his face fixed in a grimace. It's chilling to behold, the warmth and lovingness all gone.

'I'll be right back,' I say, already breaking my word. I seek out a nurse in the reception, and then dash straight back to him. I'm sat at his side again when she enters the room. I ask her if he's in pain, if they're doing everything that can be done for him. She assures me in comforting tones that he is not feeling anything. He is at rest, she says. Okay, I say. Thank you.

We are on our own. Mum is on her way; my father-in-law is picking her up. Coming from different directions, we have agreed to meet at the hospice rather than lose an hour by me collecting her. Dad must not be on his own when the moment comes.

I keep lowering my mask to kiss him on his forehead and hand, all responseless.

'I saw a Small Tortoiseshell in your garage,' I say. He moves. I'm sure of it. A flex of the cheek, an almost imperceptible motion in the hand. He is still there, somewhere, for the last butterfly of a lifetime, another gift shared. I don't tell him that it was the wing of a dead creature.

Mum arrives, looking small, lost, her heart breaking. She sits next to Dad and I cross the room so that she can speak to him without me hearing. When I rejoin her, pulling a seat alongside, I watch her pushing his soft curly hair back, pressing her head against his. He remains insensate, his presence in the room almost spectral now.

I call my brother in Japan and put him on speaker phone. He talks into the silent void, telling Dad that he's here and that he loves him. Then something remarkable happens. Dad moves – another flex of his facial muscles, and the faint noise at the back of his throat, the noise of an entire family history spiralling through his distant lungs. He was waiting for all of us to be together again – that's what we will say to each other whenever we remember this moment. He was waiting for all of us to be together again, a family.

Mum tells him he can rest now, stroking his head. Not more than a minute later, Dad takes his last breath.

Coda

I spend the night at Mum's, sleeping in my childhood bed. It's a lumpy single mattress that I have outgrown, though I seem to shrink to its expectations of me. For eighteen years, and some beyond, I would wake in this room and simply take for granted that Dad was down at the kitchen table with his grapefruit and Alpen, or out in the surrounding fields with the dogs. Today I wake to a new world, my co-ordinates in it shifted, a few steps closer to the edge.

Mum and I hug, talk, eat some breakfast, stare into the abyss of practical next-steps and instantly look the other way. Mum goes back to bed and I can think of only one thing to do.

I put on my trainers and go running through my childhood imaginary – the village green with the red phone box and post box that we used to circle on our bikes, the tennis courts that the rich old lady who lived on her own let us use, the surrounding country lanes that once seemed the very edges of the known universe – a tired and grieving man. On the horizon, at the tip of Dad's own hinterland, I see a matchstick complex of woods that contains the place of trespass where he and I saw the Wood White. I run a loop, back round to the edge of the village, and enter the warren.

The warren is a bumpy fold of two fields, each inclined to form a V, meeting where a brook runs through the seam, the second field rising towards the village church. As a child I thought of it as a half-open book, so that I was always running through stories and legend. I enter through the kissing gate and run down the hill. I am halfway across the first page when it catches my eye. There is no mistaking it. A bright flutter-by of an almost orange-hued yellow, scudding over the tussocky grass and clover. I chase it, stunned, zigzagging up and down the slant of the field, then running loop-the-loops, no match for the Clouded Yellow and its speedy flight. A dog walker passes by and eyes me – I am an oddly behaved young man running in circles, laughing and talking to himself. My first butterfly without Dad.

'Are you seeing this?'

The canopy of my parents' Wych Elm, summer 2021, the year after Dad died.

Notes

Prologue

1 When I first wrote this sentence, the all-time NBA scoring record belonged to Kareem Abdul-Jabbar, as it had my entire life (38,387 points), but it was taken by LeBron James during the writing of this book. (I reckon Dad would've guessed Michael Jordan. He's fifth.)

2 Zadie Smith, 'Some Notes on Attunement' in *Feel Free: Essays* (London: Hamish Hamilton, 2018), pp. 102, 105.

3 Ibid., p. 113.

4 Ibid.

5 'Wessex Heights', lines 13–16, *The Collected Poems of Thomas Hardy* (Ware: Wordsworth Editions, 2006), ed. Michael Irwin, pp. 290–1.

1 The Unknowing

1 The poet looking up is John Keats and the poet looking down is Thomas Hardy. 'Bright star, would I were stedfast as thou art' is the first line and title of the poem that, allegedly, Keats composed when his Italy-bound boat stopped on the Dorset

coast in September 1820; 'A hundred years . . .' is from Hardy's 'At Lulworth Cove a Century Back', which imagines looking down on Lulworth Cove and seeing Keats in that moment of last reflection, inspiration and departure. 'Bright Star', line 1, *John Keats: The Major Works* (Oxford: Oxford University Press, 2001), ed. Elizabeth Cook, p. 325; 'At Lulworth Cove', lines 19–20, *The Collected Poems of Thomas Hardy*, p. 556.

2 Hardy, 'An August Midnight', line 12, *The Collected Poems of Thomas Hardy*, p. 131.

3 Vladimir Nabokov, *Speak, Memory* (London: Penguin, 2000), p. 95.

2 4-4-2

1 *BB: A Celebration* (Barnsley: Wharncliffe Publishing Limited, 1993), ed. Tom Quinn.

2 BB, *The Quiet Fields* (London: Michael Joseph, 1981); *A Summer on the Nene* (London: Kaye & Ward, 1967), p. 9.

3 BB, *The Idle Countryman* (London: Eyre & Spottiswoode, 1944).

4 BB, *Letters from Compton Deverell* (London: Eyre & Spottiswoode, 1950).

3 Our Fathers' Studies

1 I am indebted to a wealth of rich Nabokov scholarship and biography, all of which is detailed in the bibliography. In this chapter I draw particularly from Dmitri Nabokov, 'On Revisiting Father's Room', in *Vladimir Nabokov: A Tribute: His Life, His Work, His World* (London: Weidenfeld and Nicolson, 1979), ed. Peter Quennell, pp. 129–36 (the quote is from p. 127); and Brian Boyd, *Vladimir Nabokov: The Russian Years* (London: Chatto & Windus, 1990).

2 See Vladimir Nabokov, *Strong Opinions* (London: Penguin, 2011), p. 25.

3 Quoted in Boyd, *The Russian Years*, p. 68.

4 Nabokov, *Speak, Memory*, p. 144.

5 Ibid., p. 136.

6 Ibid., p. 137.

7 Ibid.

8 Dmitri Nabokov, 'On Revisiting Father's Room', p. 126.

6 The Early Spring Fliers

1 Vladimir Nabokov, *Nabokov's Butterflies: Unpublished and Uncollected Writings* (London: Allen Lane, 2000), eds. Brian Boyd and Robert Michael Pyle, p. 164.

7 The Gift (i)

1 Nabokov, *Speak, Memory*, p. 144.

2 See Stacy Schiff, *Véra (Mrs. Vladimir Nabokov)* (New York: The Modern Library, 1999), pp. 55–6, 102.

3 See Brian Boyd, *Vladimir Nabokov: The American Years* (London: Chatto & Windus, 1992), p. 211.

4 Quoted in Boyd, *The Russian Years*, p. 192.

5 Ibid., p. 194.

6 Nabokov, *Speak, Memory*, p. 132.

7 Brian Boyd, 'Nabokov's Butterflies, Introduction', *The Atlantic*, April 2000, https://www.theatlantic.com/magazine/archive/2000/04/nabokovs-butterflies-introduction/378103/ [accessed 25/1/24].

8 Dmitri Nabokov, 'On Revisiting Father's Room', p. 128.

8 If You Go Down to the Woods Today

1 See Badger Walker, 'Out in the Forest', in *BB's Butterflies: A Celebration of One Man's Passion for the Purple Emperor* (Solihull: Roseworld, 2013), ed. Bryan Holden, p. 21. My thinking on BB has been greatly assisted by *BB's Butterflies*, as well as by Tom Quinn, *BB Remembered: The Life and Times of Denys Watkins-Pitchford* (Shrewsbury: Swan Hill Press, 2006).

2 Words from BB, *Brendon Chase* (London: Methuen, 1978), p. 135.

3 Matthew Oates, *His Imperial Majesty: A Natural History of the Purple Emperor* (London: Bloomsbury, 2020), p. 47.

4 Ibid., p. 49.

5 *BB's Butterflies*, p. 137.

6 Ibid., pp. 190–1.

7 Oates, *His Imperial Majesty*, p. 47.

8 *BB's Butterflies*, p. 118.

9 A Momentary Vacuum

1 My thinking on gifts has been shaped by Lewis Hyde, *The Gift: How the Creative Spirit Transforms the World* (Edinburgh: Canongate, 2012); Robert Macfarlane, *The Gifts of Reading* (London: Penguin, 2016); and, above all, Ali Smith, *Artful* (London: Hamish Hamilton, 2012).

2 Quoted in Quinn, *BB Remembered*, p. 42.

3 See BB, *A Child Alone: The Memoirs of 'BB'* (London: Michael Joseph, 1978), p. 17.

4 Ibid., pp. 22 and 24.

5 *BB's Butterflies*, p. 126.

6 Nabokov, *Speak, Memory*, pp. 102–3.

7 *BB's Butterflies*, p. 67.

8 BB, *A Child Alone*, p. 18.
9 Quoted in Quinn, *BB Remembered*, p. 83.
10 Oates, *His Imperial Majesty*, p. 19.
11 Ibid., p. 23.
12 Ibid., pp. 24–5.
13 Ibid., p. 38.

10 Dad the Obscure

1 BB, *A Child Alone*, pp. 69–70.
2 *BB's Butterflies*, p. 66.
3 Ibid., p. 104.
4 Ibid., p. 63.
5 Thomas Hardy, *Jude the Obscure* (London: Penguin, 1998), p. 213.

11 The Gift (ii)

1 Vladimir Nabokov, *The Gift*, translated by Michael Scammell and Dmitri Nabokov (London: Penguin, 2017), p. 94.
2 Vladimir Nabokov, *Lectures on Literature* (San Diego: Harvest, 1980), p. 87.
3 Nabokov, *The Gift*, p. 104.
4 From 'Father's Butterflies', an addendum to *The Gift*, p. 376.
5 Ibid., p. 104.
6 Ibid., p. 137.
7 Ibid.

12 Magic Carpet Ride

1 See Saul Bellow, *Humboldt's Gift* (London: Penguin, 2007), p. 262.

2 On forestry management and the Purple Emperor, see Oates, *His Imperial Majesty*, pp. 44, 53.

3 These words, from 'birds, plants, trees . . .', are from BB, *A Child Alone*, pp. 68–9.

13 The Lowick, Sudborough and Slipton Parish Newsletter

1 *BB's Butterflies*, p. 74.

2 Badger Walker in *BB's Butterflies*, p. 24.

3 Nabokov, *Speak, Memory*, p. 102.

14 The Purple Prince

1 https://www.youtube.com/watch?v=6SFNW5F8K9Y [accessed 25/1/24].

2 The following account is informed by 'The Day Prince's Guitar Wept the Loudest', Finn Cohen, *The New York Times*, 28 April 2016, https://www.nytimes.com/2016/04/28/arts/music/prince-guitar-rock-hall-of-fame.html [accessed 25/1/24].

16 The Boxer

1 As well as continuing to be informed by Boyd's two-volume biography of Nabokov, this chapter also draws upon Robert Roper, *Nabokov in America: On the Road to Lolita* (New York: Bloomsbury, 2015); and Andrew Field, *Nabokov: His Life in Part* (London: Hamish Hamilton, 1977).

2 *Nabokov's Butterflies*, p. 236.

3 Nabokov, *The Gift*, p. 401.

4 See Boyd, *The Russian Years*, p. 158, and Nabokov's own account of his cousin in chapter 10 of *Speak, Memory*.

5 *Nabokov's Butterflies*, p. 526.

17 Holly Blue

1 For an engaging account of trying to see all the UK butterfly species in one year, see Patrick Barkham, *The Butterfly Isles: A Summer in Search of Our Emperors and Admirals* (London: Granta, 2010).

19 Mr Blue and Mrs Woolf

1 Virginia Woolf, 'Old Bloomsbury', *Moments of Being* (London: Pimlico, 2002), ed. Jeanne Schulkind, p. 58.

2 Virginia Woolf, *The Diary of Virginia Woolf* (London: The Hogarth Press, 1977), p. 295.

3 In writing this chapter I found Benjamin Bagocius's 'Queer Entomology: Virginia Woolf's Butterflies' very illuminating – *Modernism/Modernity* (November 2017), 24:4, pp. 723–50. Hermione Lee's *Virginia Woolf* (London: Vintage, 1997) was also informative.

4 'Erratic' and 'irregular' from 'Old Bloomsbury' (p. 58); 'fantastic & very sensitive' from *The Diary of Virginia Woolf*, p. 295. Bagocius is particularly compelling on the significance of Woolf's descriptions of butterfly movement in his reading of gender fluidity in her work.

5 Woolf, *The Diary of Virginia Woolf*, p. 295.

6 Lee, *Virginia Woolf*, p. 140.

7 Quoted by Lee in her introduction to *To the Lighthouse* (London: Penguin, 2000), xvii.

8 Ibid., p. 54.

9 Ibid.

10 Ibid., p. 186.

11 Ibid., p. 12.

20 Lulworth Skipper Revisited

1 Ali Smith, *Artful*, pp. 126–7.

2 Thomas Hardy, *The Return of the Native* (London: Penguin, 1999), p. 247.

3 Thomas Hardy, *Tess of the D'Urbervilles* (London: Penguin, 2003), p. 143.

4 Ali Smith, *Artful*, p. 126.

21 Silver-studded Blue

1 *Nabokov's Butterflies*, p. 385.

2 Ibid., p. 289.

3 On Nabokov's entomological pursuits in America, see Roper, *Nabokov in America*; Boyd, *The American Years*; *Nabokov's Butterflies*; Kurt Johnson and Steve Coates, *Nabokov's Blues: The Scientific Odyssey of a Literary Genius* (New York: McGraw-Hill, 1999); *Fine Lines: Vladimir Nabokov's Scientific Art* (New Haven: Yale University Press, 2016), eds. Stephen H. Blackwell and Kurt Johnson.

4 Jeremy Thomas and Richard Lewington, *The Butterflies of Britain & Ireland* (Oxford: British Wildlife Publishing, 2014), p. 118.

22 What Is Man?

1 Rudyard Kipling, 'If—', lines 1–2 and line 32, https://www.poetryfoundation.org/poems/46473/if--- [accessed 25/1/24].

2 Ibid., lines 13-16.

3 E. M. Forster, *Howards End* (London: Penguin, 2000), p. 176.

4 Quoted in Edmund Gordon, *The Invention of Angela Carter* (London: Chatto & Windus, 2016), p. 215.

5 On Carter's time in Japan, see Gordon, *The Invention of Angela Carter*, pp. 137–199; Natsumi Ikoma, 'Encounter with the Mirror of the Other: Angela Carter and Her Personal Connection with Japan', *Journal of the Theoretical Humanities* (2017), 22:1, pp. 77–92; Susan Rubin Suleiman, 'The Fate of the Surrealist Imagination in the Society of the Spectacle', in *Flesh and the Mirror: Essays on the Art of Angela Carter* (London: Virago, 2007), ed. Lorna Sage, pp. 115–32; Charlotte Crofts, '"The Other of the Other": Angela Carter's "New-Fangled" Orientalism' in *Re-Visiting Angela Carter: Texts, Contexts, Intertexts* (Basingstoke: Palgrave Macmillan, 2006), ed. Rebecca Munford, pp. 87–109; Scott Dimovitz, *Angela Carter: Surrealist, Psychologist, Moral Pornographer* (Abingdon: Routledge, 2016).

6 Angela Carter, *Nothing Sacred: Selected Writings* (London: Virago, 1982), p. 28.

7 Quoted in Gordon, *The Invention of Angela Carter*, pp. 157 and 143.

8 Angela Carter, 'Poor Butterfly', in *Shaking a Leg: Collected Writings* (London: Chatto & Windus, 1997), ed. Jenny Uglow, p. 249.

9 Ibid., pp. 251–2.

10 Gordon, *The Invention of Angela Carter*, p. 164.

11 Carter, *Shaking a Leg*, p. 252.

12 You can view a facsimile of Carter's notebook for *Wise Children* at https://www.bl.uk/20th-century-literature/articles/shakespeare-and-carnival-in-angela-carters-wise-children [accessed 16/5/23]. The second quote is from Carter's 'Sugar Daddy', in *Shaking a Leg*, p. 25.

13 Angela Carter, *Wise Children* (London: Chatto & Windus, 1991), p. 216.

14 Ibid., p. 19.

15 Ibid., p. 18.

16 Ibid., p. 220.

17 Angela Carter, *The Infernal Desire Machines of Doctor Hoffman* (London: Rupert Hart-Davis, 1972), p. 190.

18 Carter, *Wise Children*, p. 230.

19 'Nabokov on Metamorphosis', *Natural History* (Jul/Aug 1999), 108:6, pp. 52–3.

20 Ibid.

24 Chalkhills and Adonises

1 *Nabokov's Butterflies*, p. 481.

2 Ibid.

3 Nabokov (with Edmund Wilson), *Nabokov-Wilson Letters* (New York: Harper and Row, 1979), ed. Simon Karlinsky, p. 264.

4 Ibid., p. 265.

5 Vladimir Nabokov, *The Annotated Lolita* (London: Penguin, 2000), ed. Alfred Appel, Jr, pp. 133 ('hot thunder'), 139 ('squall'), 10 ('picnic').

6 *Nabokov's Butterflies*, p. 481.

7 Here I have adapted details from Nabokov's 6 September 1951 letter to Elena Sikorski and an early September 1951 letter to Edmund Wilson (*Nabokov's Butterflies*, pp. 478–9).

8 The words here echo lines from Nabokov's 1958 afterword to *Lolita*: 'These are the nerves of the novel. These are the secret points, the subliminal co-ordinates by means of which the book is plotted' (*The Annotated Lolita*, p. 316).

9 Robert H. Boyle, 'An Absence of Wood Nymphs', 14 September 1959, *Sports Illustrated*, E7.

10 'Butterflies', in Vladimir Nabokov, *Collected Poems* (London: Penguin Classics, 2012), ed. Thomas Karshan, p. 55.

11 Vladimir Nabokov, *Selected Letters 1940–1977* (London: Weidenfeld and Nicolson, 1990), eds. Dmitri Nabokov and Matthew J. Bruccoli, p. 114.

25 Gossamer-Winged

1 Quote from David Yaffe, *Reckless Daughter: A Portrait of Joni Mitchell* (New York: Farrar, Straus and Giroux, 2018), p. 132. Yaffe's book has been especially informative for this chapter.

2 Ibid., pp. 132–3.

3 Ibid., p. 148.

4 Ibid., pp. 200–01.

5 https://www.youtube.com/watch?v=zeaO5UZ5OcI [accessed 25/1/24].

26 Hinterland

1 Nabokov, *The Gift*, p. 107.

2 My understanding of trespass and poaching has been informed by O. F. Brown and G. J. Roberts, *Passenham: The History of a Forest Village* (Sussex: Phillimore, 1973), and Nick Hayes, *The Book of Trespass: Crossing the Lines that Divide Us* (London: Bloomsbury, 2021).

3 Detailed in Brown and Roberts, *Passenham*, p. 108.

27 White Butterflies

1 Colin McPhedran, *White Butterflies* (Canberra: Pandanus Books, 2009), p. 45.

2 Ibid., p. 102.

3 Andrew French, 'Pensioner Needs Help to Find Home for Burmese Butterflies', *Oxford Mail*, 8 September 2019, https://www.oxfordmail.co.uk/news/17888414.pensioner-needs-help-find-home-burmese-butterflies/ [accessed 25/1/24].

28 Moth-Hunting

1 Virginia Woolf, 'The Death of the Moth', *The Death of the Moth and Other Essays* (London: The Hogarth Press, 1943), pp. 10–11.

2 Virginia Woolf, 'Reading', *Collected Essays: Volume Two* (London: The Hogarth Press, 1966), p. 25.

3 Ibid.

4 Virginia Woolf, *Jacob's Room* (London: Penguin, 1992), pp. 17–18.

5 Ibid. p. 17.

6 Woolf, 'Reading', p. 25.

7 Woolf, *Jacob's Room*, p. 18.

8 Ibid., p. 61.

9 Ibid., p. 29.

10 Ibid.

29 Legacy

1 https://www.beds-northants-butterflies.org.uk/woodlandwings.html [accessed 25/1/24].

2 Virginia Woolf, 'Character in Fiction', in *Selected Essays* (Oxford: Oxford University Press, 2009), ed. David Bradshaw, p. 37.

3 Ibid., p. 41.

4 Ibid.

5 Ibid., p. 42.

6 Nabokov, *The Annotated Lolita*, p. 224.

31 I Hug You

1 Nabokov, *The Annotated Lolita*, p. 308.

2 Ibid., p. 44.

3 Ibid., p. 104.

4 Ibid., p. 171.

5 Ibid., pp. 207, 255, 83.

6 Ibid., p. 91.

7 Ibid., p. 75.

8 Nabokov, *The Gift*, p. 110.

9 Roper, *Nabokov in America*, p. 137.

10 Nabokov, *Speak, Memory*, p. 43.

11 Boyd, *The American Years*, p. 203.

12 Véra recognised in her son's nostalgic and obsessive tendencies (not least his 'passionate clinging to every bit of his childish possessions and propensity towards accumulating "complete" sets' of toy vehicles, which Véra felt '[had] its root in that initial loss of home and toys') the 'pathetic attempt of a very small and bewildered individual to throw an anchor of his own amidst the incomprehensible'. Véra doesn't acknowledge that this analysis could easily be applied to her repeatedly exiled, orphaned, butterfly-collecting husband. (Quoted in Roper, *Nabokov in America*, p. 53.)

13 See Boyd, *The American Years*, pp. 207–08.

14 Vladimir Nabokov, *Bend Sinister* (London: Penguin, 2016), p. 167.

15 Nabokov, *Speak, Memory*, p. 232.

16 Ibid., p. 233.

17 Nabokov, *Selected Letters*, pp. 353 and 565.

32 Waking Dad

1 William Wordsworth, 'To a Butterfly', lines 1–4, *William Wordsworth: The Major Works* (Oxford: Oxford University Press, 2000), ed. Stephen Gill, p. 254.

33 Who's Afraid of Tony Soprano?

1 Virginia Woolf, *Mrs Dalloway* (London: Penguin, 2000), p. 46. While writing this I was moved to find Merve Emre and James Wood discussing this same passage in a way that chimed with my own response to it; see https://www.youtube.com/watch?v=Z02XbbYEvRA [accessed 25/1/24].

2 See Hyde, *The Gift*, pp. xxi–xxvii.

3 Virginia Woolf, *A Room of One's Own* (London: Penguin, 2000), p. 6.

4 Several reviewers and commentators have noted the Albee connection, including Philip Ringstrom, 'Not Sure What I'm Watching Anymore', 9 December 2002, https://slate.com/culture/2002/12/not-sure-what-i-m-watching-anymore.html [accessed 25/1/24]; Matt Zoller Seitz and Alan Sepinwall, *The* Sopranos *Sessions* (New York: Abrams Press, 2019), pp. 186–9.

34 Unexpected Readings

1 For more on this, see Jesmond Harding, 'Butterflies in Time of War', 13 May 2020, https://butterflyconservation.ie/wp/2020/05/13/butterflies-in-time-of-war/ [accessed 25/1/24].

35 Northamptonshire Poet

1 See John Clare's own account of his 'Journey out of Essex', in *John Clare: Major Works*, pp. 432–7. Jonathan Bate's biography of Clare, *John Clare: A Biography* (London: Picador, 2004), has informed this chapter – see pp. 451–65 for Bate's narration of the journey from Essex. Iain Sinclair's psychogeographical reconstruction of Clare's journey, *Edge of the Orison* (London: Hamish Hamilton, 2005), has also been influential.

2 Statistics from 'The State of the UK's Butterflies 2022', a report by Butterfly Conservation, https://butterfly-conservation.org/sites/default/files/2023-01/State%20of%20UK%20Butterflies%202022%20Report.pdf [accessed 25/1/24]. On 'shifting baseline syndrome' in relation to the state of insects, see Dave Goulson, *Silent Earth: Averting the Insect Apocalypse* (London: Vintage, 2022), p. 68. Other recent studies of insect decline include Oliver Milman, *The Insect Crisis: The Fall of the Tiny Empires that Run the World* (London: Atlantic Books, 2022); and Nick Haddad, *The Last Butterflies: A Scientist's Quest to Save a Rare and Vanishing Creature* (Princeton: Princeton University Press, 2019).

3 See Thomas and Lewington, *The Butterflies of Britain & Ireland*, p. 102.

4 John Clare, 'The Flitting', lines 1–4, in *John Clare: Major Works*, p. 250.

5 Ibid., lines 17–18.

6 Clare, 'The Lament of Swordy Well', lines 109–12, in *John Clare: Major Works*, p. 150.

7 Ibid., lines 93-4, p. 149.

8 On Clare's lost natures, see Alan Bewell, 'John Clare and the Ghosts of Natures Past', *Nineteenth-Century Literature* (March 2011), 65:4, pp. 548–78.

9 See Bate, *John Clare*, p. 354.

10 John Clare, 'Shadows of Taste', lines 87–90, in *John Clare: Major Works*, p. 172.

11 Ibid., lines 148–52, p. 173.

12 Clare, 'Shadows of Taste', lines 135–40, in *John Clare: Major Works*, p. 173. For a compelling reading of this poem, see Sarah Weiger, '"Shadows of Taste": John Clare's Tasteful Natural History', *John Clare Society Journal* (2008), 27, pp. 59–72.

36 Time Passes

1 The house is Lyveden New Bield, and the owner was Sir Thomas Tresham. Tresham is memorably brought to life by another Northampton writer, Alan Moore, in *Voice of the Fire* (Atlanta: Top Shelf Productions, 2009), pp. 185–201.

38 A Change in Sensibility, in Four Parts

1 *Nabokov's Butterflies*, pp. 494–5.

2 Based on a 'dream report' originally published in the *New Yorker* in 1964, reproduced in *Nabokov's Butterflies*, pp. 617–18.

3 On BB and collecting and killing, see Quinn, *BB Remembered*, p. 24.

39 Dark Vanessa

1 Dieter E. Zimmer's online compendium, *A Guide to Nabokov's Butterflies and Moths*, is a tremendous resource, with detailed entries for every species mentioned in Nabokov's writing. http://www.d-e-zimmer.de/eGuide/PageOne.htm [accessed 25/1/24]. You can find fascinating details about Nabokov and *Vanessa atalanta* here: http://www.d-e-zimmer.de/eGuide/

Lep2.1-T-Z.htm#V.atalanta [accessed 25/1/24]. On the significance of the Red Admiral in *Pale Fire* in particular, see Brian Boyd, '*Pale Fire*: The *Vanessa atalanta*', in *Nabokov at Cornell* (Ithaca: Cornell University Press, 2003), ed. Gavriel Shapiro, pp. 78–90; and Robert Dirig, 'Drawing with Words: The Toothwort White and Related Natural History Motifs in *Pale Fire*', in *Fine Lines*, eds. Blackwell and Johnson, pp. 201–15.

2 See Dirig, 'Drawing with Words', p. 211.

3 On the coded allusions, see Boyd, *The American Years*, p. 454.

4 Nabokov, *Pale Fire*, pp. 227–8.

5 Nabokov, *Strong Opinions*, p. 144.

6 See Boyd, '*Pale Fire*: The *Vanessa atalanta*', p. 87.

42 The Anxiety of Influence, in Three Parts

1 Some of the sources I have drawn upon regarding the relationship between Prince and Joni include Yaffe, *Reckless Daughter*; Matt Thorne, *Prince* (London: Faber & Faber, 2013); www.princevault.com [accessed 25/1/24]; and others detailed below.

2 Yaffe, *Reckless Daughter*, p. 188.

3 Ibid.

4 'From "Blue" to Purple: How Joni Mitchell Influenced Prince', https://weareclassicrockers.com/article/blue-purple-how-joni-mitchell-influenced-prince [accessed 25/1/24].

5 Jack Whatley, 'Why Joni Mitchell Rejected the Song Prince Had Written for Her', 24 May 2022, https://faroutmagazine.co.uk/why-joni-mitchell-rejected-the-song-prince-had-written-for-her/ [accessed 25/1/24].

6 You can find Prince's own recording of 'Emotional Pump' on Prince, *Sign O' The Times* (Super) *Deluxe Edition* (NPG Records / The Prince Estate / Warner Records, 2020).

7 Raymond Williams, *The Long Revolution* (London: Chatto & Windus, 1961), p. 64.

8 Woolf, *To the Lighthouse*, p. 54.

9 Nabokov, 'Nabokov on Metamorphosis'.

10 Carter, *Shaking a Leg*, p. 38.

11 Smith, 'Some Notes on Attunement', p. 113.

12 Yaffe, *Reckless Daughter*, p. 292.

43 Strange Meeting

1 On Clare's time in Northampton General Lunatic Asylum, see Bate, *John Clare*, pp. 466–529, from which I draw here.

2 Clare, 'Shadows of Taste', lines 150–3, in *John Clare: Major Works*, p. 173

3 Quoted in Bate, *John Clare*, p. 481.

4 'Into the nothingness of scorn and noise, – / Into the living sea of waking dreams, / Where there is neither sense of life or joys, / But the vast shipwreck of my lifes esteems; Even the dearest, that I love the best / Are strange – nay, rather stranger than the rest.' John Clare, 'I Am', lines 7–12, *John Clare: Major Works* (Oxford: Oxford University Press, 1984), p. 361.

44 Voice

1 'Luther Vandross: The Velvet Voice', Elizabeth Blair, NPR, 29 November 2010, https://www.npr.org/2010/11/29/131665902/luther-vandross-the-velvet-voice [accessed 25/1/24].

2 https://www.youtube.com/watch?v=FNk11dP86Dc [accessed 25/1/24].

3 https://www.youtube.com/watch?v=NNHBT7wjqVI [accessed 25/1/24].

4 https://www.youtube.com/watch?v=OW7uz9ktU24 [accessed 25/1/24].

45 Visitation

1 From Dmitri Nabokov's introduction to Vladimir Nabokov, *The Original of Laura* (London: Penguin, 2012), p. xv.

2 Vladimir Nabokov, *Selected Letters*, p. 562.

3 Dmitri Nabokov, 'On Revisiting Father's Room', p. 136.

Bibliography

Anonymous, 'From "Blue" to Purple: How Joni Mitchell Influenced Prince', https://weareclassicrockers.com/article/blue-purple-how-joni-mitchell-influenced-prince

Appel, Alfred, Jr. and Charles Newman (eds.), *Nabokov: Criticism, Reminiscences, Translations and Tributes* (London: Weidenfeld and Nicolson, 1971)

Bagocius, Benjamin, 'Queer Entomology: Virginia Woolf's Butterflies', *Modernism/Modernity* (November 2017), 24:4, pp. 723–50

Barkham, Patrick, *The Butterfly Isles: A Summer in Search of Our Emperors and Admirals* (London: Granta, 2010)

Bate, Jonathan, *John Clare: A Biography* (London: Picador, 2004)

BB, *The Idle Countryman* (1943) (London: Eyre & Spottiswoode, 1944)

—— *Brendon Chase* (1944) (London: Methuen, 1978)

—— *Letters from Compton Deverell* (London: Eyre & Spottiswoode, 1950)

—— *A Summer on the Nene* (London: Kaye & Ward, 1967)

—— *A Child Alone: The Memoirs of 'BB'* (London: Michael Joseph, 1978)

—— *The Quiet Fields* (London: Michael Joseph, 1981)

—— *BB: A Celebration* (Barnsley: Wharncliffe Publishing Limited, 1993), ed. Tom Quinn

—— *BB's Butterflies: A Celebration of One Man's Passion for the Purple Emperor* (Solihull: Roseworld, 2013), ed. Bryan Holden

Bellow, Saul, *Humboldt's Gift* (1975) (London: Penguin, 2007)

Bewell, Alan, 'John Clare and the Ghosts of Natures Past', *Nineteenth-Century Literature* (March 2011), 65:4, pp. 548–78

Blackwell, Stephen and Kurt Johnson (eds.), *Fine Lines: Vladimir Nabokov's Scientific Art* (New Haven: Yale University Press, 2016)

Blair, Elizabeth, 'Luther Vandross: The Velvet Voice', NPR, 29 November 2010, https://www.npr.org/2010/11/29/131665902/luther-vandross-the-velvet-voice

Boyd, Brian, *Vladimir Nabokov: The Russian Years* (London: Chatto & Windus, 1990)

—— *Vladimir Nabokov: The American Years* (London: Chatto & Windus, 1992)

—— 'Nabokov's Butterflies, Introduction', *The Atlantic*, April 2000,https://www.theatlantic.com/magazine/archive/2000/04/nabokovs-butterflies-introduction/378103/

—— '*Pale Fire*: The *Vanessa atalanta*', in *Nabokov at Cornell*, ed. Gavriel Shapiro, pp. 78–90

Boyle, Robert H., 'An Absence of Wood Nymphs', 14 September 1959, *Sports Illustrated*, E7

Brown, O. F. and G. J. Roberts, *Passenham: The History of a Forest Village* (Sussex: Phillimore, 1973)

Carter, Angela, *The Infernal Desire Machines of Doctor Hoffman* (London: Rupert Hart-Davis, 1972)

—— *Nothing Sacred: Selected Writings* (London: Virago, 1982)

—— *Wise Children* (London: Chatto & Windus, 1991)

—— *Shaking a Leg: Collected Writings* (London: Chatto & Windus, 1997), ed. Jenny Uglow

Clare, John, *John Clare: Major Works* (Oxford: Oxford University Press, 2004), eds. Eric Robinson and David Powell

Cohen, Finn, 'The Day Prince's Guitar Wept the Loudest', *The New York Times*, 28 April 2016, https://www.nytimes.com/2016/04/28/arts/music/prince-guitar-rock-hall-of-fame.html

Crofts, Charlotte, '"The Other of the Other": Angela Carter's "New-Fangled" Orientalism', in *Re-Visiting Angela Carter: Texts, Contexts, Intertexts* (Basingstoke: Palgrave Macmillan, 2006), pp. 87–109, ed. Rebecca Munford

Deleuze, Gilles, *The Fold: Leibniz and the Baroque* (London: Continuum, 2011), translated by Tom Conley

Dimovitz, Scott, *Angela Carter: Surrealist, Psychologist, Moral Pornographer* (Abingdon: Routledge, 2016)

Dirig, Robert, 'Theme in Blue: Vladimir Nabokov's Endangered Butterfly', in *Nabokov at Cornell*, ed. Gavriel Shapiro, pp. 205–18

—— 'Drawing with Words: The Toothwort White and Related Natural History Motifs in *Pale Fire*', in *Fine Lines*, eds. Stephen Blackwell and Kurt Johnson, pp. 201–15

Emre, Merve and James Wood, 'The Annotated Mrs. Dalloway, Live from NYPL', https://www.youtube.com/watch?v=Z02XbbYEvRA

Feldman, Jessica R., *Gender on the Divide: The Dandy in Modernist Literature* (Ithaca: Cornell University Press, 1993)

Field, Andrew, *Nabokov: His Life in Part* (London: Hamish Hamilton, 1977)

Forster, E. M., *Howards End* (1910) (London: Penguin, 2000)

Fox, R., E. B. Dennis, K. M. Purdy, I. Middlebrook, D. B. Roy, D. G. Noble, M. S. Botham, and N. A. D. Bourn, *The State of the UK's Butterflies 2022*. Wareham, UK: Butterfly Conservation, 2023. https://butterfly-conservation.org/sites/default/files/2023-01/State%20of%20UK%20Butterflies%202022%20Report.pdf

French, Andrew, 'Pensioner Needs Help to Find Home for Burmese Butterflies', *Oxford Mail*, 8 September 2019, https://www.oxfordmail.co.uk/news/17888414.pensioner-needs-help-find-home-burmese-butterflies/

Gordon, Edmund, *The Invention of Angela Carter* (London: Chatto & Windus, 2016)

Goulson, Dave, *A Buzz in the Meadow* (London: Jonathan Cape, 2014)

—— *Silent Earth: Averting the Insect Apocalypse* (London: Vintage, 2022)

Haddad, Nick, *The Last Butterflies: A Scientist's Quest to Save a Rare and Vanishing Creature* (Princeton: Princeton University Press, 2019)

Harding, Jesmond, 'Butterflies in Time of War', 13 May 2020, https://butterflyconservation.ie/wp/2020/05/13/butterflies-in-time-of-war/

Hardy, Thomas, *Far from the Madding Crowd* (1874) (London: Penguin, 2003)

—— *The Return of the Native* (1878) (London: Penguin, 1999)

—— *Tess of the D'Urbervilles* (1891) (London: Penguin, 2003)

—— *Jude the Obscure* (1895) (London: Penguin, 1998)

—— *The Collected Poems of Thomas Hardy* (Ware: Wordsworth Editions, 2006)

Hayes, Nick, *The Book of Trespass: Crossing the Lines that Divide Us* (London: Bloomsbury, 2021)

Hopkins, Harry, *The Long Affray: The Poaching Wars in Britain* (London: Faber and Faber, 2008)

Hyde, Lewis, *The Gift: How the Creative Spirit Transforms the World* (Edinburgh: Canongate, 2012)

Ikoma, Natsumi, 'Encounter with the Mirror of the Other: Angela Carter and Her Personal Connection with Japan', *Journal of the Theoretical Humanities* (2017), 22:1, pp. 77–92

Irwin, Michael, 'Insects in Hardy's Fiction', *The Thomas Hardy Journal* (Oct 1994), 10:3, pp. 54–63

Johnson, Kurt and Steve Coates, *Nabokov's Blues: The Scientific Odyssey of a Literary Genius* (New York: McGraw-Hill, 1999)

Keats, John, *John Keats: The Major Works* (Oxford: Oxford University Press, 2001), ed. Elizabeth Cook

Lee, Hermione, *Virginia Woolf* (London: Vintage, 1997)

Macfarlane, Robert, *The Wild Places* (London: Granta, 2008)

—— *Landmarks* (London: Hamish Hamilton, 2015)

—— *The Gifts of Reading* (London: Penguin, 2016)

Magrs, Paul, 'Boys Keep Swinging: Angela Carter and the Subject of Men', in *The Infernal Desires of Angela Carter: Fiction, Femininity and Feminism* (London: Routledge, 1997), eds. Joseph Bristow and Trev L. Broughton, pp. 342–65

McPhedran, Colin, *White Butterflies* (Canberra: Pandanus Books, 2009)

Marren, Peter, *Rainbow Dust: Three Centuries of Delight in British Butterflies* (London: Square Peg, 2015)

Martin, Brett, *Difficult Men: From* The Sopranos *and* The Wire *to* Mad Men *and* Breaking Bad*: Behind the Scenes of a Creative Revolution* (London: Faber and Faber, 2013)

Martinez, Juan, 'A Fold of the Marquisette: Nabokov's Lepidoptery in Visual Media', in *The Goalkeeper: The Nabokov*

Almanac (Boston: American Studies Press, 2010), ed. Yuri Leving, pp. 158–76

Matthews, Sean, 'Change and Theory in Raymond Williams's Structure of Feeling', *Pretexts: Literary and Cultural Studies* (2001), 10:2, pp. 179–94

Milman, Oliver, *The Insect Crisis: The Fall of the Tiny Empires that Run the World* (London: Atlantic Books, 2022)

Moore, Alan, *Voice of the Fire* (Atlanta: Top Shelf Productions, 2009)

Morgenstern, Barry, 'The Self-Conscious Narrator in *Jacob's Room*', *Modern Fiction Studies* (Autumn 1972), 18:3, pp. 351–61

Nabokov, Dmitri, 'On Revisiting Father's Room', in *Vladimir Nabokov: A Tribute: His Life, His Work, His World* (London: Weidenfeld and Nicolson, 1979), ed. Peter Quennell, pp. 129–36

—— 'A Few Things That Must Be Said on Behalf of Vladimir Nabokov', in *Nabokov's Fifth Arc* (Austin: University of Texas Press, 1982), eds. J .E. Rivers and Charles Nicol, pp. 35–42

——'On Returning to Ithaca', in *Nabokov at Cornell*, ed. Gavriel Shapiro, pp. 277–84

Nabokov, Vladimir, *King, Queen, Knave* (1968) (London: Penguin, 2010); first published in Russian as *Korol', Dama, Valet* (1928)

—— *Laughter in the Dark* (1961) (London: Penguin, 2010); first published in Russian as *Kamera Obscura* (1933)

—— *The Gift*, translated by Michael Scammell and Dmitri Nabokov (London: Penguin, 2017), p. 94; first published in Russian as *Dar* (1938)

—— *Bend Sinister* (1947) (London: Penguin, 2016)
—— *The Annotated Lolita* (London: Penguin, 2000), ed. Alfred Appel, Jr (*Lolita* was first published 1955)
—— *Pnin* (1957) (London: Penguin, 2000)
—— *Pale Fire* (1962) (London: Penguin, 2000)
—— *Collected Stories* (1965) (London: Penguin, 2010)
—— *Speak, Memory: An Autobiography Revisited* (1967) (London: Penguin, 2000)
—— *Ada, or Ardor: A Family Chronicle* (London: Weidenfeld and Nicolson, 1969)
—— *Strong Opinions* (1973) (London: Penguin, 2011)
—— Nabokov, Vladimir and Edmund Wilson, *Nabokov-Wilson Letters* (New York: Harper and Row, 1979), ed. Simon Karlinsky
—— *Lectures on Literature* (San Diego: Harvest, 1980)
—— *Selected Letters 1940–1977* (London: Weidenfeld and Nicolson, 1990), eds. Dmitri Nabokov and Matthew J. Bruccoli
—— 'Nabokov on Metamorphosis', *Natural History* (Jul/Aug 1999), 108:6, pp. 52–3
—— *Nabokov's Butterflies: Unpublished and Uncollected Writings* (London: Allen Lane, 2000), eds. Brian Boyd and Robert Michael Pyle
—— *The Original of Laura* (2009) (London: Penguin, 2012), ed. Dmitri Nabokov
—— *Collected Poems* (London: Penguin Classics, 2012), ed. Thomas Karshan

Oates, Matthew, *In Pursuit of Butterflies: A Fifty-Year Affair* (London: Bloomsbury, 2015)
—— *His Imperial Majesty: A Natural History of the Purple Emperor* (London: Bloomsbury, 2020)

Quinn, Tom, *BB Remembered: The Life and Times of Denys Watkins-Pitchford* (Shrewsbury: Swan Hill Press, 2006)
Ringstrom, Philip, 'Not Sure What I'm Watching Anymore', 9 December 2002, https://slate.com/culture/2002/12/not-sure-what-i-m-watching-anymore.html
Roeg, Nicolas, *The World is Ever Changing* (London: Faber and Faber, 2013)
Roper, Robert, *Nabokov in America: On the Road to Lolita* (New York: Bloomsbury, 2015)
Schiff, Stacy, *Véra (Mrs. Vladimir Nabokov)* (New York: The Modern Library, 1999)
Seitz, Matt Zoller and Alan Sepinwall, *The Sopranos Sessions* (New York: Abrams Press, 2019)
Senderovich, Savely, and Yelena Shvarts, '*Lolita* the Butterfly. Nabokov's Private Aesthetics', *Nabokov Studies* (2020), 17, pp. 61–83
Shapiro, Gavriel (ed.), *Nabokov at Cornell* (Ithaca: Cornell University Press, 2003)
Sinclair, Iain, *Edge of the Orison* (London: Hamish Hamilton, 2005)
Smith, Ali, *Artful* (London: Hamish Hamilton, 2012)
Smith, Zadie, *Feel Free: Essays* (London: Hamish Hamilton, 2018)
Suleiman, Susan Rubin, 'The Fate of the Surrealist Imagination in the Society of the Spectacle', in *Flesh and the Mirror: Essays on the Art of Angela Carter* (London: Virago, 2007), ed. Lorna Sage, pp. 115–32
Thomas, Jeremy and Richard Lewington, *The Butterflies of Britain & Ireland* (Oxford: British Wildlife Publishing, 2014)
Thorne, Matt, *Prince* (London: Faber and Faber, 2013)
Tomalin, Claire, *Thomas Hardy: The Time-Torn Man* (London: Viking, 2006)

Walker, Badger, 'Out in the Forest', in *BB's Butterflies: A Celebration of One Man's Passion for the Purple Emperor* (Solihull: Roseworld, 2013), ed. Bryan Holden, pp. 17–24

Weiger, Sarah, '"Shadows of Taste": John Clare's Tasteful Natural History', *John Clare Society Journal* (2008), 27, pp. 59–72

Whatley, Jack, 'Why Joni Mitchell Rejected the Song Prince had Written for Her', 24 May 2022, https://faroutmagazine.co.uk/why-joni-mitchell-rejected-the-song-prince-had-written-for-her/

Williams, Raymond, *The Long Revolution* (London: Chatto & Windus, 1961)

—— *The Country and the City* (1973) (London: Vintage, 2016)

—— *Marxism and Literature* (Oxford: Oxford University Press, 1977)

—— *Culture and Materialism* (1980) (London: Verso, 2005)

Wood, Michael, *The Magician's Doubts: Nabokov and the Risks of Fiction* (London: Pimlico, 1995)

Woolf, Virginia, *Jacob's Room* (1922) (London: Penguin, 1992)

—— *Mrs Dalloway* (1925) (London: Penguin, 2000)

—— *To the Lighthouse* (1927) (London: Penguin, 2000)

—— *A Room of One's Own* (1929) (London: Penguin, 2000)

—— *The Death of the Moth and Other Essays* (London: The Hogarth Press, 1943)

—— *Collected Essays: Volume Two* (London: The Hogarth Press, 1966)

—— *Moments of Being* (London: Pimlico, 2002), ed. Jeanne Schulkind (1976)

—— *The Diary of Virginia Woolf* (London: The Hogarth Press, 1977), ed. Anne Olivier Bell

—— *A Passionate Apprentice: The Early Journals 1897–1909* (London: The Hogarth Press, 1990), ed. Mitchell A. Leaska

—— *Selected Essays* (Oxford: Oxford University Press, 2009), ed. David Bradshaw

Wordsworth, William, *William Wordsworth: The Major Works* (Oxford: Oxford University Press, 2000), ed. Stephen Gill

Yaffe, David, *Reckless Daughter: A Portrait of Joni Mitchell* (New York: Farrar, Straus and Giroux, 2018)

Zimmer, Dieter E., *A Guide to Nabokov's Butterflies and Moths.* Web version, 2012. http://www.d-e-zimmer.de/eGuide/PageOne.htm.

Websites Consulted:

Butterfly Conservation, https://butterfly-conservation.org/

Butterflies of Myanmar, https://www.inaturalist.org/projects/butterflies-of-myanmar

Prince Vault, https://princevault.com/index.php?title=Main_Page

UK Butterflies, https://www.ukbutterflies.co.uk/index.php

Acknowledgements

While the narrative of this book, barring a few flights of fancy, does not spread its wings beyond 2020, my desire to be with butterflies has only increased in the years since, and I have enjoyed innumerable conversations with other butterfliers out in the field. Butterfly lovers, I've discovered, are a generous bunch, keen to pass on their experiences and knowledge, as though the thrill of private moments with butterflies demands to be shared. Gifts are an essential theme of this book, and I would like to thank those strangers who have stopped to talk with me during my pursuits and, without realising it, encouraged me deeper into the fold.

This book could never have taken its final form without the gifts of those who read it in its larval phase. First and foremost, I'd like to thank Sos Eltis. Ever since I wrote a shoddy essay on Thomas Hardy for her in my first week at university in 2005, Sos has patiently read almost everything I have written, for which a simple thank you is not sufficient. (Perhaps an apology is more appropriate!) Sos, you are a difference-maker in so many ways. Thank you also to Steven Morrison, an exemplar of collegiality, generosity and fine literary sense; and to Kevin Harvey, who selflessly read the first draft in the shadow of his own loss. I am grateful to Sos, Steven and Kevin for allowing me to re-view my sensibility through their richer and more discerning ones.

I am also indebted to a plethora of scholars, critics and writers, from whom my research has drawn. Their works are all acknowledged in the endnotes and bibliography, but I must give extra acknowledgement to Brian Boyd's magisterial two-volume biography of Vladimir Nabokov, Robert Roper's always compelling *Nabokov in America*, Tom Quinn's informative *BB Remembered*, and Jeremy Thomas and Richard Lewington's indispensable *The Butterflies of Britain & Ireland*, on which I have depended for so much detail and insight.

Ten years after the publication of my last book, my writerly confidence was very low when Jessica Woollard took this book under her wing and gave me the uplift I so desperately needed. Thank you, Jessica, and to Esme Bright and the wider team at David Higham too. To then have the belief and advocacy of two incredible, indefatigable editors, Jason Arthur and Masie Cochran, has been unbelievable good fortune. Thank you, Jason and Masie, for ensuring the final imago saw its light of day. For expertly seeing the book into the world, thank you to Lamorna Elmer, Christine Lo and everyone at Granta in the UK, and Win McCormack and all the team at Tin House in the US. Thank you to Jack Alexander for his perceptive and sensitive copy edit (not least for pointing out that cheesecake is not on the Very Hungry Caterpillar's binge list), Gesche Ipsen and Kate Shearman for their careful proofreads, and Anna Morrison for the book's beautiful set of wings. Thank you also to the University of Nottingham and my talented colleagues.

I can't imagine how this book reads for my mum and brother, but they have given me nothing but permission, trust and love, for which I am deeply grateful. When someone dies, we lose them in our own unique, personal ways, so that the loss of someone is really a multitude of losses. This book is an account (and a limited one at that) of *my* loss, but the loss for them has been monumental and distinct too. While I hope this book doesn't in any way obtrude on that, I do hope it can be some comfort.

Finally, I owe so much to Carli, my wife. I wrote this book not only in the wake of *my* father's death but in the aftermath of hers (Carli's dad died five months after mine). Carli, I hope you have felt as supported and loved through it all as I have by you. This book is in memory of your father as well.

Our children have taught me the infinitude of love. Kit was just under two when Dad died. When Joss was born, two years later, friends and relatives, with good intentions, would imply that new life (and by extension, new love) can somehow replace or fill in for that which has been lost. But the capacity for love does not work to limit. New love joins old love, adds to it, grows it. My dear Kit and dear Joss, it will serve me right if you have no time for your dad's literary pursuits, given how I once had no time for *my* dad's naturalist ones. But, if when you are older you decide to read this book, I hope that you will know your granddad through it. He had the names of all the trees, birds and butterflies for you.

Index